Microsoft® EXCHANGE 5.0

Step by Step

Catapult

Microsoft Press

PUBLISHED BY
Microsoft Press
A Division of Microsoft Corporation
One Microsoft Way
Redmond, Washington 98052-6399

Library of Congress Cataloging-in-Publication Data pending.

Printed and bound in the United States of America.

1 2 3 4 5 6 7 8 9   WCWC   2 1 0 9 8 7

Distributed to the book trade in Canada by Macmillan of Canada, a division of Canada
Publishing Corporation.

British Cataloging-in-Publication Data pending.

Microsoft Press books are available through booksellers and distributors worldwide. For further
information about international editions, contact your local Microsoft Corporation office. Or
contact Microsoft Press International directly at fax (206) 936-7329.

For Catapult, Inc.
Managing Editor: Diana Stiles
Writer: Karen A. Deinhard
Project Editor: Armelle O'Neal
Technical Editor: R. Alan Spring
Production/Layout Editor: Anne Kim
Indexer: Julie Kawabata

For Microsoft Press
Acquisitions Editor: Susanne M. Freet
Project Editors: Maureen Williams
Zimmerman; Laura Sackerman

Microsoft® EXCHANGE 5.0

Step by Step

Other titles in the *Step by Step* series:

Microsoft Access 97 Step by Step
Microsoft Excel 97 Step by Step
Microsoft FrontPage 97 Step by Step
Microsoft Internet Explorer 3.0 Step by Step
Microsoft Office 97 Integration Step by Step
Microsoft Outlook 97 Step by Step
Microsoft PowerPoint 97 Step by Step
Microsoft Team Manager 97 Step by Step
Microsoft Windows 95 Step by Step
Microsoft Windows NT Workstation version 4.0 Step by Step
Microsoft Word 97 Step by Step

Step by Step books are also available for the Microsoft
Office 95 programs.

Catapult, Inc. & Microsoft Press

Microsoft Exchange 5.0 Step by Step has been created by the professional trainers and writers at Catapult, Inc., to the exacting standards you've come to expect from Microsoft Press. Together, we are pleased to present this self-paced training guide, which you can use individually or as part of a class.

Catapult, Inc., is a software training company with years of experience in PC and Macintosh instruction. Catapult's exclusive Performance-Based Training system is available in Catapult training centers across North America and at customer sites. Based on the principles of adult learning, Performance-Based Training ensures that students leave the classroom with confidence and the ability to apply skills to real-world scenarios. *Microsoft Exchange 5.0 Step by Step* incorporates Catapult's training expertise to ensure that you'll receive the maximum return on your training time. You'll focus on the skills that can increase your productivity the most while working at your own pace and convenience.

Microsoft Press is the book publishing division of Microsoft Corporation. The leading publisher of information about Microsoft products and services, Microsoft Press is dedicated to providing the highest quality computer books and multimedia training and reference tools that make using Microsoft software easier, more enjoyable, and more productive.

Table of Contents

*Quick*Look Guide xi

Finding Your Best Starting Point xv

Finding Your Best Starting Point in This Book xvi • What
Is Microsoft Exchange? xvii • What Is Electronic
Mail xviii • Corrections, Comments, and Help xix • Visit
Our World Wide Web Site xix

Installing and Using the Practice Files xxi

Using the Practice Files xxiii • Need Help with the
Practice Files? xxviii

Conventions and Features in This Book xxix

Conventions xxix • Other Features of This Book xxx

Part 1 Learning Messaging Basics

Lesson 1   Creating and Sending Messages 3

Working in the Viewer 5 • Creating and Addressing
Messages 6 • Sending Messages 10 • Adding Delivery
Options 16 • Editing Message Text 17 • Inserting Files in
Messages 21 • One Step Further: Sending a Blind Carbon
Copy 25 • Lesson Summary 27

Lesson 2   Processing Incoming Messages 29

Locating and Reading Messages 30 • Browsing Through
Messages 33 • Replying to Messages 35 • Forwarding
Messages 37 • Saving Attachments 38 • Deleting
Messages 39 • One Step Further: Saving the Address of the
Sender of an Incoming Message 40 • Lesson Summary 41

Lesson 3   Organizing Messages 43

Sorting Messages 44 • Working with Folders 46 •
Finding Specific Messages 49 • Printing Messages 52 •
One Step Further: Customizing Toolbars 53 • Lesson
Summary 55

Part 1   *Review & Practice*   57

Table of Contents

Part 2   **Increasing Your Productivity**

Lesson 4   **Automating Repetitive Tasks** 63

Grouping Messages 64 • Creating Custom Views 67 •
Processing Messages Using the Inbox Assistant 69 •
Inserting Text Automatically Using AutoSignature 72 •
One Step Further: Filtering Messages 75 • Lesson
Summary 77

Lesson 5   **Communicating Remotely** 79

Managing Messages Using the Out Of Office
Assistant 80 • Delegating Access to Another User 84 •
Working Offline 89 • One Step Further: Signing and
Sealing Messages 100 • Lesson Summary 105

Lesson 6   **Integrating with Microsoft Office** 107

Sending a Document to Another User 108 • Linking
Microsoft Excel Data to a Microsoft Word
Document 110 • Distributing a Document to Multiple
Users 113 • One Step Further: Modifying a Message
Template Using Microsoft Word 117 • Lesson
Summary 120

Part 2   Review & Practice   *123*

Part 3   **Extending Your Messaging Capabilities**

Lesson 7   **Customizing Forms** 129

Creating Forms by Using Sample Forms 130 • Installing a
Form 136 • One Step Further: Creating New Forms 138 •
Lesson Summary 141

Lesson 8   **Using Public Folders** 145

Viewing a Public Folder 146 • Creating a Public
Folder 149 • Posting Information in a Public
Folder 153 • Opening a Public Folder Quickly 160 • One
Step Further: Creating a Moderated Folder 161 • Lesson
Summary 163

Lesson 9   Connecting to Exchange Through a Web Browser **167**

Accessing Your Exchange Mailbox on the World Wide
Web 169 • Working with Public Folders on the World
Wide Web 179 • One Step Further: Using the Out Of Office
Assistant 182 • Lesson Summary 185

Part 3   Review & Practice   **187**

Part 4   Working with Microsoft Schedule+

Lesson 10   Organizing Your Personal Calendar **193**

Creating and Editing Appointments 194 • Adding
Events 204 • Printing Schedules 205 • Customizing
Schedule+ Options 206 • One Step Further: Preparing a
Schedule for Viewing on the World Wide Web 208 •
Lesson Summary 210

Lesson 11   Managing Tasks **213**

Creating a To Do List 214 • Organizing Tasks 218 •
Creating Your Contact List 221 • One Step Further:
Creating a Recurring Task 227 • Lesson Summary 229

Lesson 12   Planning Meetings **233**

Viewing Your Schedule in the Planner 234 • Setting Up
Meetings 236 • One Step Further: Viewing Your Mail from
Schedule+ 245 • Lesson Summary 246

Part 4   Review & Practice   **249**

Appendix

Additional Configurations and Setups **257**

Using Exchange with a Different Configuration 258 •
Additional Setup Procedures 259

Glossary **263**

Index **271**

QuickLook Guide

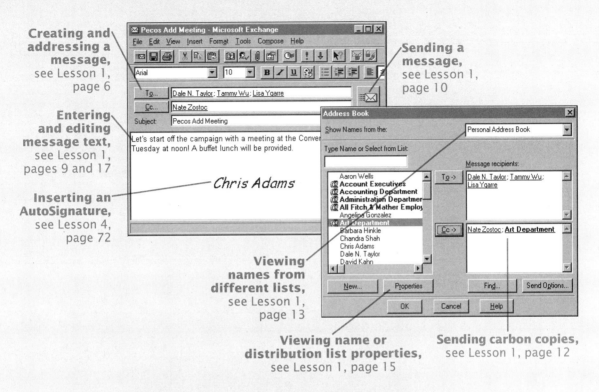

Creating and addressing a message, see Lesson 1, page 6

Entering and editing message text, see Lesson 1, pages 9 and 17

Inserting an AutoSignature, see Lesson 4, page 72

Sending a message, see Lesson 1, page 10

Viewing names from different lists, see Lesson 1, page 13

Viewing name or distribution list properties, see Lesson 1, page 15

Sending carbon copies, see Lesson 1, page 12

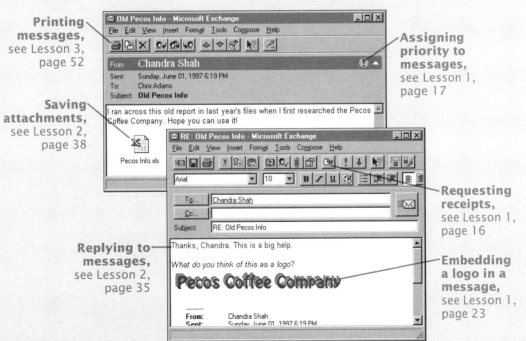

Printing messages, see Lesson 3, page 52

Saving attachments, see Lesson 2, page 38

Replying to messages, see Lesson 2, page 35

Assigning priority to messages, see Lesson 1, page 17

Requesting receipts, see Lesson 1, page 16

Embedding a logo in a message, see Lesson 1, page 23

Viewing mail using your Web browser, see Lesson 9, page 169

Deleting messages, see Lesson 2, page 39

Working with folders, see Lesson 3, page 46

Creating a personal view, see Lesson 4, page 68

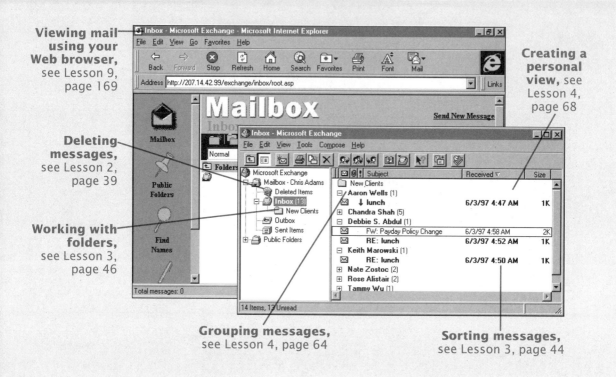

Grouping messages, see Lesson 4, page 64

Sorting messages, see Lesson 3, page 44

Using Remote Mail to view a list of messages, see Lesson 5, page 93

Marking messages for action while working offline, see Lesson 5, page 96

Creating an automatic reply, see Lesson 5, page 81

Managing messages using the Out Of Office Assistant, see Lesson 5, page 80

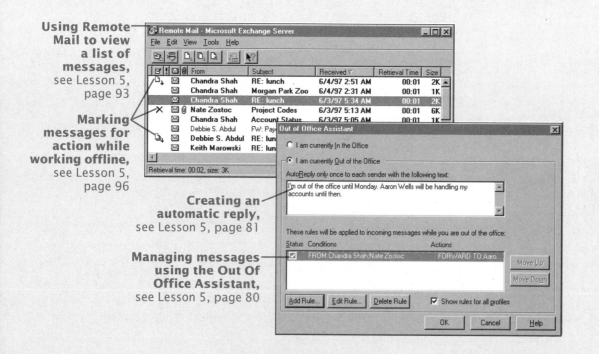

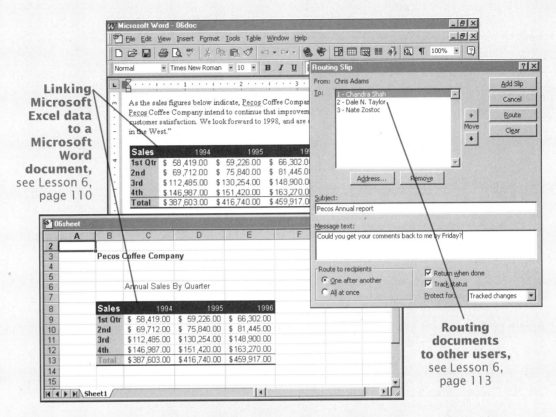

Linking Microsoft Excel data to a Microsoft Word document, see Lesson 6, page 110

Routing documents to other users, see Lesson 6, page 113

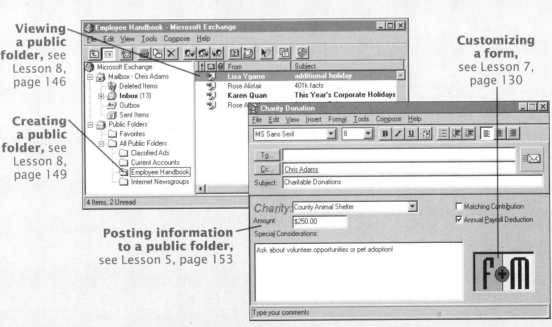

Viewing a public folder, see Lesson 8, page 146

Creating a public folder, see Lesson 8, page 149

Customizing a form, see Lesson 7, page 130

Posting information to a public folder, see Lesson 5, page 153

*Quick*Look Guide

Recording information about personal and business contacts, see Lesson 11, page 223

Setting recurring appointments, see Lesson 10, page 200

Recording events, see Lesson 10, page 204

Creating and editing appointments, see Lesson 10, page 194

Creating a To Do List and organizing tasks, see Lesson 11, pages 214 and 218

Creating tentative and private appointments, see Lesson 10, page 202

Viewing schedules in the Planner, see Lesson 12, page 234

Scheduling meetings with the Planner, see Lesson 12, page 236

Requesting a meeting, see Lesson 12, page 240

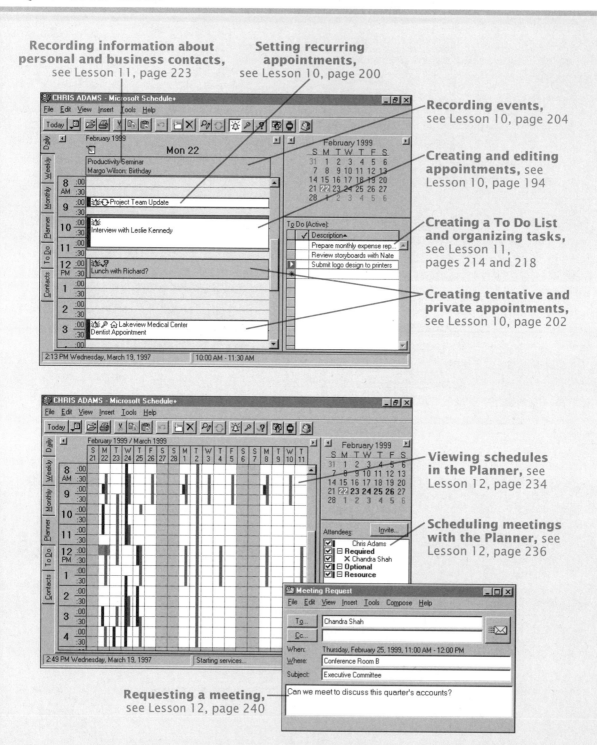

xiv

Finding Your Best Starting Point

Microsoft Exchange 5.0 is a powerful messaging program that you can use to efficiently plan, schedule, organize, and communicate information. *Microsoft Exchange 5.0 Step by Step* shows you how to use Microsoft Exchange to simplify your work and increase your productivity. With this book, you can learn Microsoft Exchange at your own pace and at your own convenience or you can use it in a classroom setting.

 IMPORTANT   This book is designed for use with Microsoft Exchange 5.0 for the Windows 95 and Windows NT version 4.0 operating systems. The Exchange 5.0 Client and Exchange 5.0 Server business communications software are vastly different and more full-featured than the Microsoft Exchange for Windows 95 or Windows NT client that is included with the operating system. When we use the term "Exchange" in this book, we are referring to the Exchange 5.0 Client connected to an Exchange 5.0 Server that is functioning as your mail server.

To find out what software you're running, you can check the product package or you can start Exchange, click the Help menu at the top of the screen, and click About Microsoft Exchange. If your software is not compatible with this book, a Step by Step book for your software is probably available. Many of the Step by Step titles are listed on the second page of this book. If the book you want isn't listed, please visit our World Wide Web site at http://mspress.microsoft.com or call 1-800-MSPRESS for more information.

Finding Your Best Starting Point in This Book

This book is designed for readers learning Microsoft Exchange for the first time and for more experienced readers who want to learn and use the new features in Exchange. Use the following table to find your best starting point in this book.

If you are	Follow these steps
Switching... from Lotus Notes from Lotus Organizer	1 Install the practice files as described in "Installing and Using the Practice Files." 2 Learn basic skills for using Microsoft Exchange by working through Lessons 1 through 3. Then you can work through Lessons 4 through 12 in any order. To work through Lessons 4 through 12, you must be using Exchange 5.0 with a Microsoft Exchange Server.

If you are	Follow these steps
Upgrading... from Microsoft Mail from Microsoft Exchange 4.0	1 Install the practice files as described in "Installing and Using the Practice Files." 2 Complete the lessons that cover the topics you need. You can use the table of contents and the *Quick*Look Guide to locate information about general topics. You can use the index to find information about a specific topic or feature.

If you are	Follow these steps
Referencing... this book after working through the lessons	1 Use the index to locate information about specific topics, and use the table of contents and the *Quick*Look Guide to locate information about general topics. 2 Read the Lesson Summary at the end of each lesson for a brief review of the major tasks in the lesson. The Lesson Summary topics are listed in the same order as they are presented in the lesson.

What Is Microsoft Exchange?

With Microsoft Exchange, it's easy to communicate information quickly to others in your organization. For example, if you want to give your co-worker a memo, you could print the memo, and then leave it on her desk. If your co-worker is in another building or a branch office, you could fax the memo to her. However, if you use Microsoft Exchange you can send the memo as electronic mail, called e-mail, without leaving your computer. In addition, you can receive e-mail and faxes from your co-workers directly on your computer. Exchange is a powerful messaging program used not only for e-mail, but for scheduling, document sharing, conferencing, and other forms of electronic groupware communication.

More and more companies are efficiently communicating and gathering information online. Exchange is designed to keep you connected with other people, especially within your company. With Exchange and a modem with a phone line, you can use your mailbox to organize and access all your messages and faxes in one convenient location, regardless of the messaging programs used to create and send them. In addition, you can use Exchange to share information with other people by using public folders.

The collection of computers known as a Microsoft Exchange *enterprise* is made up of *client* computers, a *domain server* computer, and a *Microsoft Exchange Server*. The minimum configuration for an enterprise is a client, a domain server, and a Microsoft Exchange Server, although the domain server and the Exchange Server can be the same computer, as is the case in the following illustration.

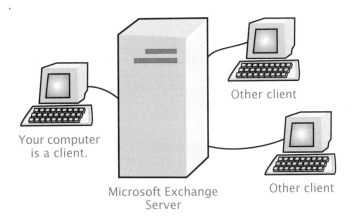

Your computer is a client.

Microsoft Exchange Server

Other client

Other client

This client/server messaging system provides workgroups, such as an organization, with a method for accessing and exchanging information using programs such as Exchange and Schedule+. A system administrator installs and configures the Exchange Server and adds new users.

What Is Electronic Mail?

Electronic mail, or *e-mail*, is your computer's version of the postal service or interoffice mail. Instead of hand-delivering printed documents, you send the information online, through the network, to other computer users. With e-mail, you can send messages to and receive messages from other people who have access to an e-mail service.

The Windows NT-based Exchange Server acts as a post office, containing all user mailboxes and handling messages. Messages you receive are stored on the Exchange Server and appear in your own electronic mailbox on the Exchange Server. The following illustration shows how the Microsoft Exchange Server connects your mailbox to other mailboxes.

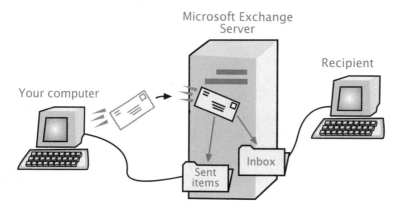

When you send a message, a copy of your message is stored on the Microsoft Exchange Server. A pointer to the message is placed in each recipient's Inbox and in your Sent Items folder.

With Exchange, you are not limited to just text in your messages—documents, video, sound, and graphic images can be inserted in your messages or sent directly as separate files. You can send carbon copies of your messages or forward them to other people. When you receive a message from another person, you can reply to it, forward it, or delete it; you can also have Exchange do this for you automatically.

Corrections, Comments, and Help

Every effort has been made to ensure the accuracy of this book and the contents of the practice files disk. Microsoft Press provides corrections and additional content for its books through the World Wide Web at:

http://mspress.microsoft.com/support

If you have comments, questions, or ideas regarding this book or the practice files disk, please send them to us.

Send e-mail to:

mspinput@microsoft.com

Or send postal mail to:

Microsoft Press

Attn: Step by Step Series Editor

One Microsoft Way

Redmond, WA 98052-6399

Please note that support for the Microsoft Exchange software product itself is not offered through the above addresses. For help using Exchange, you can call Microsoft Technical Support at 1-800-936-5900 on weekdays between 6 a.m. and 6 p.m. Pacific time.

Visit Our World Wide Web Site

We invite you to visit the Microsoft Press World Wide Web site. You can visit us at the following location:

http://mspress.microsoft.com

You'll find descriptions for all of our books, information about ordering titles, notice of special features and events, additional content for Microsoft Press books, and much more.

You can also find out the latest in software developments and news from Microsoft Corporation by visiting the following World Wide Web site:

http://microsoft.com

We look forward to your visit on the Web!

Installing and Using the Practice Files

The disk inside the back cover of this book contains practice files that you'll use as you perform the exercises in the book. For example, when you're learning how to read and organize your e-mail, you'll move several of the practice files—in this case, sample e-mail messages—into your Inbox, and then open, read, and respond to them. By using the practice files, you won't waste time creating the samples used in the lessons—instead, you can concentrate on learning how to use Microsoft Exchange. With the files and the step-by-step instructions in the lessons, you'll also learn by doing, which is an easy and effective way to acquire and remember new skills.

IMPORTANT   Before you break the seal on the practice disk package, be sure that this book matches your version of the software. This book is designed for use with Microsoft Exchange 5.0 for the Windows 95 and Windows NT version 4.0 operating systems.

To find out what software you're running, you can check the product package or start the program, and then on the Help menu at the top of the screen, click About Microsoft Exchange. If your program is not compatible with this book, a Step by Step book matching your product is probably available. For a complete list of our books, please visit our World Wide Web site at http://mspress.microsoft.com or call 1-800-MSPRESS for more information.

Microsoft Exchange 5.0 Step by Step

Install the practice files on your computer

Follow these steps to install the practice files on your computer's hard disk so that you can use them with the exercises in this book.

1   If your computer isn't on, turn it on now.

2   If you're using Windows NT, press CTRL+ALT+DEL to display a dialog box asking for your username and password. If you are using Windows 95, you will see this dialog box if your computer is connected to a network.

3   Type your username and password in the appropriate boxes, and then click OK. If you see the Welcome dialog box, click the Close button.

4   Remove the disk from the package inside the back cover of this book.

5   Insert the disk in drive A or drive B of your computer.

6   On the task bar at the bottom of your screen, click the Start button.

    The Start menu appears.

Click Start...   ...and then click Run.

7   On the Start menu, click Run.

    The Run dialog box appears.

8   In the Open box, type **a:setup** (or **b:setup** if the disk is in drive B). Don't add spaces as you type.

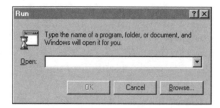

9   Click OK, and then follow the instructions on the screen.

    The setup program window appears with recommended options preselected for you. For best results in using the practice files with this book, accept these preselected settings.

xxii

10 When the files have been installed, remove the disk from your drive and replace it in the package inside the back cover of the book.

A folder called Exchange 5.0 SBS Practice has been created on your hard disk, and the practice files have been put in that folder.

Microsoft
Press
Welcome

Camcorder
Files On The
Internet

NOTE In addition to installing the practice files, the Setup program has created two shortcuts on your Desktop. If your computer is set up to connect to the Internet, you can double-click the Microsoft Press Welcome shortcut to visit the Microsoft Press Web site. You can also connect to this Web site directly at http://mspress.microsoft.com

You can double-click the Camcorder Files On The Internet shortcut to connect to the *Microsoft Exchange 5.0 Step by Step* Camcorder files Web page. This page contains audiovisual demonstrations of how to do a number of tasks in Exchange, which you can copy to your computer for viewing. You can connect to this Web site directly at http://mspress.microsoft.com/products/1417/

Using the Practice Files

The lessons in this book are built around a scenario that simulates a real work environment, so you can easily apply the skills you learn to your own work. For this scenario, imagine that you're Chris Adams, an account executive at the Fitch & Mather advertising agency. You are currently starting to work on an advertising campaign for your newest client, the Pecos Coffee Company. Some of your tasks include communicating with your clients, as well as with the creative director, the media planner, and others on your team—such as graphic artists and copy writers.

You'll use Exchange to send messages and communicate within the corporate office. You'll use Microsoft Schedule+ to create and send schedules and other important information throughout the agency and to your clients at the Pecos Coffee Company.

The screen illustrations in this book might look different than what you see on your computer, depending on how your computer has been set up and because you will be using your own mailbox.

Creating a Profile

Before you can start using Exchange, you must have a user profile. Your profile contains information about customized options that you can use while you are working in Exchange, including your password and a list of available information services. Your default profile will probably be set up for you by your system administrator.

Before you begin, it is strongly recommended that you perform the following steps to create an additional profile for a fictitious person, Chris Adams. Creating this profile will give you a clean environment in which you can practice performing tasks. In addition, what you see on your screen will more closely match the illustrations in this book as you work through the lessons.

Create a practice profile

Mail And Fax

1   Click the Start button, point to Settings, and then click Control Panel.

2   Double-click the Mail And Fax icon.

3   On the Services tab, be sure that Microsoft Exchange Server is selected, and then click the Show Profiles button

    The Mail and Fax dialog box appears.

4   Click Add.

    The Inbox Setup Wizard starts.

5   Be sure that the Use the Following Information Services option button is selected, and then verify that only the Microsoft Exchange Server check box is selected.

    Microsoft Exchange Server should be the only information service selected for the purposes of this book. If any other check boxes are selected, clear them.

6   Click Next.

7   In the Profile Name box, type **Chris Adams** and then click Next.

If you are not sure of the name of your Microsoft Exchange Server, ask your system administrator.

8   Type the name of your Microsoft Exchange Server, and then press TAB.

9   In the Mailbox box, type your username, and then click Next.

    You are asked if you travel with your computer.

10   Verify that the No option button is selected, and then click Next.

    You are prompted to select a personal address book.

Create a practice personal address book

1   Select the word "mail" in mailbox.pab, and then type **chrisa**

    Chrisabox.pab is the practice personal address book.

2   Click Next. Be sure that the Do Not Add Inbox To The StartUp Group option button is selected, and click Next.

    Microsoft Exchange will not be started automatically when you start Windows 95 or Windows NT.

3   Click Finish.

    The practice profile and personal address book for Chris Adams are created.

4   Close all the open dialog boxes and windows.

> **NOTE**   After you have completed the lessons in this book, you can remove the Chris Adams profile and the personal address book by following the steps in "Uninstalling the Practice Files," later in this section.

Change your mailbox profile settings

Inbox

1   On the Desktop, double-click the Inbox icon.

Microsoft Exchange starts.

2   On the Tools menu, click Options.

The Options dialog box appears.

3   On the General tab, click the Prompt For A Profile To Be Used option button, and then click OK.

Every time you log on to Microsoft Exchange, you will be prompted to select a profile.

4   On the file menu, click Exit And Log Off.

Microsoft Exchange closes and you are logged off.

Importing the Personal Address Book

Before you start Lesson 1, you must import a personal address book from the practice disk. It includes employees of the fictional company Fitch & Mather and will serve as Chris Adams' personal address book. Importing the address book will allow you to work through the lessons in this book without having to modify the list of users in your own Address Book. In this book, you will use both this imported personal address book and your own company's global address list to simulate sending the interoffice messages as Chris Adams.

Log on to Microsoft Exchange

Because personal address books are not stored on the Microsoft Exchange Server, you need to log on to Exchange using the Chris Adams profile before you can import the personal address book.

1   On the Desktop, double-click the Inbox icon.

Microsoft Exchange starts. The Choose Profile dialog box appears.

2   Click the Profile Name down arrow, and then click Chris Adams.

3   Click OK, and be sure that the Inbox folder is open.

Import the practice personal address book

Follow these steps to copy the practice personal address book to your computer's hard disk so that you can use it with the lessons.

1   On the File menu, click Import.

2   Click the Look In down arrow, and then click drive C.

3   Double-click the Exchange 5.0 SBS Practice folder.

4   Click sbs.pab, click Open, and then click OK.

   The personal address book is imported into Chris Adams' mailbox.

5   Click OK.

6   On the File menu, click Exit And Log Off.

   Microsoft Exchange closes and you are logged off.

 IMPORTANT   Keep in mind that as you work through the lessons, you will receive Undelivered Receipts when you send messages to the fictitious users from the imported personal address book.

Importing the Schedule+ Contact List

Before you start Lesson 11, you need to import the Schedule+ Contact List from the practice disk. This list contains contact information that you view and modify in the "Adding Contacts" section of Lesson 11.

Start Schedule+

If Exchange is already running, the Choose Profile dialog box will not appear.

1   Click Start, point to Programs, and then click Microsoft Schedule+.

   The Choose Profile dialog box appears.

2   Click the down arrow, click Chris Adams, and then click OK.

   The Microsoft Schedule+ dialog box appears if you have not used Schedule+ before. The I Want To Create A New Schedule File option button is selected.

3   Click OK.

   The Select Local Schedule dialog box appears. The Schedule folder appears automatically in the Save In box.

4   In the File Name box, type your name, and then click Save.

   A Schedule+ file with your name opens. The current date appears in the Daily view.

5   Click the Contacts tab.

Import the practice Schedule+ Contact List

1   On the File menu, point to Import, and then click Schedule+ Interchange.

    The Import Schedule+ Interchange dialog box appears.

2   Click the Look In down arrow, and then click drive C.

3   Double-click the Exchange 5.0 SBS Practice folder, and then double-click the Lesson 11 folder.

4   Click Lesson 11, and then click Open.

    The practice Contact List is imported into your Schedule+ file.

5   On the File menu, click Exit And Log Off.

    If a dialog box appears, click Yes.

Start Microsoft Exchange

1   On the Desktop, double-click the Inbox icon.

    Microsoft Exchange starts. The Choose Profile dialog box appears.

2   Click the Profile Name down arrow, and then click Chris Adams.

    For the purposes of this book, you use the profile for Chris Adams that you created earlier in this section.

3   Click OK, and then be sure that the Inbox folder is open.

    The Viewer window appears.

Uninstalling the Practice Files

After you have completed the lessons in this book, you can remove the practice files.

Uninstall the practice files

In this exercise you delete the Exchange 5.0 SBS practice files. If you want to work through the lessons in this book again, you can reinstall the file from the practice disk inside the back cover of this book.

1   Click Start, point to Settings, and then click Control Panel.

2   Double-click the Add/Remove Programs icon.

3   Select Microsoft Exchange 5.0 Step by Step from the list, and then click Add/Remove.

    A confirmation message appears.

4   Click Yes.

    The practice files are uninstalled.

5   Click OK to close the Add/Remove Programs Properties dialog box.

6   Close the Control Panel window.

Need Help with the Practice Files?

Every effort has been made to ensure the accuracy of this book and the contents of the practice files disk. If you do run into a problem, Microsoft Press provides corrections for its books through the World Wide Web at:

http://mspress.microsoft.com/support

We also invite you to visit our main Web page at:

http://mspress.microsoft.com

You'll find descriptions for all of our books, information about ordering titles, notices of special features and events, additional content for Microsoft Press books, and much more.

Conventions
and Features
in This Book

You can save time when you use this book by understanding, before you start the lessons, how instructions, keys to press, and so on are shown in the book. Please take a moment to read the following list, which also points out helpful features of this book.

Conventions

■ Hands-on exercises for you to follow are given in numbered lists of steps (1, 2, and so on). An arrowhead bullet (➤) indicates an exercise that has only one step.

■ Text that you are to type appears in **bold**.

■ A plus sign (+) between two key names means that you must press those keys at the same time. For example, "Press ALT+TAB" means that you need to hold down the ALT key while you press TAB.

The icons on the next page identify the different types of supplementary material.

	Note labeled	Alerts you to
	Note	Additional information for a step.
	Tip	Suggested additional methods for a step or helpful hints.

Note labeled	Alerts you to
Important	Essential information that you should read before continuing with the lesson.
Troubleshooting	Possible error messages or computer difficulties and their solutions.
Warning	Possible data loss and tells you how to proceed safely.
Demonstration	Skills that are demonstrated in audio-visual files available on the World Wide Web.

Other Features of This Book

- You can learn about techniques that build on what you learned by trying the optional One Step Further exercise at the end of each lesson.

- You can get a quick reminder of how to perform the tasks you learned by reading the Lesson Summary at the end of each lesson.

- You can quickly determine what online Help topics are available for additional information by referring to the Help topics listed at the end of each lesson. The Help system provides a complete online reference to Microsoft Exchange.

- You can practice the major skills presented in the lessons by working through the Review & Practice section at the end of each part.

- If you have Web browser software and access to the World Wide Web, you can view audiovisual demonstrations of how to perform some of the more complicated tasks in Exchange by downloading supplementary files from the Web. Double-click the Camcorder Files On The Internet shortcut that was created on your Desktop when you installed the practice files for this book, or connect directly to http://mspress.microsoft.com/products/1417/. The Web page that opens contains full instructions for copying and viewing the demonstration files.

Part 1

Learning Messaging Basics

Lesson 1
Creating and Sending Messages   3

Lesson 2
Processing Incoming Messages   29

Lesson 3
Organizing Messages   43

Review & Practice   57

Creating and Sending Messages

Estimated time
30 min.

In this lesson you will learn how to:

- Create and address messages.
- Enter and edit message text.
- Attach files to messages.
- Send messages.

Using Microsoft Exchange, it's easy to communicate and exchange information with others in your organization. For example, if you want to give one of your co-workers a memo, you could print the memo and leave it on her desk. If she's in another building, you could fax it to her. However, if you use Exchange, you can send the memo via electronic mail, called *e-mail,* without leaving your computer. Similarly, you can receive e-mail from your co-workers directly on your computer.

Sending your messages using e-mail has many advantages over other forms of communication. You can use e-mail for anything that you might use paper mail or the telephone for, such as sending reports, new hire announcements, or correspondence regarding a project. If you need to send copies of a message to other people, you can easily add more recipients to your message or forward it to others. Sending e-mail messages is the quickest way to communicate—after a message is sent, the recipient gets it in seconds or minutes, depending on the speed at which it is processed. Because you send e-mail over a network of computers, you can communicate online exclusively, saving time and paper.

To learn more about using other Internet service providers, see Appendix B.

You can exchange e-mail with others in your organization as well as send messages to and receive messages from people all over the world using the *Internet*. The Internet is a vast system of linked computers, a worldwide "network of networks" that connects educational institutions, research organizations, businesses, government entities, and millions of private individuals. E-mail is the most commonly used service of the Internet, allowing people to exchange messages with others who use e-mail. Anyone with a computer, and a modem or access to a network can send e-mail across the Internet through an Internet service provider, such as The Microsoft Network (MSN). Internet access providers supply the link between the Internet user and the Internet supercomputers.

Companies often use a smaller, private *intranet* to distribute and share information with only the people in their organization. Using an intranet is similar to working across the Internet, except that only authorized personnel can use it. Certain types of information, such as employee mailboxes, are protected by a password or other security measures to ensure that only authorized users can view their contents.

IMPORTANT   The exercises in this lesson assume that a mailbox has been set up for you by your system administrator, if you are on a network.

Setting the Scene

You are an account executive who has just landed a new account, the Pecos Coffee Company, and need to start communicating with your client and co-workers. Now that your company, the Fitch & Mather advertising agency, has upgraded everyone's operating system to Microsoft Windows 95 or Microsoft Windows NT version 4.0, you want to start using Exchange 5.0 to send information efficiently. In this lesson, you'll learn how to create, address, and send e-mail messages to others within your company as well as how to send e-mail externally using the Internet.

Before you begin working through this lesson, you'll start Exchange and choose the Chris Adams profile. You can also use Exchange without a profile or with another profile, but it is recommended that you use the Chris Adams profile so that the exercises and illustrations in this book will match what you see on your screen.

IMPORTANT   If you haven't imported the personal address book or created the Chris Adams profile yet, refer to "Installing and Using the Practice Files," earlier in this book. If you don't know your Microsoft Exchange username or password, contact your system administrator for further help.

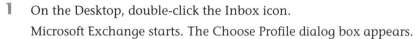

Start Microsoft Exchange

Inbox

1 On the Desktop, double-click the Inbox icon.

Microsoft Exchange starts. The Choose Profile dialog box appears.

2 Click the down arrow, and then click Chris Adams.

For the purposes of this book, you'll use the Chris Adams profile.

3 Click OK, and then be sure that the Inbox folder is open.

The Viewer window opens. If you see folders in the left half of the Viewer, skip step 4. If you do not see the Viewer toolbar, on the View menu, click Toolbar.

*Show/Hide
Folder List*

4 On the Viewer toolbar, click the Show/Hide Folder List button.

The built-in folders appear. You are ready to start this lesson.

Working in the Viewer

After you start Microsoft Exchange, the *Viewer* window appears. The Viewer is the central location from which you send, receive, and organize your messages. The left half of Viewer (the *folder list*) contains an alphabetical list of available folders, and the right half (the *folder contents list*) displays the contents of each folder, including messages and subfolders. If a folder contains messages, the number of unread items appears to the right of the folder name and the total number of items appears on the status bar.

By default, the first time you start Exchange, the Inbox folder is open. This folder contains messages sent to you by other users. Unread messages appear in bold type while messages that have been read appear in normal type. Additionally, a number of folders are built in. The following table des-cribes built-in folders that are automatically created for each mailbox.

Folder	Description
Deleted Items	Temporarily stores the messages that you delete until you permanently delete them or quit Exchange.
Inbox	Stores the messages you receive.
Outbox	Temporarily holds messages that you send until they are delivered to recipients.
Sent Items	Stores copies of the messages you have sent.

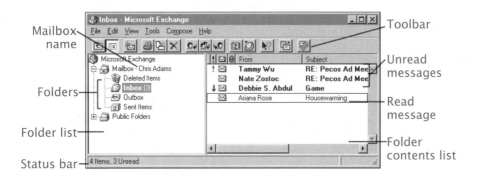

Mailbox name — Toolbar

Folders

Folder list

Status bar

Unread messages

Read message

Folder contents list

Creating and Addressing Messages

When you want to send a message using Exchange, you begin by creating a new message. When you click the New Message button, a blank form called the *New Message form* appears. This form serves as a template to help you compose your message and identify the recipients.

Create a message

In this exercise, you create an e-mail message.

New Message

You can also click New Message on the Compose menu.

1 On the Viewer toolbar, click the New Message button.

   A blank message appears.

2 On the View menu, click Toolbar.

   The New Message toolbar appears. Your message should look similar to the following illustration.

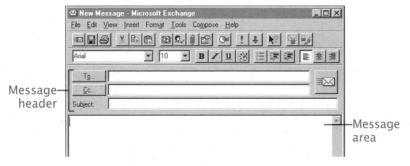

Message header

Message area

NOTE To match the illustrations in this book, be sure that you are not using Microsoft Word as your e-mail editor. To do this, on the Compose menu, click WordMail Options, and then clear the Enable Word As E-Mail Editor check box.

Addressing Messages Using the Global Address List

Before you start writing the text of your message, you address it by entering recipient names in the To area located at the top of the *message header*. This is similar to a traditional memo where the recipients are identified at the top. In Exchange, you use the *Address Book* to find all users to whom you can send messages and identify the recipients of your messages. Within the Address Book are address lists—you have at least two address lists: the global address list and your personal address book.

The *global address list* contains a directory of all users in your company or organization. All the users in an organization make up a *Microsoft Exchange enterprise*. For example, at Fitch & Mather, all the employees are listed in the global address list, including out-of-state employees. Every user in your company has access to the global address list, but depending on how your mailbox is configured, your global address list might look different from other users'. The system administrator creates and maintains the global address list for your enterprise.

The New Message form contains several blank boxes that you fill in with information. Information is required in some of these boxes, such as the To box, while information is optional in others, such as the Subject box. Although the Subject box is optional, typing a subject line helps the recipient quickly identify the contents of your message.

You can address a message in two ways. You can click either the Address Book button or the To and Cc buttons located next to each box, and then select names from the list of possible recipients. You can also address a message by typing names directly into the box and separating each name with a semicolon (;). If you type the names, they are automatically checked against the Address Book before the message is sent.

 TIP   If you address your message by typing recipients' names, you can manually verify the names before you send your message. To do this, click the Check Names button on the New Message Form toolbar. If a name was typed incorrectly or isn't recognized, or if more than one name matches the one you typed, you are prompted to select the correct name or to create a new address.

Address a message using the global address list

In this exercise, you open the Address Book to find your own name in your organization's global address list, and then add yourself as the recipient of the message you're creating. Although you would not normally send a message to yourself, this will give you a chance to practice sending a message.

NOTE If you are using the standard Exchange client that comes with Windows 95 and your global address list is empty, select any name from the practice personal address book or create a new entry. However, the message will be returned as undeliverable because the name of the recipient is ficticious.

1 Click the To button.

The Address Book dialog box appears. The names of people in your organization appear in the global address list; therefore, your Address Book dialog box will look different from the following illustration.

If you type the first few letters of a name here, the Address Book automatically moves to that name.

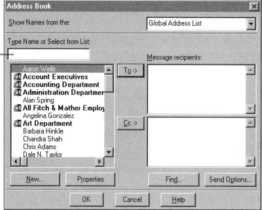

2 Scroll to locate your name, click your name, and then click To.

3 Click OK.

Your message reappears with your name in the To box. Your message should look similar to the following illustration.

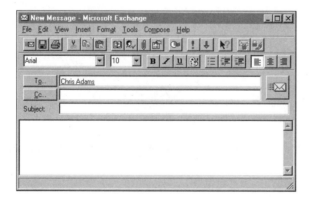

TIP If you are using the Exchange 5.0 client, you can view your mailbox name and Internet address. To do this, click your name in the global address list, click Properties, and then click the E-mail Addresses tab. The SMTP (Simple Mail Transport Protocol) address is the format commonly used on the Internet, such as chrisa@fitch&mather.com.

Entering Message Text

Now that you have identified the recipient of your message, you are ready to enter the subject and type the text in the message area. The topic of e-mail messages is summarized in the Subject box to help recipients classify and organize their messages.

Enter the message text

In this exercise, you type the subject of your message, and then add the main text of the message.

 IMPORTANT If you make a mistake while typing, you can click Undo on the Edit menu to delete what you typed or undo any formatting.

1 Click in the Subject box.

2 Type **Congratulations** and then press TAB.

Pressing TAB moves the insertion point to the next box.

3 Type **I can now send messages!**

Your message should look similar to the following illustration.

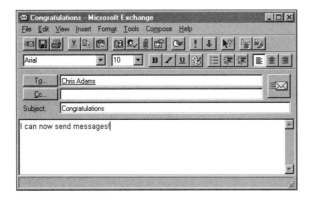

Sending Messages

Now that you have addressed and composed a message, you are ready to send it. When you *send* a message, it is moved to the Outbox, where it is temporarily stored until it's delivered. It isn't necessary for a recipient to be present when the message is received; the message is stored in the recipient's mailbox until he or she starts Exchange. If your e-mail cannot be delivered because of a network problem or incorrect address, you will receive a notification message.

Send a message

In this exercise, you send the message you just composed.

 NOTE   If you are not using the Exchange 5.0 Client, the New Message form will not contain a second, larger Send button on the right half of the form in addition to the one located on the New Message Form toolbar.

Send

The name appearing in the From column will be your mailbox name.

> On the New Message Form toolbar, click the Send button.
>
> After a few moments, a copy of your message is placed in the Sent Items folder, and your message is delivered to your Inbox. When you receive a new message, a message icon appears on the taskbar. You will learn how to open and read messages in Lesson 2. Your Viewer window should look similar to the following illustration.

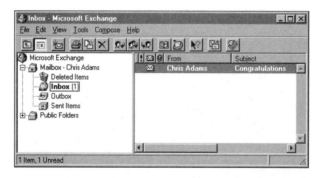

 TIP   If you accidentally click the Send button and don't want to send the message after all, quickly double-click the Outbox folder, and then double-click the message, if it has not already been delivered.

Using Your Personal Address Book

In addition to your organization's global address list, your Address Book contains a *personal address book* (PAB). If you regularly send messages to someone who isn't listed on the global address list, you can add that person's name and address to your personal address book. For example, if you communicate with people outside of your company, such as clients, you can add their addresses to your personal address book. Because only you have access to your personal address book, you create and maintain it.

As an account executive, you have to communicate with your clients and team members, such as the graphic artist and the copywriter who work on the creative materials. You are planning a meeting to introduce your team members to your new client, the Pecos Coffee Company. You need to give everyone advance notice of the meeting, and an e-mail message is the quickest way to accomplish this.

Address a message using your personal address book

Now that you know how to create and send messages, you use your personal address book to address your message to the members of your team at Fitch & Mather.

 IMPORTANT Your imported personal address book contains names of employees at the fictional Fitch & Mather agency. Throughout the lessons in this book, you'll be instructed to select names from this personal address book, instead of the global address list. However, if you were actually working at Fitch & Mather, you would select names from the global address list.

New Message

You can also click the Address Book button on the New Message Form toolbar.

Multiple recipients are separated by a semicolon.

1 On the Viewer toolbar, click the New Message button.

   A blank message appears.

2 Click the To button.

   The Address Book dialog box appears. By default, the names in the global address list are listed.

3 In the upper-right corner of the Address Book dialog box, click the Show Names From The down arrow, and then click Personal Address Book.

   Names from the practice personal address book you imported are shown.

4 Click Dale N. Taylor, and then click To.

5 Scroll downward, click Tammy Wu, and then click To.

   Your message will be sent to Dale N. Taylor, the graphic artist, and Tammy Wu, the copywriter. The Address Book dialog box should look similar to the following illustration.

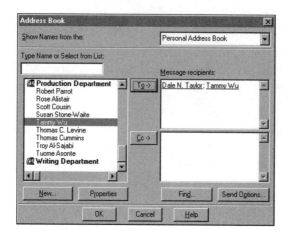

6   Click OK.

Your message reappears with the names you selected in the To box.

Sending Messages to Multiple Recipients Using Carbon Copies

A carbon copy (cc) is also known as a courtesy copy.

Now that your message is addressed to the principal recipients who will attend the Pecos Coffee Company meeting, you can easily send additional copies, called *carbon copies*, of the message to additional people who should be informed of the meeting, but whose presence is not required.

Send a carbon copy

In this exercise, you send a carbon copy of your message to the creative director and the media planner so that they are aware of your meeting with Pecos Coffee Company.

1   Click the Cc button.

The Address Book dialog box appears.

2   Click the Show Names From The down arrow, and then click Personal Address Book.

3   Click Lisa Ygarre, and then click Cc.

4   Click Nate Zostoc, and then click Cc.

A carbon copy of the message will be sent to Lisa Ygarre, the media planner, and Nate Zostoc, the creative director.

5   Click OK.

The New Message form reappears with the names you selected in the Cc box.

Sending Messages to Multiple Recipients Using Distribution Lists

If you frequently send messages to a group of people, such as a work team or a committee, you can use a *distribution list* from your Address Book to reach all the recipients at once rather than selecting or typing each person's name. There are two kinds of distribution lists. A distribution list (DL) is created for use by an entire organization. A *personal distribution list* (PDL) is created by an individual for personal use.

Distribution lists are identified by bold type and appear only in your organization's global address list. To view the names of all the people included in a particular distribution list, you can select the distribution list name and view the properties. Distribution lists are created and maintained by your system administrator. For example, the system administrator at Fitch & Mather created a distribution list called "Account Executives" so that anyone in the company who wants to e-mail all the account executives at once can simply address their message using this distribution list.

You can create your own personal distribution lists, which are stored and appear only in your personal address book. As the owner, you create, maintain, and delete your own personal distribution lists as well as add and remove members. Personal distribution lists appear in bold type in your personal address book.

Entries in your personal address book can include recipients who use other e-mail or messaging systems, such as Microsoft Internet Mail or CompuServe. The most common way to send e-mail to someone outside of your company is through the Internet.

Use a distribution list

In this exercise, you send a copy of the message to the Art Department distribution list so that all the copywriters and graphic artists at Fitch & Mather will be informed of the Pecos Coffee Company meeting.

1   Click the Cc button.

    The Address Book dialog box appears.

2   Click the Show Names From The down arrow, and then click Personal Address Book.

Distribution lists appear in bold with an icon to the left of their name.

3   Click the Art Department distribution list, and then click Cc.

    The distribution list you selected appears in the Cc box.

NOTE   Some people to whom you have addressed the message are also part of the Art Department distribution list, but they will only receive one copy of your message because Exchange recognizes the duplication.

Create a personal distribution list

For the meeting, you also need to invite your clients, the owners of the Pecos Coffee Company, Hazel and Joe Pecos. In this exercise, you create a personal distribution list.

1 In the Address Book dialog box, click New.

The New Entry dialog box appears.

2 Under Select The Entry Type, click Personal Distribution List.

3 Under Put This Entry, be sure that Personal Address Book is selected, and then click OK.

The New Personal Distribution List Properties dialog box appears.

4 In the Name box, type **Pecos Coffee Company**

"Pecos Coffee Company" will be the name of this personal distribution list.

Add members to a personal distribution list

In this exercise, you add members to the Pecos Coffee Company personal distribution list.

 NOTE   The Internet addresses that you will be entering in the following exercises are fictitious. Your messages will be returned to you as undeliverable. If you have an Internet address and want to try sending e-mail over the Internet, try using your own Internet address. If you are not sure whether or not you are connected to the Internet, contact your system administrator.

1 In the New Personal Distribution List Members dialog box, click Add/Remove Members.

The Edit Members Of Pecos Coffee Company dialog box appears.

2 Click New.

The New Entry dialog box appears. You can select entry types using other mail programs, such as Microsoft Mail, or an Internet address.

3 Select Internet Address, and then click OK.

The New Internet Address Properties dialog box appears.

4 In the Display Name box, type **Joe Pecos** and then press TAB.

5 Type **jpecos@pecoscoffee.com**

The Internet address for Joe Pecos is added. Your dialog box should look similar to the following illustration.

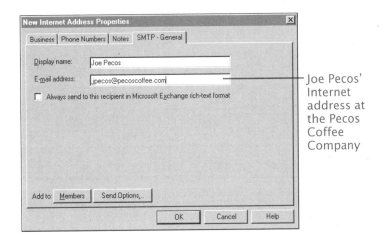

Joe Pecos' Internet address at the Pecos Coffee Company

6 Click Members.

The entry is added to your personal distribution list in your personal address book.

7 Repeat steps 1 through 3 to create an Internet address for Hazel Pecos.

8 In the Display Name box, type **Hazel Pecos**, press TAB, type **hpecos@pecoscoffee.com** and then click the Members button.

The entry is added to your personal distribution list in your personal address book. Your personal distribution list is complete.

9 In the New Personal Distribution List Properties dialog box, click To.

The New Message form reappears with the personal distribution list you selected in the To box.

 TIP You can verify that your message will be sent to all members of a distribution list by viewing the distribution list properties. To do this, use the right mouse button to click the Pecos Coffee Company entry in the To box, and then click Properties on the shortcut menu.

Adding Delivery Options

Before you send your e-mail, you need to decide how to handle the message and how you want others to respond. You can select several options that will affect the delivery of your message.

TIP When you add recipients to your personal address book, you can specify Internet delivery *encoding* options on a per-recipient basis. For example, you can specify that one recipient receive your message encoded as plain text or using uuencode, while another recipient receives it as MIME (Multipurpose Internet Mail Extensions). To specify the delivery options when you create a new address entry, click Send Options in the dialog box. If you request a Read Receipt for a message sent to a user of another mail system, you must keep a copy of the message in you Sent Items folder for the Read Receipt to include the recipient name.

Attaching Receipts to Messages

You can attach both a Delivery Receipt and a Read Receipt to your message by clicking the Properties button, and then selecting both check boxes.

If you want to make sure that your message was successfully sent, you can attach a *Delivery Receipt* so that a notification is sent to you when the recipient receives the message. To know when the message was opened by the recipient, you can attach a *Read Receipt* so that notification is sent to you when the recipient opens the message. Receipts are similar to sending registered mail and are useful if your message is time-sensitive. If a recipient deletes your message without opening it, you will receive a Not Read Receipt to notify you that your message was deleted without being read.

Attach a Read Receipt

In this exercise, you attach a Read Receipt to your message to make sure that all the recipients received and read the message. Since you are sending your message to fictional users, you will receive an Undelivered Receipt.

Read Receipt

 On the New Message Form toolbar, click the Read Receipt button.

TIP You can automatically request receipts for all outgoing messages. To do this, on the Tools menu, click Options. Click the Send tab, and then under Request That Receipt Be Sent When, select the The Item Has Been Delivered check box and/ or the The Item Has Been Read check box.

Assigning Priorities to Messages

You can also assign a priority to your message so that the recipient can instantly know the importance of your message before opening it. By default, messages are sent with a normal priority, but you can tag them with a low or a high priority, depending on their importance. For example, you want the recipients of your message regarding the Pecos Coffee Company meeting to know that the message requires immediate attention, so you assign it a high priority.

After you send a message, recipients are able to identify the priority level by looking at the message header in their Inbox. Messages with a high priority have a red bold exclamation point next to the message header while messages with a low priority have a blue downward-pointing arrow. Normal priority messages do not have a symbol next to the message header.

Assign high priority to a message

In this exercise, you let the recipients know that your message is important by assigning it a high priority.

*Importance:
High*

> On the New Message Form toolbar, click the "Importance: High" button.

 TIP   You can quickly set all types of delivery options for your message at once. To do this, click the Properties button on the New Message Form toolbar, and then select the appropriate delivery options.

Editing Message Text

Now that you have identified the recipients of your message and the delivery options, you can finish the message by entering a subject and typing the message itself in the blank area located at the bottom of the New Message form. Messages can be brief or lengthy—the message area expands as you type.

You can enter and edit text in your message, just as you would using a word processor, such as Microsoft Word. In Exchange, you can use the BACKSPACE or DELETE keys to delete text, move or copy text by dragging and dropping as well as reverse an action using the Undo command on the Edit menu.

Enter and edit the message text

In this exercise, you type the subject of your message, and then add and edit the message text.

1   Click in the Subject box.
2   Type **Pecos Ad Meeting** and then press TAB.

The insertion point moves to the message area.

3   Type **Let's strat off the campaign with a lunch buffet meeting at the Convention Hall on Monday at noon!**

Be sure to type the word "start" incorrectly. You will check the spelling of your message in a later exercise.

4   Double-click the word "buffet."

The word "buffet" is selected.

5   Press DELETE.

6   Double-click the word "Monday," and then type **Friday**

7   Click before the word "Convention," type **new** and then press the SPACEBAR.

Your message should look similar to the following illustration.

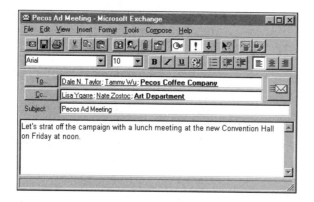

Checking the Spelling of Messages

You can use the spell checker in Exchange to identify and correct spelling errors in your messages. It is a good idea to check the spelling of all your outgoing messages, whether or not you think you made any mistakes. When you start the spell checker, your message is checked from the beginning. If you don't want to check the spelling of the entire message, you can select part of it, even just one word. The text in the Subject box is also checked for spelling, but recipient names are ignored.

If the spelling of a word isn't recognized when you check your message, you can correct it. If the spelling of the word is correct as is, but the spell checker does not recognize it, you can add it to the dictionary, or ignore the word and proceed. In addition to misspelled words, duplicated words are recognized and the second word can be deleted using the spell checker. The buttons used in the Spelling dialog box are listed in the following table.

Use this button	To
Ignore	Ignore only that occurrence of a word in a message.
Ignore All	Ignore all instances of a word in a message.
Change	Change only that occurrence of a word in a message.
Change All	Change all instances of a word in a message.
Add	Add the word to the dictionary for future reference.
Suggest	Display a list of proposed spellings or words.
Options	Set options for spell checks.
Undo Last	Reverse the last spell check change.
Cancel	Cancel the spell check.
Help	Open the Help topic on the Spelling dialog box.

TIP You can have all the messages automatically checked for spelling before they are sent. To do this, click Options on the Tools menu, click the Spelling tab, and then select the Always Check Spelling Before Sending check box.

Spell check your message

In this exercise, you check your message for spelling, especially since you know that you made at least one spelling error.

1   On the Tools menu, click Spelling.

The spell checker starts. The Spelling dialog box appears and the word "strat" is not recognized by the dictionary.

2   Click Suggest.

Several suggested words appear in the Suggestions box.

3   Be sure that the word "start" is selected in the Suggestions box, and then click Change.

The next unrecognized word, "Pecos," appears in the Change To box.

4   Click Ignore.

A message appears indicating that the spelling check is complete.

5   Click OK.

TIP You can have the spell checker always suggest words for unrecognized words. To do this, click Options on the Tools menu, click the Spelling tab, and then select the Always Suggest Replacements For Misspelled Words check box.

Formatting Text for Impact

In Exchange, you can format your message text to emphasize its content and create interest, just like you would in a word processing program. For example, you can choose from a series of *fonts*, or format text as bold or italic to create a different look. You can also add bullets to highlight and separate the main points of your message as well as change the color of the text.

To format text, you first select the text you want to format, and then apply the formatting. If you do not select any text before you format, the formatting you define will be applied to any text you type after the insertion point. Only the text in the message area can be formatted.

You can change the appearance and attributes of your message text using the buttons on the Formatting toolbar or the Font command on the Format menu. You can also modify paragraph formatting such as alignment, indentation, and bullets.

At Fitch & Mather, you have several messages to send. You want your messages to be effective and interesting, so you decide to experiment with text formatting.

Format text

You can also press CTRL+END.

1   Click at the end of the message text, and then press ENTER twice.

2   Type the following text, pressing ENTER after each line.

The agenda

Round Up Roast

Brown Cow Creamer

Tumbleweed Tea

3   Select the text "The agenda."

4   On the Formatting toolbar, click the Italic button.

Italic

The text is italicized.

5   Select the text "Round Up Roast" through "Tumbleweed Tea."

6   On the Formatting toolbar, click the Color button.

Color

A color palette appears.

7   Click Green.

The text is formatted with the color green.

 NOTE   You must have a color printer to print text in color. If you use a black and white printer to print colored text, the text will appear in shades of gray.

Format the paragraph

Bullets

Increase Indent

1   On the Formatting toolbar, click the Bullets button.

      Bullets are added next to the text.

2   On the Formatting toolbar, click the Increase Indent button.

      The text is indented to the right.

3   Click anywhere in the text.

      Your message should look similar to the following illustration.

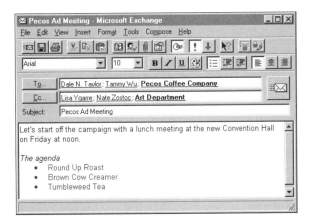

Inserting Files in Messages

Now that you have learned the basics of sending messages, you are ready to take advantage of some additional Exchange capabilities. In addition to typing your own text in messages, you can send files to other people by inserting files into your messages. Suppose you have information in a Word document that you want a colleague in another city to look at. You could print the document and mail it, but this would take time and might be costly. With Exchange, you can send the file by inserting it into a message. Your colleague will then receive the file within minutes instead of days.

This feature lets you share information with other users through messages rather than printing a file or copying the data and pasting it in a message. You can include information by *embedding* a file in your message or *attaching* a file to your message.

Embedding is helpful if you want the message recipients to be able to view information without making changes to it. However, if you want the recipients to be able to easily copy a file to their hard disk, you should attach the file to your message. If the recipients have the program that was used to create an attached

21

file or a program installed on their computers that recognizes the file type, they can double-click the icon in the message to open and edit the file.

You can also attach a file as a text-only file, although no text formatting will be retained. This is especially useful if the text you want to send is heavily formatted and the recipient's postoffice cannot read formatted text files. This can occur when sending files over the Internet or to non-Microsoft Exchange Server mail systems.

Some good reasons for choosing whether to embed or attach objects in messages are listed in the following table.

When you want to	Do this in your message
Allow the recipient to view the information in a file without opening a program.	Embed the file as an object
Allow the recipient to view the information in a file using a program, but still want to condense the amount of space used by the object.	Embed the file as an icon
Allow the recipient to view and edit all or part of the information contained in a file without affecting the original.	Embed the file as an object
Allow the recipient to view and edit all or part of the information contained in a file so that the original file is updated.	Embed the file as a linked object
Send a file to a recipient who uses an e-mail system that doesn't support embedded objects.	Attach the file to the message
Send an object so that it can be easily copied to hard disk by the recipient.	Attach the file to the message
Send a rich text formatted file to a recipient who isn't able to view heavily formatted documents.	Attach the file to the message as a text-only file

You will learn more about linking objects in Lesson 6.

Sending Objects in Messages

To insert a file directly into a message, you can embed the file as an *object*. Objects can include files of any type or even parts of files. You can insert one of several object types, depending on what programs you have installed on your computer. For example, you could insert a Microsoft Excel spreadsheet, a Microsoft Paint graphic, or a Word document. When you embed an object in a message, the recipient can view the object without opening the program in which it was created. If the recipients of a message don't have the program that you used to create the object installed on their computer, they can still view the data in the message, but they won't be able to edit or modify it.

Within a message, an embedded object can be shown directly or it can be represented by an icon. If a large embedded object is displayed in the message, it can take up a lot of room. Embedding an object as an icon helps minimize the amount of space that the object takes up when the recipients view the message. However, if they don't have the program that was used to create the embedded file installed on their computer and you send the embedded file as an icon, the recipients will only be able to see the icon, not any of the file's content.

If the recipients want to modify the embedded object, they can double-click it to open the object in the program in which it was created. For example, if you sent a graphic logo, the recipients can double-click the logo in your message to open Paint.

Embed a graphic object

For a demonstration of how to embed a graphic object, double-click the Camcorder Files On The Internet short-cut on your Desktop or connect to the Internet address listed on p.xxx.

You want feedback from your co-workers on a graphic that you have selected for the Pecos Coffee Company campaign. In this exercise, you embed the graphic in your message so that your co-workers can quickly view the graphic, and then return their comments on it.

1 Click at the beginning of the message text.

2 On the Insert menu, click Object.

The Insert Object dialog box appears.

3 Click the Create From File option button.

You are embedding an existing bitmap image file.

4 Click Browse.

The Browse dialog box appears.

5 Open the Exchange 5.0 SBS Practice\Lesson01 folder located on your hard drive.

6 Click the Pecos Text bitmap image, and then click Insert.

7 Click OK.

The embedded bitmap image appears in the message area.

8 Press ENTER.

Your message should look similar to the following illustration.

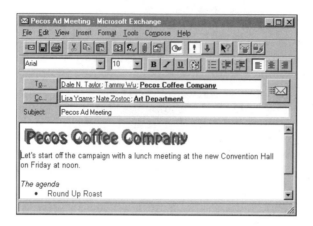

Attaching Files to Messages

For a demonstration of how to attach a file to a message, double-click the Camcorder Files On The Internet shortcut on your Desktop or connect to the Internet address listed on p.xxx.

Suppose you want to send a spreadsheet with Pecos Coffee Company data to a co-worker. Because the file contains a lot of information, you know that embedding it would make your message too large to read. By attaching the spreadsheet to your message, only an icon appears and your co-worker can view the spreadsheet by double-clicking the attachment icon. The program that was used to create the attachment will open, or if the recipient doesn't have the program, one that recognizes the data will open. Attached files can include graphics, spreadsheets, word processing documents, or even other messages. Messages with attached files are identified with a paper clip icon in the folder contents list.

You want to include information that is currently stored in a Microsoft Excel spreadsheet on your hard disk on your client, Pecos Coffee Company, in your message. To save time and paper, you attach the spreadsheet to your message.

Attach a file

Insert File

To send a file as text-only, click the Text Only option button.

1 Press CTRL+END.

The insertion point moves to the end of the message.

2 Type **I'm attaching a file with last year's data.** and then press ENTER.

3 On the New Message toolbar, click the Insert File button.

The Insert File dialog box appears.

4 Be sure that the Lesson01 folder is open, and then click the Pecos Data workbook.

5 Under Insert As, be sure that the An Attachment option button is selected.

The entire formatted file will be inserted as an attachment.

To open an attached file, you double-click the icon in the message.

6 Click OK.

The attached file appears as an icon. Your message should look similar to the following illustration.

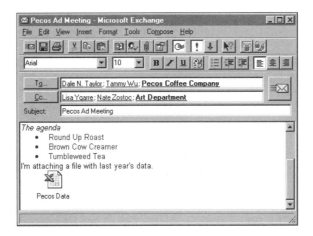

Send your message

In this exercise, you send your completed Pecos Ad Meeting message.

Send

▶ Click the Send button.

After a moment, your message with the attached worksheet is sent and a copy is placed in your Sent Items folder. You should receive several Undelivered Receipts from your system administrator, including one for the fictional Internet addresses. If you receive a message stating that you have no transport provider, click OK. This means that your network has not been set up for Internet messaging.

> **NOTE** If you'd like to build on the skills that you learned in this lesson, you can perform the exercises presented in the following section, One Step Further. Otherwise, skip to "Finish the lesson."

One Step Further: Sending a Blind Carbon Copy

A blind carbon copy (Bcc) is similar to a carbon copy, except that only the blind carbon copy recipient and the sender of the message are aware that it is being sent to additional recipients.

Other recipients listed in the To and Cc boxes can't see the blind carbon copy recipients and if they reply to your message, the Bcc recipients will not be included. This can be helpful if you just want to notify someone, but you don't think they need to be involved in further discussion relating to your original message.

Send a blind carbon copy

In this exercise, you send a price quote to your clients at the Pecos Coffee Company. You include a blind carbon copy to the CEO and CFO of your company, Floyd F. Fitch and Marilyn M. Mather, so that they're aware of the major business correspondence regarding the client's account.

New Message

1   On the Viewer toolbar, click the New Message button.

    A blank message appears.

2   In the To box, type **Pecos Coffee**

3   On the View menu, click Bcc Box.

    The optional Bcc box appears below the Cc box.

4   In the Bcc box, type **floyd; marilyn**

Check Names

5   On the New Message Form toolbar, click the Check Names button.

    The message is addressed to the Pecos Coffee Company distribution list, Floyd F. Fitch, and Marilyn M. Mather.

6   On the View menu, click Bcc Box.

    The Bcc box is hidden. It will not appear the next time you create a new message.

7   In the Subject box, type **Ad Offer**

8   In the message area, type **Your ad layout will be discounted by 15% if paid up front.**

Send

9   Click the Send button.

    Your message is sent. Recipients at Pecos Coffee Company will not be aware that Floyd and Marilyn were included in your message, and if either Joe or Hazel Pecos replies to your message, Floyd and Marilyn will not be copied. You should receive an Undelivered Receipt from the system administrator.

Finish the lesson

Follow these steps to delete the practice messages you created in this lesson.

 WARNING   Because you are logged on to Microsoft Exchange with your own username, be sure you delete only the practice files and messages you added or created during this lesson.

1   In the Inbox folder, select the practice messages you used in this lesson, and then press DELETE.

2   Close all open windows, except Microsoft Exchange.

3   If you want to continue to the next lesson, click the Inbox folder in the folder list.

4   If you are finished using Microsoft Exchange for now, on the File menu, click Exit And Log Off.

You are logged off Microsoft Exchange and the Viewer window closes.

Lesson Summary

To	Do this	Button
Create a message	Click the New Message button.	
View the Address Book	Click the To button.	
Address a message	Click the To button, select recipient names from the global address list or personal address book, and then click To.	
Send a message	Click the Send button.	
Send a carbon copy	Click the Cc button, select recipient names, and then click Cc.	
Use a distribution list	In the Address Book dialog box, select the distribution list you want, and then click To, Cc, or Bcc.	
Create a personal distribution list	In the Address Book dialog box, click New Entry, click Personal Distribution List, and then click OK. Type the distribution list name, and then click Add/Remove Members. Click New, and then type a name and an address or select recipient names.	
Add an Internet address to your personal address book	In the Address Book dialog box, click New, click Internet Address, click OK, and then type a name and an Internet address.	
Attach a receipt	On the File menu, click Properties. Select the Delivery Receipt or the Read Receipt check box, or both.	

To	Do this	Button
Assign a high or low priority to a message	Click the "Importance: High" or "Importance: Low" button.	
Edit message text	In the message area, place the insertion point in the appropriate location, and add or delete text.	
Check the spelling of a message	On the Tools menu, click Spelling, and then accept or reject the proposed changes.	
Format text and paragraphs in a message	Select the text to format, and then use the appropriate buttons on the Formatting toolbar.	
Embed an object in a message	On the Insert menu, click Object. Click the Create From File option button, select the Display As Icon check box to embed the object as an icon, and then click Browse. Locate and click the filename, and then click Open.	
Attach a file to a message	Create or open a message. Click the Insert File button, click the file, and then click the An Attachment option button.	

For online information about	On the Help menu, click Microsoft Exchange Help Topics, click the Index tab, and then type
Using the Address Book	**Address Book**
Using the global address list	**Addressing**
Using a personal address book	**Personal address book**
Creating carbon copies	**Cc box** *or* **Bcc box**
Adding Internet addresses	**Internet**
Using or creating distribution lists	**Distribution lists** *or* **personal distribution lists**
Attaching delivery receipts	**Receipts** *or* **read receipt**
Assigning priorities	**Priority** *or* **high importance** *or* **low importance**
Checking spelling	**Spelling checker** *or* **checking spelling**
Formatting text	**Formatting text**
Embedding objects	**Embedded objects**
Attaching files	**Attachments** *or* **inserting: files**
Sending messages	**Sending messages**

Processing Incoming Messages

Estimated time
25 min.

In this lesson you will learn how to:

- Locate and open messages.
- Browse through messages.
- Reply to and forward messages.
- Save attachments.
- Delete messages.

You probably have already received new messages from other people or are aware that messages have been sent to you. Now, you need to be able to do more than just read messages; you need to find out what you can with them.

At Fitch & Mather, your team has been working on the Pecos Coffee Company campaign for a few days. You have received several messages inquiring about the scope of the project and ideas for the campaign. In this lesson, you will learn how to quickly respond to your messages so that you can be prepared for the kick-off meeting with your clients.

IMPORTANT   If you haven't imported the personal address book or created the Chris Adams profile yet, refer to "Installing and Using the Practice Files," earlier in this book. If you don't know your Microsoft Exchange username or password, contact your system administrator for further help.

Start Microsoft Exchange

Inbox

1   On the Desktop, double-click the Inbox icon.

Microsoft Exchange starts. The Choose Profile dialog box appears.

2   Click the down arrow, and then click Chris Adams.

For the purposes of this book, you'll use the Chris Adams profile.

3   Click OK, and then be sure that the Inbox folder is open.

The Viewer window opens. You are ready to set up your Inbox for this lesson.

Set up your Inbox for this lesson

1   Click the Start button. Point to Programs, and then click Windows Explorer or Windows NT Explorer.

2   In the left side of the window, titled All Folders, click drive C.

3   In the right side of the window, titled Contents Of, double-click the Exchange 5.0 SBS Practice folder.

4   Double-click the Lesson02 folder.

The contents of the practice folder appear.

5   Use the right mouse button to click an open area on the taskbar, and then, on the shortcut menu, click Tile Horizontally or Tile Windows Horizontally.

The Exploring–Lesson02 and Inbox–Microsoft Exchange windows are tiled.

6   With the Exploring–Lesson02 window active, on the Edit menu, click Select All.

The number of unread messages in a folder appears in parentheses next to the folder name.

7   Drag the selected files to the right side of the Inbox–Microsoft Exchange window.

The practice files are copied, and you are ready to start the lesson.

8   Close the Exploring–Lesson02 window, and then resize the Inbox–Microsoft Exchange window to its previous size.

Locating and Reading Messages

After you start Microsoft Exchange, you use the Viewer window to identify and manage the incoming messages that have been automatically placed in your Inbox folder.

Viewing Folders to Locate Messages

You can easily assess the messages in the folder contents list by reading the message headers. Each message header identifies the sender, the subject, and when the message was sent. Messages that have not been opened are in bold type, while messages that have been opened are in regular type. By default, your Viewer window includes the following four built-in folders as follows.

Folder	Icon	Folder Description
Deleted Items folder		Messages that you delete are moved to the Deleted Items folder. By default, when you log off of Exchange, the Deleted Items folder is emptied and the messages it contains are permanently deleted.
Inbox folder		When you receive an incoming message, an icon appears on the status bar by default, indicating that a new message has been delivered to your Inbox. You can also be notified by a chiming sound, a notification message, and by your mouse pointer changing briefly to a small message icon. All the messages sent to you by other people are delivered to your Inbox folder; these messages remain in this folder until you move or delete them.
Outbox folder		The Outbox is the temporary storage area for outgoing messages until they are delivered.
Sent Items folder		By default, a copy of each message you send is placed in your Sent Items folder, so it is not necessary to add your name to the Cc box in each message you send to retain a copy. You can view the contents of the Sent Items folder by double-clicking the folder icon. All sent mess- ages are stored in the Sent Items folder until you delete or move them.

TIP You can be automatically notified each time you get a message. To do this, on the Tools menu, click Options, click the General tab, and then select the Display A Notification Message check box.

Using the Viewer window, you can easily locate incoming messages, already sent messages, outgoing messages, or deleted messages. In Lesson 3, you will learn how to organize your messages within existing folders and how to create new folders.

Explore your mailbox folders

In this exercise, you open your built-in folders to identify where different messages are stored.

1   In the folders list, click the Deleted Items folder.

If you have completed Lesson 1 and have not logged off of Exchange, the messages you deleted at the end of Lesson 1 appear in the Deleted Items folder. Otherwise, no messages appear.

2   In the folders list, click the Outbox folder.

The Outbox folder shouldn't contain any messages, because none have been sent recently.

3   Click the Sent Items folder.

If you have completed Lesson 1, the messages you sent appear in the Sent Items folder.

4   Click the Inbox folder.

The practice messages appear.

 TIP   When you receive incoming messages, a message icon appears on the taskbar. If Exchange is not the active window, you can quickly open your Inbox to view new messages by double-clicking the message icon.

Reading Messages

Each message you open appears in the Read Message form, which allows you to view the sender, the date and time it was sent, and all the recipients.

Open a message

In this exercise, you open and read a reply to the Pecos Ad Meeting message.

1   In the Inbox folder, double-click the "RE: Pecos Ad Meeting" message from Tammy Wu.

A reply to the message you sent in Lesson 1 opens. Your message should look similar to the following illustration.

The message header indicates the sender, the date and time it was sent, and the recipients of the message.

Click here to shorten the message header.

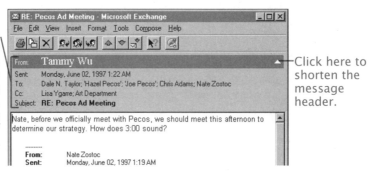

You can also click Close on the File menu.

2   On the "RE: Pecos Ad Meeting" window, click the Close button.

The message closes.

View a receipt

1   In the Inbox folder, double-click the "Undeliverable: Pecos Ad Meeting" receipt from the System Administrator.

The Undelivered Receipt shows the subject information, the date and time you sent the message, the names of the recipients who did not receive the message, and the date and time they could not be reached. Your Undelivered Receipt should look similar to the following illustration.

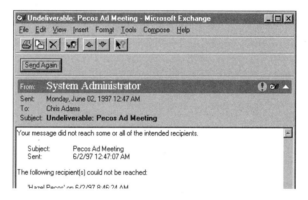

2   On the "Undeliverable: Pecos Ad Meeting" window, click the Close button.

The message closes.

Browsing Through Messages

As you look in the Viewer window, you can see that icons appear to the left of messages. Different kinds of messages have different icons associated with them to help identify different types of messages. For example, an icon representing e-mail containing an attachment looks like an envelope with a paper clip, while a Read Receipt icon looks like a postage meter stamp with a green checkmark. Some of the different icons used to identify messages in the folder contents list are listed in the following table.

Icon	Description
✉	E-mail with high priority
✉	E-mail with low priority

Icon	Description
✉ 📎	E-mail with an attached file
➡	Postmark for Delivery Receipt
⊘	Postmark for Undelivered Receipt
✓	Postmark for read messages
✗	Postmark for unread messages

In the folder contents list, columns divide the message header by priority, item type, attachment, sender, subject, received date, and size. By default, messages are sorted by date, with the most recent message at the top of the list. You will learn how to sort the messages differently in Lesson 3.

Instead of opening and closing each message individually, you can quickly browse through your messages by opening a message, and then clicking the Next or Previous button on the Read Message Form toolbar. When you open a message that is a reply or a forward, the original message text is appended to the bottom of the message by default.

Browse through messages

A number of replies to the "Pecos Ad Meeting" message you sent have been delivered to your Inbox and appear in bold type because they haven't yet been read. In this exercise, you browse through your messages, including the replies to your "Pecos Ad Meeting" message.

1 Be sure that the messages in your Inbox are sorted by date, with the most recent message at the top of the list.

   If your messages are not sorted properly, click the Received column button in the right half of the Viewer window until they are.

2 In your Inbox, double-click the "RE: Pecos Ad Meeting" message from Tammy Wu.

   This message should be the first practice message. Tammy Wu's reply appears at the top of the Read Message form.

3 Scroll downward and read the entire message.

   Following Tammy Wu's reply is Nate Zostoc's reply to your message.

Next

4 On the Read Message Form toolbar, click the Next button until the "RE: Pecos Ad Meeting" message from Nate Zostoc appears.

   If the Read Message Form toolbar does not appear, click Toolbar on the View menu. Nate Zostoc's reply to the original message that you sent appears at the top of the Read Message form.

5   Click the Next button to read the following messages:

From	Content
Nate Zostoc	Read Receipt indicating the date and time that Nate read the "Pecos Ad Meeting" message
Debbie S. Abdul	"Game" message
Dale N. Taylor	"RE: Pecos Ad Meeting" message containing a graphic object
Dale N. Taylor	Read Receipt indicating the date and time that Dale read the "Pecos Ad Meeting" message
System Administrator	"Undeliverable: Pecos Ad Meeting" message
Chris Adams	"Congratulations!" message
Chandra Shah	"Old Pecos Info" message
Ariana Rose	"Housewarming" message
Joe Pecos	"Meeting" message

Previous

6   On the Read Message Form toolbar, click the Previous button until the "RE: Pecos Ad Meeting" message from Dale N. Taylor appears.

Replying to Messages

Many messages that you receive require a reply. Reply messages are identified by the letters "RE" in the Subject box. When replying to messages with multiple recipients, you need to decide whether you want to respond to only the sender or to all recipients. When you send your reply, the message you're replying to is automatically closed and your reply text is formatted in blue by default.

TIP You can change the reply settings so that the original message text is not included in replies. To do this, on the Tools menu, click Options. Click the Read tab, and then clear the Include The Original Text When Replying check box.

Replying to the Sender

If you want to respond to a message you have received, you can create a new message, add the recipient and the subject, and then try to recall the details of the original message. A much faster way to respond is to select or open a message, and then use the Reply To Sender button.

Reply to a sender

In this exercise, you reply to Dale N. Taylor's message regarding his logo for the Pecos Coffee Company campaign.

Reply To Sender

1 On the Read Message Form toolbar, click the Reply To Sender button.

The New Message form appears. The To and Subject boxes are automatically filled in, with the subject preceded by "RE:" Dale's message is now indented below the message area where you will type your reply.

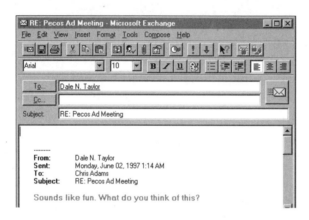

2 Type **This logo looks great! Bring your design to the kick-off meeting.**

3 Click the Send button.

Your reply is sent to Dale N. Taylor.

Send

Replying to All Recipients

When you use the Reply To Sender button, you respond only to the person who sent the original message. But if you want to respond to all the recipients listed in the original message, you can use the Reply To All button.

 NOTE If you reply to all recipients and the original message included blind carbon copy recipients, the blind carbon copy recipients will not receive a copy of your reply.

Reply to all recipients

In this exercise, you reply to Tammy Wu's message.

1 Click the "RE: Pecos Ad Meeting" message from Tammy Wu.

You do not have to open a message to send a reply.

Reply To All

2 On the Viewer toolbar, click the Reply To All button.

The New Message form appears. The To and Subject boxes are automatically filled in.

3 Type **I'm interested in attending the strategy meeting.**

4 Click the Send button.

Your reply is sent to all recipients of the original message. You will receive an Undeliverable Receipt because the recipient names are fictitious.

NOTE If the original message to which you are replying contained an attachment and if you want the recipients of your reply to be able to see the attachment, you need to forward the message rather than reply to it. If you reply to a message that contains an attachment, only the filename will appear in your reply message, not the file itself.

Forwarding Messages

Sometimes you receive messages that you think another person should also see. Or you might not be the best person to reply to the message. When this happens, you can forward a copy of the message to a new recipient rather than retype the message or show a printout of the message to the person who needs to see it. You can forward a message to several people or add carbon copy recipients, just as you can in any other message. Keep in mind that just as you can forward messages that you receive from other people, others can forward your messages to whomever they want.

Forwarded messages are similar to replies in that the original message is appended at the end of the message. If you want to precede the message with text, you can type additional information before the appended message. For example, you can type background information on a forwarded message so that the recipient can handle the message without asking you why you're forwarding it. Forwarded messages are identified by the letters "FW" in the Subject box.

Forward a message

In this exercise, you forward the message containing Dale's artwork to Tammy Wu, the copywriter assigned to the Pecos Coffee Company account.

Forward

1 Click the "RE: Pecos Ad Meeting" message from Dale N. Taylor.

2 On the Viewer toolbar, click the Forward button.

The New Message form appears with the Subject box filled in.

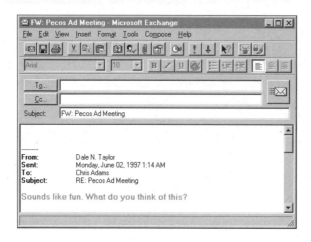

3 In the To box, type **Tammy**

4 On the Send Form toolbar, click the Check Names button.

Check Names

You can also press CTRL+K to check names.

The name "Tammy Wu" automatically appears after it is checked against the Address Book.

5 Click in the message area, and then type **Can you draft some slogans before Friday's meeting?**

6 Click the Send button.

Send

Dale's message is forwarded to Tammy. You will receive an Undeliverable Receipt because the recipient name is fictitious.

Saving Attachments

Messages with attached files are identified with a paper clip icon in the folder contents list.

Suppose you receive a message that contains an important attachment and you want to save the file so that you can work with it in a different program, such as Microsoft Word or Microsoft Excel. Instead of double-clicking the attachment to open the program and the file, and then saving the file to your hard disk, you can directly save the attachment in any folder on your computer or network. After the attached file is opened, you can view, edit, or print it just like any other file.

Save an attachment

Your co-worker, Chandra Shah, sent you a message containing a Microsoft Excel workbook. In this exercise, you save the workbook file attached to Chandra's message.

1 In the Inbox folder, double-click the "Old Pecos Info" message from Chandra Shah.

The message opens.

2 Click the attachment icon to select it.

If you accidentally double-click the icon and open Microsoft Excel, on the File menu, click Exit.

3 On the File menu, click Save As.

The Save As dialog box appears.

4 Click the Save In down arrow, and then click Desktop.

5 Be sure that the Save These Attachments Only option button and the Pecos Info.xls file are selected.

6 Click Save.

The workbook is saved on the Desktop.

7 On the Old Pecos Info window, click the Close button.

The message closes.

 TIP If you start composing a message, but can't complete its drafting until a later time, you can save an entire message in a message format (.MSG). To do this, on the File menu, click Save. When you use the Save command to save a message, it is automatically saved in message format in your Inbox. You can also save messages as a text file (.TXT) or rich text format file (.RTF) to any location on your computer using the Save As command on the File menu.

Deleting Messages

When you have finished reading and taking actions, such as replying to or forwarding your messages, it is a good idea to decide whether you want to save or delete your messages. If you save all the messages you receive, they'll require a lot of storage space and will be harder to organize. If you no longer need a message, you should delete it.

Because deleted messages are moved to the Deleted Items folder temporarily, if you change your mind about deleting a message, you can still retrieve it. However, by default, when you log off of Exchange, items stored in the Deleted Items folder are deleted permanently.

 TIP You can empty the Deleted Items folder at any time before you log off of Exchange. To do this, use the right mouse button to click the Deleted Items folder, and then, on the shortcut menu, click Empty Folder.

Delete a message

In this exercise, you delete messages that you no longer need from your Inbox.

Delete

1 Be sure the "Old Pecos Info" message from Chandra Shah is selected.

2 On the Viewer toolbar, click the Delete button.

The message is moved from the Inbox to the Deleted Items folder.

View the Deleted Items folder

1 In the folders list, click the Deleted Items folder.

The contents of your Deleted Items folder, including Chandra's message, appear.

2 Click the Inbox folder.

The contents of the Inbox appear in the folder contents list.

 TIP You can change your Deleted Items folder to work like the Recycle Bin so that deleted messages are stored and not permanently removed until you explicitly delete them. To do this, on the Tools menu, click Options, click the General tab, and then clear the Empty The 'Deleted Items' Folder Upon Exiting check box.

One Step Further: Saving the Address of the Sender of an Incoming Message

If you receive a message from someone and you want to save that person's address for future reference, you can easily add it to your personal address book.

Save an address to your personal address book

In this exercise, you read a message from your out-of-state friend, Ariana Rose. Because you want to keep her new address, you add it to your personal address book.

1 In your Inbox, open the Housewarming message from Ariana Rose.

2 In the From area, use the right mouse button to click the name "Ariana Rose."

A shortcut menu appears.

3 Click Add To Personal Address Book.

4 On the Housewarming window, click the Close button.

The message closes.

View your personal address book

Address Book

1 On the Viewer toolbar, click the Address Book button.

The Address Book dialog box appears.

2 In the upper-right corner of the Address Book dialog box, click the Show Names From The down arrow, and then select Personal Address Book.

Ariana Rose's name now appears in your personal address book.

3 On the Address Book window, click the Close button.

Finish the lesson

Follow these steps to delete the practice messages you created in this lesson.

⚠ WARNING Because you are logged on to Microsoft Exchange with your own username, be sure to delete only the practice files and messages you added or created during this lesson.

1 In your Inbox and Sent Items folders, delete the practice messages you used in this lesson.

2 Delete the Pecos Info icon from your Desktop.

3 Close all open windows, except Microsoft Exchange.

4 If you want to continue to the next lesson, click the Inbox folder in the folder list.

5 If you are finished using Microsoft Exchange for now, on the File menu, click Exit And Log Off.

You are logged off Microsoft Exchange and the Viewer window closes.

Lesson Summary

To	Do this	Button
View the contents of a folder	Click the folder in the folder list.	
Open a message	Double-click the message.	
Browse to the next message	Open the message. On the Read Message Form toolbar, click the Next button.	⬇
Browse to the previous message	Open the message. On the Read Message Form toolbar, click the Previous button.	⬆

To	Do this	Button
Reply to a message	Click or open the message. On the Read Message Form toolbar, click the Reply To Sender button.	![Reply To Sender button]
Reply to all recipients	Click or open the message. On the Read Message Form toolbar, click the Reply To All button.	![Reply To All button]
Forward a message	Click or open the message. On the Read Message Form toolbar, click the Forward button.	![Forward button]
Check names	Type a recipient. On the toolbar, click the Check Names button.	![Check Names button]
Save an attached file	Click or open the message. On the File menu, click Save As. Click the Save These Attachments Only option button, and then select where to save the attached file.	
Delete a message	Click or open the message. On the toolbar, click the Delete button.	![Delete button]

For online information about	On the Help menu, click Microsoft Exchange Help Topics, click the Index tab, and then type
Viewing items in your Inbox	**Opening: messages**
Working with incoming messages	**Incoming mail**
Replying to messages	**Replying**
Forwarding messages	**Forwarding messages**
Saving attachments	**Saving: attachments** *or* **attachments: saving**
Deleting messages	**Deleting: messages** *or* **Deleted Items folder**
Using the Address Book	**Address Book**

Organizing Messages

Estimated time
30 min.

In this lesson you will learn how to:

- Sort messages.
- Work with folders.
- Find specific messages.
- Print messages.

By now, you have received several messages. Although you can let your messages accumulate in your Inbox, you'll find that organizing your messages will allow you to quickly find them later. Depending on your preferences and work habits, you can organize your folders in several different ways. For example, you can create folders for different types of messages, and then move your messages into the appropriate folders.

In this lesson, you'll organize the messages in your Inbox. Then, you'll create a folder specifically for your new client, Pecos Coffee Company, so that you can save all the messages that deal with your new account in one place. You will also find and print messages.

IMPORTANT If you haven't imported the personal address book or created the Chris Adams profile yet, refer to "Installing and Using the Practice Files," earlier in this book. If you don't know your Microsoft Exchange username or password, contact your system administrator for further help.

Start Microsoft Exchange

Inbox

1 On the Desktop, double-click the Inbox icon.

Microsoft Exchange starts. The Choose Profile dialog box appears.

2 Click the down arrow, and then click Chris Adams.

For the purposes of this book, you'll use the Chris Adams profile.

3 Click OK, and then be sure that the Inbox folder is open.

The Viewer window appears. You are ready to set up your Inbox for this lesson.

Set up your Inbox for this lesson

For more detailed instructions on how to set up your Inbox, see Lesson 2.

1 In Windows Explorer or in Windows NT Explorer, open the Exchange 5.0 SBS Practice\Lesson03 folder.

2 Tile the Exploring–Lesson03 and Inbox–Microsoft Exchange windows.

3 Drag the files from the Exploring–Lesson03 window to the right side of the Inbox–Microsoft Exchange window, and then close the Exploring–Lesson03 window.

The practice files are copied to your Inbox and you are ready to start this lesson.

Sorting Messages

For a demonstration of how to sort messages, double-click the Camcorder Files On The Internet shortcut on your Desktop or connect to the Internet address listed on p. xxx.

You can organize the messages stored in your Inbox by sorting them. The information in the message header is used to sort messages by column, such as Sender, Subject, and Received Date. Depending on the type of information in the column, messages can be sorted in ascending or descending order. An ascending sort lists data from A to Z, from the lowest to the highest number, or from the earliest to the latest date. A descending sort lists data from Z to A, from the highest to the lowest number, or from the latest to the earliest date. A down arrow in a column heading indicates that messages are sorted in descending order while an up arrow indicates an ascending sort.

To change how your messages are sorted, you can click a column heading. For example, if you click the Received Date column heading, the messages get sorted in ascending order to show the oldest message at the top of the list. The current sort settings are saved with each folder. When you reopen a folder, the messages will be sorted based on the settings defined the last time you viewed the folder's contents. You can have different sort orders for different folders.

Sort messages

In this exercise, you experiment with sorting to find a good way to organize the different types of messages stored in your Inbox.

1 On the Inbox–Microsoft Exchange window, click the Maximize button.

By default, messages in your Inbox should be sorted by date, in descending order, so that the most recent message appears at the top of the list.

You can also sort messages by clicking Sort on the View menu.

2 In the folder contents list, click the From column heading.

The messages are sorted in ascending order by sender. Your screen should look similar to the following illustration.

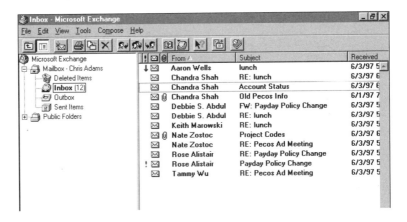

3 Click the From column heading again.

The messages are sorted in descending order by sender.

The letters "RE" and "FW" are ignored when sorting.

4 Click the Subject column heading.

The messages are sorted in ascending order by subject.

5 Click the Subject column heading again.

The messages are sorted in descending order by subject. Your screen should look similar to the following illustration.

TIP You can modify how usernames are listed in your personal address book. For example, if the From column is sorted according to first name, you can change the properties to sort by last name. To do this, on the Tools menu, click Services, select Personal Address Book, click Properties, and then click the Last Name or the First Name option button. However, this will not affect how names are listed in the global address list—those names are sorted according to the way they were entered by the system administrator.

Working with Folders

Because you now have several messages that deal with your client, the Pecos Coffee Company, you want to organize them into separate folders. When you are finished with the account, you will be able to remove the folder and streamline your working environment.

Creating Folders

You can also organize your mailbox by creating additional folders. After you have created a folder, you can move or copy messages from other folders into it. You can also create subfolders within a folder, such as your Inbox, to further organize your messages. All the folders in your mailbox are shown in the folders list in the left half of the Viewer window.

You can delete folders you create. However, when you delete a folder, you also delete all subfolders and messages contained within the folder. Just as with messages, if you accidentally delete a folder, you can recover it and the messages it contains from the Deleted Items folder before you log off of Microsoft Exchange. Built-in folders, such as the Inbox and Sent Items folders, cannot be deleted.

Folders can look different depending on their type or the current selection. Near the top of your folders list is an *information store*, which is a container for folders. Your Exchange profile can contain several information stores: private folders, personal folders, and public folders. Depending on the services you are using with Exchange, you might have additional information stores. Some of the icons used to identify folders and information stores in Exchange are listed in the following table.

Icon	Description
	Folder
	Open folder
	Information store

Icon	Description
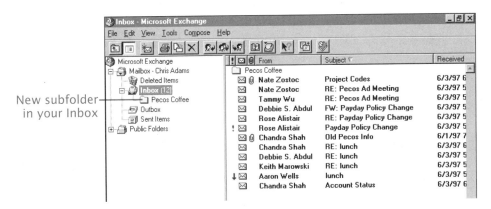	Plus sign indicates collapsed folder with subfolders that are not displayed.
	Minus sign indicates open folder with displayed subfolders.

Create a folder

In this exercise, you create a folder in your Inbox to store messages related to the Pecos Coffee Company account.

1 In the folders list, click the Inbox folder.

   By selecting the Inbox, you specify where to create the new folder.

2 On the File menu, click New Folder.

   The New Folder dialog box appears.

3 In the Folder Name box, type **Pecos Coffee** and then click OK.

   A subfolder of the Inbox folder is created. Your folders list should look similar to the following illustration.

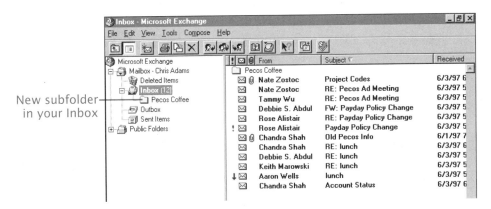

New subfolder in your Inbox

Move a group of messages to a folder

Now that you have created a folder for storing messages related to the Pecos Coffee Company account, you can move messages into it. In this exercise, you sort messages by subject, and then move the appropriate messages to the Pecos Coffee folder.

1 Click the Subject column heading.

   The messages are sorted in ascending order by subject.

2 Drag the "Old Pecos Info" message from Chandra Shah into the Pecos Coffee folder in the folders list.

   The message is moved to the Pecos Coffee folder.

*To select mul-
tiple consecutive
messages, click
a message,
hold down
SHIFT, and then
click another
message. To
select multiple
nonconsecutive
messages,
hold down CTRL
instead.*

3 Drag both "RE: Pecos Ad Meeting" messages from Nate Zostoc and
Tammy Wu to the Pecos Coffee folder.

4 In the folders list, click the Pecos Coffee folder.

Now all messages regarding the Pecos Coffee Company account are
located in one folder. Your screen should look similar to the following
illustration.

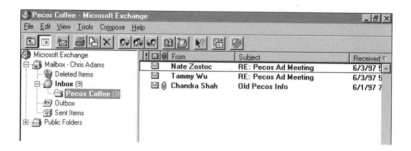

Using Columns

In addition to being able to sort messages using the columns in each folder, you
can add or remove columns as well as change the column width to further help
you organize your messages. For example, if you want to only show the priority
of incoming messages and the sender's name, you can display on the Priority
and Sender columns, and hide the rest of the columns in your Inbox. If the
sender's name or the subject is too long to be fully displayed, you can resize the
From and Subject columns to make them wider. Just as with sorting, any modifications you make to columns in a particular folder remain applied to that
folder until you change its organization or format again.

Add a column

In this exercise, you add a To column to your Pecos Coffee folder so that you
can see to whom the messages were sent without opening them.

1 On the View menu, click Columns.

The Columns dialog box appears.

2 In the Available Columns list, scroll downward, click To, and then click
Add.

The To column now appears at the top of the Show The Following list.

3 Click Move Down three times.

The To column will appear between the Attachment and From
columns.

4 Click OK.

The To column appears in the Pecos Coffee folder.

Resize a column

1   Place the mouse pointer over the split bar between the To and From columns.

The pointer changes to a double-arrow.

2   Drag the column border about 1 inch to the right.

You can now see more of the recipients names in the To column. Your screen should look similar to the following illustration.

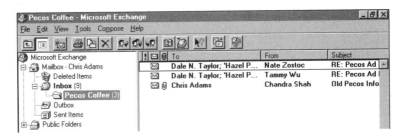

Restore the default columns

1   On the View menu, click Columns.

The Columns dialog box appears.

2   Click Reset, and then click OK.

The default columns are restored to the Pecos Coffee folder.

NOTE   You can remove a column without resetting the default columns. To do this, on the View menu, click Columns. Click the column to remove in the Show The Following list, and then click Remove.

Finding Specific Messages

Sometimes you know you have a specific message somewhere in your mailbox, but you can't find it and you don't want to read every message header in every folder. You can easily locate items, such as messages and folders, using the Find command to specify one or more search conditions to use. For example, you can search for messages that were sent by your supervisor after a specific date or messages that don't include your supervisor as a recipient.

Any items that match your search criteria appear in the lower half of the Find dialog box; you can then open any item by double-clicking its name. You can work with messages in the lower half of the Find dialog box just like you would in the folder contents list. For example, you can sort, reply, print, or delete messages from within the dialog box. Any customized columns or sort orders applied to the folder you're searching in also apply to messages in the Find dialog box.

Find a message

In this exercise, you first find all the messages that you received from Chandra Shah, then narrow the search by looking for messages sent by Chandra regarding the Pecos Coffee Company account, and finally open a message directly from within the Find dialog box.

1 In the folders list, click the Inbox folder.

You will search for messages in your Inbox and its subfolder, the Pecos Coffee folder.

You can also press CTRL+SHIFT+F.

2 On the Tools menu, click Find Items.

The Find Items dialog box appears. The Inbox appears at the top of the dialog box because it is the active folder.

3 Under Find Items That Meet The Following Conditions, click From.

The Address Book dialog box appears.

4 In the upper-right corner of the Address Book dialog box, click the Show Names From The down arrow, and then select Personal Address Book.

If you type the first few letters of a username, the Address Book automatically moves to that name.

5 Double-click Chandra Shah, and then click OK.

The Find dialog box reappears.

6 Click Find Now.

Your Inbox is searched, and after a few moments, three messages from Chandra Shah appear. Two messages were found in the Inbox and one was found in the Pecos Coffee folder. Your dialog box should look similar to the following illustration.

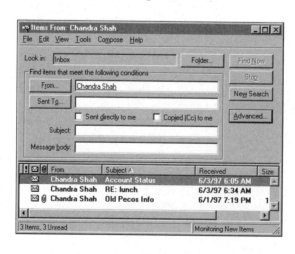

*Search condition
text is not case
sensitive.*

7   Click in the Message Body box, and then type **pecos**

This condition will help narrow the search to messages that not only were sent by Chandra Shah but also contain the text "pecos" in the body of the message.

8   Click Find Now.

Your Inbox is searched, and after a few moments, one message from Chandra Shah appears.

9   Double-click the "Old Pecos Info" message from Chandra Shah.

The message appears.

10   On the "Old Pecos Info" window, click the Close button.

The message closes. The Find dialog box reappears.

Find items with attachments

In this exercise, you try another search condition to find only messages that contain attachments.

1   Click New Search.

All information is cleared from the Find dialog box.

2   Click Advanced.

3   Select the Only Items With Attachments check box, and then click OK.

The Find dialog box reappears. All messages with attachments stored in your Inbox folder and its subfolder will be found.

4   Click Find Now.

After a moment, two messages with attachments appear. The Find dialog box should look similar to the following illustration.

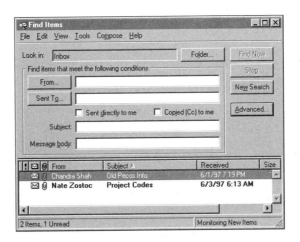

5 Click the Close button.

 TIP By default, the folder that is searched is the one that is currently active. To search another folder without closing the Find Items dialog box, click the Folder button, and then select the folder you want.

Printing Messages

You can easily print a hard copy of a message using Exchange. Any message in any folder can be printed. You can print several messages at a time or print more than one copy of a message. When you print multiple messages, you can print one message per page or print several messages on a page.

If you want to print a message that contains an attachment, you can print the attached item if your computer recognizes its file format and a program that can open the attachment is installed on your computer. If the message contains an embedded object, such as a graphic, the object will be printed as it appears in the message.

Print a message

 IMPORTANT You must have a printer installed to print messages and complete the rest of the exercises in this lesson. If you don't, skip to either "One Step Further" or "Finish the lesson."

In this exercise, you print the message from Rose Alistair, the Human Resources director, because you want to have a hard copy of the message to post in your office.

1 Click the "Payday Policy Change" message from Rose Alistair.

2 On the Viewer toolbar, click the Print button.

Print

The message prints using the last print settings. If you want to modify the print settings, on the File menu, click Print.

3 On the "Payday Policy Change" message, click the Close button.

 TIP To print multiple messages, click a message, hold down CTRL and click each additional message, and then on the File menu, click Print. If you want each message to begin on a new page, select the Start Each Item On A New Page check box in the Print dialog box.

Print an attached file

In this exercise, you print Chandra's message and the spreadsheet attached to it.

You can also press CTRL+P.

1   In the folder list, click the Pecos Coffee folder.

2   Click the "Old Pecos Info" message from Chandra Shah.

3   On the File menu, click Print.

    The Print dialog box appears.

4   Under Options, select the Print Attachments check box.

5   Under Copies, verify that 1 appears in the Number Of Copies box.

    You can click the up arrow to print additional copies.

If you don't have Microsoft Excel installed on your computer, click Cancel.

6   Click OK.

    Microsoft Excel starts and another Print dialog box appears.

7   Click OK.

    The message and the attached file print.

 NOTE   If you'd like to build on the skills that you learned in this lesson, you can perform the exercises presented in the following section, One Step Further. Otherwise, skip to "Finish the lesson."

One Step Further: Customizing Toolbars

Suppose you frequently use a command, but its button does not appear on the Viewer toolbar. You can add the command as a button on the Viewer toolbar so that you can quickly perform the task without using menus.

You can add a button anywhere on the Viewer toolbar. You can also add separators to add space between sets of buttons. This helps you group buttons on a toolbar according to a common task theme. For example, the Reply To Sender, Reply To All, and Forward buttons are grouped together with a separator on each side because these buttons are all used to respond to messages.

Add a toolbar button

Because you use the File Properties command frequently to view message properties, you add it as a button to the Viewer toolbar.

You can also double-click a blank toolbar area.

1   On the Tools menu, click Customize Toolbar.

    The Customize Toolbar dialog box appears.

2   In the Available Buttons list, scroll down, and then click File–Properties.

You can also drag buttons from the Available Buttons box to the Toolbar Buttons box.

3 Click Add.

The File–Properties button is added as the second-to-last button in the Toolbar Buttons list located in the right half of the dialog box. Buttons are added before the selected item in the Toolbar Buttons list.

4 On the Customize Toolbar dialog box, click the Close button.

The Properties button now appears on the Viewer toolbar.

 Properties button

Use the new button

1 Verify that the "Old Pecos Info" message from Chandra Shah is selected.

2 On the Viewer toolbar, click the Properties button you just added.

The Properties dialog box appears.

Properties

3 Click OK.

Restore the toolbar

In this exercise, you return the Viewer toolbar to its original settings.

1 On the Tools menu, click Customize Toolbar.

2 Click Reset, and then click the Close button.

The default Viewer toolbar is restored.

 TIP You can manipulate existing buttons on a toolbar without opening the Customize Toolbar dialog box. To move a toolbar button, hold down SHIFT, and then drag the button to a new location. To delete a button, hold down SHIFT, and then drag the button off the toolbar.

Finish the lesson

Follow these steps to delete the practice messages you created in this lesson.

 WARNING Because you are logged on to Microsoft Exchange with your own username, be sure you delete only the practice files and messages you added or created during this lesson.

1   In your Inbox and Sent Items folders, delete the practice messages you used in this lesson, including the Pecos Coffee subfolder.

2   Close all open windows, except Microsoft Exchange.

3   If you want to continue to the next lesson, click the Inbox folder in the folder list.

4   If you are finished using Microsoft Exchange for now, on the File menu, click Exit And Log Off.

You are logged off Microsoft Exchange and the Viewer window closes.

Lesson Summary

To	Do this	Button
Sort messages within a folder	In the folder contents list, click the column heading for a category.	
Create a folder	Click the information store in which you want to create the new folder or the folder in which you want to create a subfolder. On the File menu, click New Folder, and then type a name.	
Find an item	On the Tools menu, click Find Items. Select the folder and the search conditions you want, and then click Find Now.	
Print a message	Click or open the message. On the toolbar, click the Print button. *or* On the File menu, click Print, and then select the printing options you want.	
Print an attached file	Click or open the message. On the File menu, click Print, and then select the Print Attachments check box.	

For online information about	On the Help menu, click Microsoft Exchange Help Topics, click the Index tab, and then type
Sorting messages	**Sorting: overview**
Creating folders	**Creating: folders**
Deleting folders	**Deleting: folders**
Finding messages	**Finding: messages** *or* **searching messages**
Printing messages	**Printing: messages**
Printing attachments	**Printing: attachments**

Review & Practice

You will review and practice how to:

Estimated time
20 min.

- Open and browse quickly through messages.
- Print a message.
- Create, address, and send a message.
- Attach a file to a message.
- Forward a message.
- Create a folder.
- Sort messages.

Before you move on to Part 2, which covers increasing your productivity using some of Microsoft Exchange enhanced capabilities, you can practice the skills you learned in Part 1 by working through this Review & Practice section. You will open and browse through messages, forward messages, as well as create, address, and send messages. You will also sort messages, create a folder, and print a message.

Scenario

As a busy account executive, you find that your workload is too heavy to meet the demands of several clients. Using Exchange helps you manage your workload more efficiently, but you still need additional support. So, you ask the Human Resources manager if you can hire an administrative assistant.

Step 1: Open and Browse Through Messages

You have received a number of messages that you want to quickly check before sending your message to Human Resources. You notice a message from Lisa Ygarre containing information you need for your meeting with the Pecos Coffee Company. In this step, you open and browse through messages, and then print Lisa's message.

1 Drag the practice messages in the R&P1 folder to your Inbox folder. (Hint: For detailed instructions on setting up your Inbox for this Review & Practice section, see the beginning of Lesson 2.)

2 Sort the practice messages by sender.

3 Open the first practice message. Browse through all your practice messages and find the "RE: Pecos Logo" message from Lisa Ygarre.

4 Print Lisa Ygarre's message. Close the message.

For more information on	See
Opening a message	Lesson 2
Browsing through messages	Lesson 2
Sorting messages	Lesson 3
Printing messages	Lesson 3

Step 2: Create, Address, and Send a Message

You just came back from your meeting with the Pecos Coffee Company and are ready to draft your message to Human Resources. In this step, you create and address a message, attach a file to it, and then send the message.

1 Create a new message and address it to the Human Resources department distribution list. Send a carbon copy to Nate Zostoc, your supervisor.

2 Type **Personnel request** as the message subject.

3 Assign a high priority to your message and request a Read Receipt.

4 Type the following text as the message text:

I am requesting an assistant to help me. A draft of the job description is attached.

5 Check the spelling.

6 Attach the Duties file from the Exchange 5.0 SBS Practice\R&P1 folder at the end of your message.

7 Send the message.

For more information on	See
Creating messages	Lesson 1
Addressing messages	Lesson 1
Assigning priorities	Lesson 1
Attaching receipts	Lesson 1
Checking spelling	Lesson 1
Attaching files	Lesson 1
Sending messages	Lesson 1

Step 3: Forward Messages

To speed up your online communication with the Art team working on the Pecos Coffee Company account, you create a personal distribution list that includes the creative director and the media planner. You then reply to a message concerning the new slogans using your newly created personal distribution list. In this step, you create a distribution list and forward a message.

1   Create a new personal distribution list named "Senior Art Staff." Add Lisa Ygarre and Nate Zostoc as members of the distribution list.

2   Locate the "RE: Pecos Logo" message from Tammy Wu, and then forward Tammy's message to Lisa and Nate using the "Senior Art Staff" personal distribution list.

3   In the message area, type **This is a great start!** and then send the message.

For more information on	See
Creating personal distribution lists	Lesson 1
Forwarding messages	Lesson 2

Step 4: Sort Messages and Work with Folders

Because you receive many messages during the course of a day, you need to create more folders in which to file your messages. You start by creating a folder for messages related to personnel issues because you anticipate more correspondence on this topic. In this step, you create a folder, move a message to that folder, and then sort messages.

1   Sort messages in your Inbox in ascending order by subject.

2   Create a subfolder in your mailbox and name the folder Personnel.

3   Open your Sent Items folder. Move the "Personnel Request" message that you sent to the Human Resources department to the Personnel folder.

For more information on	See
Sorting messages	Lesson 3
Creating folders	Lesson 3

Finish the Review & Practice

Follow these steps to delete the practice messages you created and used in this Review & Practice.

 ⚡ **WARNING** Because you are logged on to Microsoft Exchange with your own username, be sure to delete only the practice files and messages you added or created during this Review & Practice.

1 In your Inbox and Sent Items folders, delete the practice messages you used in this lesson, including the Personnel subfolder.

2 Close all open windows, except Microsoft Exchange.

3 If you want to continue to the next lesson, click the Inbox folder in the folder list.

4 If you are finished using Microsoft Exchange for now, on the File menu, click Exit And Log Off.

You are logged off Microsoft Exchange, and the Viewer window closes.

Increasing Your Productivity

Lesson 4
Automating Repetitive Tasks   63

Lesson 5
Communicating Remotely   79

Lesson 6
Integrating with Microsoft Office   107

Review & Practice   123

Automating Repetitive Tasks

Estimated time
25 min.

In this lesson you will learn how to:

- Group messages.
- Create and save custom views.
- Process incoming messages using the Inbox Assistant.
- Insert text automatically using AutoSignature.

Now that you have learned the basics of creating, sending, and organizing messages in your Inbox, you are ready to expand your skills and discover more efficient ways to manage your messages. For example, if you have spent some time organizing your messages, you can save your settings as a view, and then apply that view to another folder. You can even automate the process of routing your incoming mail using the Inbox Assistant.

In this lesson, you will learn how to automate routine tasks and organize your folders further by grouping messages. You will also learn how to use the Inbox Assistant to apply custom rules to your mailbox and use an AutoSignature to quickly sign your outgoing messages.

Set up your Inbox for this lesson

Before you begin working through this lesson, you'll log on to Microsoft Exchange and choose the Chris Adams profile. You can also use your own profile, but it is recommended that you use the Chris Adams profile so that the exercises and illustrations in this book will more closely match what you see on your screen.

IMPORTANT Because this lesson explores the interactive aspects of Microsoft Exchange, you'll need to recruit some help from a co-worker on your network in order to complete the following exercises.

To complete the exercises in this lesson, you must be using Microsoft Exchange 5.0 Client with Microsoft Exchange Server. If you are not, skip this lesson.

For more detailed instructions on how to set up your Inbox, see Lesson 2.

1 Start Microsoft Exchange using the Chris Adams profile.

2 Copy the practice messages from the Exchange 5.0 SBS Practice\Lesson04 folder to your Inbox folder.

You are ready to start this lesson.

Grouping Messages

To learn more about sorting, see Lesson 3.

Earlier you learned how to sort messages using one category of information at a time. But suppose you want to sort messages using more than one criterion at a time. You can *group* messages to sort them using up to five criteria at once. For example, you can group messages to sort by sender, then by subject, and then by date. By grouping messages, you define the level of detail used to display your messages in any folder.

Because you can organize your messages in several ways, the following table lists the different methods available for organizing messages, and helps you decide which method to use depending on your goals.

Use this	If you want to organize messages
Sort	Based on one column heading in ascending or descending order, such as by Received Date.
Group	According to specific categories, such as Subject or Importance. You also use grouping to display messages in outline form.
Filter	According to specific criteria, such as message subjects containing the word "Pecos."

Grouped messages are organized in an outline form, using the sort criteria you select, with the first sort farthest to the left. Each category can be collapsed or expanded to show more or less detail. A plus sign indicates that a category is collapsed and any information below it is hidden—a minus sign indicates that the category is expanded.

For a demonstration of how to group messages, double-click the Camcorder Files On The Internet shortcut on your Desktop or connect to the Internet address listed on p. xxx.

Group messages

As an account executive, you organize your Inbox to easily find information about your clients. You will group messages using two sort orders: first by sender in ascending order, and then by received date in descending order, so that the most recent messages appear at the top.

1 In the folders list, click the Inbox folder.

By selecting a folder, you indicate where you want the grouping to be applied.

2 On the View menu, click Group By.

The Group By dialog box appears.

3 Click the Group Items By down arrow, and then click From.

The name of the message sender is referenced in the From column. The default sort order for the From column is ascending.

4 Under Then Sort Items By at the bottom of the dialog box, be sure that Received and the Descending option button are selected.

By default, the messages are sorted by received date in descending order. Your dialog box should look similar to the following illustration.

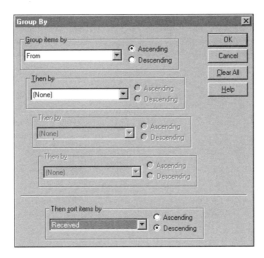

5 Click OK.

After a moment, the messages in your Inbox are grouped according to sender, because this was the first sort order selected.

Categories in bold type contain unread messages.

6 Click the plus sign (+) next to Aaron Wells.

The category expands to show a message from Aaron Wells.

7 Click the minus sign (–) next to Aaron Wells.

The category collapses and the message is hidden.

The letters "RE" and "FW" are not taken into account when you sort.

8 Click the plus sign (+) next to Chandra Shah.

The category expands to show five messages. The messages are sorted using the second sort order that you specified—by received date in descending order. Your screen should look similar to the following illustration.

Regroup messages

In this exercise, you change the way your messages are grouped in your Inbox by using three sort criteria: first by sender, then by subject, and then by received date. This will allow you to organize messages first by sender, and then by subject and date.

1 On the View menu, click Group By.

The Group By dialog box appears with the settings you selected.

2 Under Group Items By, be sure that From is selected.

3 Click the first Then By down arrow, and then click Subject.

The default sort order for the Subject column is ascending.

4 Under Then Sort Items By, at the bottom of the dialog box, be sure that Received and the Descending option button are selected, and then click OK.

The messages in your Inbox are grouped first according to sender, then subject, and finally received date.

5 Click the plus sign (+) next to Chandra Shah.

The category expands to show four subjects, because subject was the second sort criteria selected.

6 Click the plus sign (+) next to the Lunch category.

The category expands to show two messages, sorted in descending order by received date, because received date was the third sort criteria selected.

TIP You can quickly view or hide all categories and grouped messages. To do this, on the View menu, click Expand All or Collapse All.

Browse through unread grouped messages

In this exercise, you open a message and use a toolbar button to locate the rest of your unread messages, whether or not they are in the same group.

1 Double-click the first message from Chandra Shah.

   The "RE: Lunch" message opens.

2 On the Read Message Form toolbar, click the Next Unread button.

   The next unread message, another "RE: Lunch" message from Chandra, appears.

Next Unread

3 Close the "RE: Lunch" message.

Creating Custom Views

To learn more about filtering messages, complete the One Step Further section at the end of this lesson.

After you have customized the organization of your messages, you can save those custom settings as a *view*. You can then apply the view to other folders in your mailbox to display the messages they contain using the same settings. Before you create a view, you specify how you want to group, sort, or filter messages to display only the information you need. For example, you can group messages by specific categories using several sort criteria, such as by sender, and then by received date. When a view is applied to a folder, the messages it contains will be organized based on the view settings, until another view is applied.

NOTE If a view contains several types of settings, filters are applied first, then group settings, and then sort criteria.

You will learn more about public folders in Lesson 8.

There are two types of views: personal and folder. *Personal views* are applied to any or all folders in your mailbox—any personal view you create is available only to you. *Folder views* are applied to individual folders and are only available in the folder in which the view was defined. Folder views are commonly used for public folders. Up to now, you have been working in Normal view. It is a personal view in which messages are displayed by sender, subject, and received date in a particular order. The available views for a folder are listed at the bottom of the View menu. In the following exercises, you will create and work with personal views. Exchange comes with five built-in personal views described in the following table.

This built-in personal view	Displays messages
Normal	Sorted by received date in descending order
Group By From	Grouped by sender
Group By Subject	Grouped by subject
Group By Conversation Topic	Grouped by conversation topic, starting with the most recent, regardless of the subject
Unread By Conversation	Grouped by conversation topic, starting with the most recent (unread messages only)

Built-in personal views cannot be modified or deleted.

Create a personal view

In this exercise, you create a folder view based on the grouped categories currently applied to your Inbox so that you can quickly apply those settings to other folders.

1 On the View menu, click Define Views.

The Define Views dialog box appears.

2 Click New.

The New View dialog box appears. Under Description, the settings that you selected for the Inbox folder are listed.

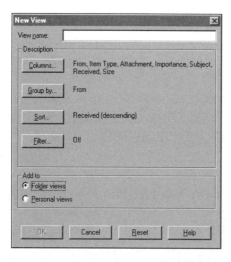

3 In the View Name box, type **Custom Grouping**

4 Under Add To, be sure that the Folder Views option button is selected.

5 Click OK, and then click Close.

Apply views

Now that you have saved the settings you defined earlier as a folder view, you first apply it, and then reapply the Normal view.

1   In the folders list, click the Inbox folder.

By selecting the Inbox folder, you specify where to apply the view.

2   On the View menu, point to Personal Views, and then click Normal.

The Normal view is applied to the Inbox.

3   On the View menu, point to Folder Views, and then click Custom Grouping.

The folder view you created is applied to your Inbox folder.

Processing Messages Using the Inbox Assistant

Most of the routine tasks you perform while using your Inbox can be automated. For example, if you receive daily progress report messages from your project team, you can specify that all incoming messages with the subject "Progress Report" be moved to a specific folder. This set of conditions and instructions is called a *rule*. The *Inbox Assistant* uses rules to process incoming messages. You can create rules that move, respond to, or delete incoming messages that meet specific conditions, such as messages from a certain client. You can even forward entire messages or forward messages as an attachment in one message, rather than as individual messages.

IMPORTANT   If you are working with Exchange offline, you cannot create rules using the Inbox Assistant. Your computer must be connected to a Microsoft Exchange Server to create rules for incoming messages.

For a demonstration of how to set a rule, double-click the Camcorder Files On The Internet shortcut on your Desktop or connect to the Internet address listed on p. xxx.

As an account executive, you receive frequent messages from the Fitch & Mather Production department. Since these messages are not related to your current projects, they do not require your immediate attention. You want to automatically move any incoming Production messages to their own folder so that they don't clutter up your Inbox.

Set a rule

In this exercise, you set a rule to automatically move all the incoming messages from the Production department into a new folder. Because you want to be notified of moved messages, you create a message that will notify you of each move operation.

1   On the Tools menu, click Inbox Assistant.

The Inbox Assistant dialog box appears.

2   Click Add Rule.

The Edit Rule dialog box appears.

3   Under When A Message Arrives That Meets The Following Conditions, click From.

The Choose Sender dialog box appears.

4   Click the Show Names From The down arrow, and then select Personal Address Book.

5   Scroll downward, and then double-click Production Department.

The Production Department distribution list is added to the To box.

6   Click the Show Names From The down arrow, and then select Global Address List.

7   Double-click your own name, and then click OK.

You are including your own name so that you can test the rule by sending a message to yourself. The Edit Rule dialog box reappears.

8   Under Perform These Actions, select the Alert With check box, and then click Action.

If you have a sound card and want to be notified by a sound, click the Sound button, and then select a sound file (.WAV).

9   Type **You have a message from Production** and then click OK.

The Edit Rule dialog box reappears.

 NOTE   If you create multiple rules, the order in which they are processed is based on the order in which they appear in the Edit Rules dialog box. Messages can be processed by more than one rule, unless you select the Do Not Process Subsequent Rules check box.

Create a folder

In this exercise, you create a new folder in which the messages sent to you by members of the Production department will be moved.

1   Under Perform These Actions, select the Move To check box, and then click Folder.

The Move Message To dialog box appears.

2   Click the plus sign (+) next to your mailbox to expand it, and then click the Inbox folder.

3   Click New Folder.

The New Folder dialog box appears.

4 In the Folder Name box, type **Production** and then click OK.

A subfolder named Production appears under the Inbox folder.

5 Click the plus sign (+) next to your Inbox, click the Production folder you just created, and then click OK.

The Production folder is selected as the folder where incoming messages from people in the Production department are to be moved.

6 Click OK.

The Inbox Assistant dialog box reappears. The rule that you created is selected. Your screen should look similar to the following illustration.

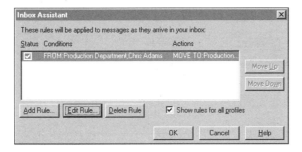

7 Click OK.

The rule for messages from the Production department is now in effect.

8 On the View menu, point to Personal Views, and then click Normal.

The Normal view is applied to the Inbox.

> **IMPORTANT** When you create a rule, it takes effect immediately. If you do not want the rule to be applied to your incoming messages, disable the rule by clearing the check box next to the rule in the Inbox Assistant dialog box. If you want to enable the rule again at a later time, select the check box next to the rule in the Inbox Assistant dialog box.

Test the rule

In this exercise, you test the rule you just created by sending yourself a message. Because you included your name as a member of the Production team when you created the rule, your message will be moved automatically to the Production folder, and you will be notified.

New Message

1 On the Viewer toolbar, click the New Message button.

2 In the To box, type your name.

3 In the Subject box, type **Inbox Assistant Test**

Send

4   Click the Send button.

Your message is sent and delivered to your Production folder because the rule in effect moves any messages sent to you by any member of the production team to your Production folder. After a few moments, a New Items Of Interest dialog box appears, indicating that an incoming message has been moved to the Production folder.

5   Click Read.

The message you sent appears.

6   Close the "Inbox Assistant Test" message.

7   In the New Items Of Interest dialog box, click the Close button.

TIP   Any rules you create are associated with the current profile, in this case, your practice profile for Chris Adams. You can continue using these rules in another profile by moving them. To do this, in the Inbox Assistant dialog box, use the right mouse button to click the rule in your current profile that you want, and then click Move Rule To This Profile.

Edit the rule

1   On the Tools menu, click Inbox Assistant.

The Inbox Assistant dialog box appears.

2   Be sure that the "From: Production" rule you created is selected, and then click Edit Rule.

The Edit Rule dialog box appears.

3   Select your name in the From box, press DELETE, and then click OK.

Your name is removed from the rule.

4   Click OK again.

Inserting Text Automatically Using AutoSignature

You have probably seen people use rubber stamps on paper documents to enter repetitive information, such as a signature or a received date. Using Exchange, you can create an *AutoSignature* entry that works much like a stamp. If you use a standard phrase repeatedly, such as your name and company name, you can create an AutoSignature entry to quickly and efficiently insert the phrase at the end of your messages.

You can format your AutoSignature entry to create a consistent look. For example, if you always write your messages using the Times New Roman font, you can format your AutoSignature entries to all use Times New Roman.

When you create an AutoSignature, it is stored in your mailbox and is available to all messages that you send. After you create your entry, you use the AutoSignature command to insert it into the active message. If you want to change the formatting of an AutoSignature entry, you can easily edit it and save your modifications, instead of recreating the AutoSignature from scratch. You can also add text, attachments, and graphics to an AutoSignature entry.

Create an AutoSignature entry

In this exercise, you create an AutoSignature entry to automatically insert your company name, Fitch & Mather, and address as a message header in all the messages you send to your clients.

1   On the Tools menu, click AutoSignature.

    The AutoSignature dialog box appears.

2   Click New.

    The New AutoSignature dialog box appears.

3   In the Name box, type **FM** and then press TAB.

    FM will be the name of the AutoSignature.

4   Type the following text, pressing ENTER after each line:

    Fitch & Mather

    511 54th Boulevard SE

    Bellevue, WA 98531

Format an AutoSignature entry

In this exercise, you format an AutoSignature entry and define its placement on the documents in which it will be inserted.

You can press CTRL+A to select all the AutoSignature text.

1   Select all the text you just typed.

2   Click Font.

    The Font dialog box appears.

3   Select Times New Roman in the Font box, Italic in the Font Style box, 12 in the Size box, and then click OK.

    The New AutoSignature dialog box reappears.

4   Click Paragraph.

    The Paragraph dialog box appears.

5   Under Alignment, click the Center option button, and then click OK.

    The New AutoSignature dialog box should look similar to the following illustration.

6   Click OK, and then, on the AutoSignature dialog box, click the Close button.

An AutoSignature entry named FM is created.

Test the AutoSignature entry

In this exercise, you test the AutoSignature entry you just created.

New Message

1   On the Viewer toolbar, click the New Message button.

2   In the To box, type your name.

3   In the Subject box, type **AutoSignature Test**

4   Click in the message area, type **Just testing** and then press ENTER twice.

5   On the Tools menu, click AutoSignature.

The AutoSignature dialog box appears.

6   Under Selections, be sure that FM is selected, and then click Insert.

The AutoSignature entry is inserted. Your message should look similar to the following illustration.

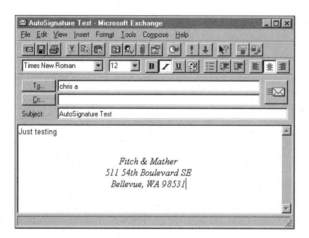

Send

7   Click the Send button.

After a few moments, the message is delivered.

> **TIP**   You can edit your AutoSignature. To do this, on the Tools menu, click AutoSignature, click the AutoSignature you want to modify, and then click Edit.
>
> You can automatically insert an AutoSignature at the end of all your outgoing messages. To do this, click the AutoSignature, click Set As Default, and then select the Add The Default Selection To The End Of Outgoing Messages check box.

NOTE If you'd like to build on the skills that you learned in this lesson, you can perform the exercises presented in the following section, One Step Further. Otherwise, skip to "Finish the lesson."

One Step Further: Filtering Messages

If you want to display only certain messages in a folder, you can apply a *filter* to it. Any messages that don't match the criteria you define are hidden temporarily. For example, if you want to show only messages from your manager in your Inbox, you can filter the messages by sender.

When a filter is applied to a folder, a filter icon appears on the status bar. If a view includes a filter, it is applied to the folder first, before any other criteria. For example, if messages in a folder are sorted or grouped and a filter is applied, the messages are filtered first, and then sorted or grouped. Filtering messages is similar to sorting and grouping messages, except that the messages you filter out are hidden from view.

Filter messages

In this exercise, you apply a filter to your Inbox so that you only view messages about the upcoming payday policy change.

1   In the folder list, click the Inbox folder.

By selecting a folder, you indicate where you want the filter to be applied.

2   On the View menu, click Filter.

The Filter dialog box appears.

3   Click in the Subject box, type **payday** and then click OK.

The filter is applied, and only messages with the subject "payday" appear in the Inbox. Your Viewer window should look similar to the following illustration.

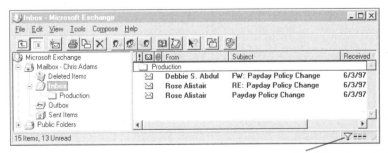

The Filter icon indicates that a filter is applied to the current folder.

75

Remove the filter

Now that you have viewed and read the messages about paydays, you want to remove the filter.

1   On the View menu, click Filter.

The Filter dialog box appears.

2   Click Clear All.

All information is cleared in the dialog box.

3   Click OK.

The filter is removed and all the messages appear again. The filter icon is removed from the status bar.

Finish the lesson

Follow these steps to delete the practice messages you created in this lesson.

 WARNING   Because you are logged on to Microsoft Exchange with your own username, be sure you delete only the practice files and messages you added or created during this lesson.

1   In your Inbox and Sent Items folders, delete the practice messages you used in this lesson, including the the Production subfolder.

2   Delete the rule that you created in this lesson by clicking Inbox Assistant on the Tools menu, selecting the rule, and then clicking Delete Rule. Click Yes when prompted to confirm the deletion.

3   Remove the AutoSignature you created in this lesson by clicking AutoSignature on the Tools menu, selecting the AutoSignature, and then clicking Remove. Click Yes when prompted to confirm the deletion.

4   Delete the view you created in this lesson by clicking Define Views on the View menu, selecting Custom Grouping, and then clicking Delete. Click Yes when prompted to confirm the deletion.

5   Close all open windows, except Microsoft Exchange.

6   If you want to continue to the next lesson, click the Inbox folder in the folder list.

7   If you are finished using Microsoft Exchange for now, on the File menu, click Exit And Log Off.

You are logged off Microsoft Exchange and the Viewer window closes.

Lesson Summary

To	Do this
Group messages using two sort orders	On the View menu, click Group By, click the Group Items By down arrow, and then click a category. Click the Then By down arrow, and then click a category.
Expand grouped messages	Click the plus sign (+) next to a grouped category. *or* On the View menu, click Expand All.
Collapse grouped messages	Click the minus sign (–) next to a grouped category. *or* On the View Menu, click Collapse All.
Create a personal view	On the View menu, click Define Views, and then click New. Type a name, and then customize the folder by defining sort, group, or filter criteria.
Apply a view	Click the folder to which you want to apply a view. On the View menu, click Personal Views or Folder Views, and then click the view.
Create a rule using the Inbox Assistant	On the Tools menu, click Inbox Assistant. Select a rule, click Add Rule, and then modify the options for incoming messages.
Modify a rule using the Inbox Assistant	On the Tools menu, click Inbox Assistant. Click Edit Rule, and then click the options you want for incoming messages.
Create an AutoSignature entry	On the Tools menu, click AutoSignature. Click New, type a name for your entry, press TAB, and then enter your text.

To	Do this
Insert an AutoSignature entry	With your message open, on the Tools menu, click AutoSignature. Click the AutoSignature entry you want, and then click Insert.
Edit an AutoSignature entry	On the Tools menu, click AutoSignature. Click the AutoSignature entry you want, click Edit, and then make the changes you want.

For online information about	On the Help menu, click Microsoft Exchange Help Topics, click the Index tab, and then type
Viewing messages in folders	**Views** or **Personal Views command**
Grouping messages	**Grouping: messages in views** or **Group By command**
Creating personal views	**Creating: views** or **personal views**
Using the Inbox Assistant	**Inbox Assistant** or **rules**
Using AutoSignature	**AutoSignature** or **signature line**

Communicating Remotely

Estimated time
40 min.

In this lesson you will learn how to:

- Process mail using the Out Of Office Assistant.
- Reply automatically to messages.
- Delegate access to another user.
- Connect to Microsoft Exchange remotely.

So far, you have learned how to use Microsoft Exchange in a networked environment, such as your office, where your computer is directly connected to a local area network on which the Microsoft Exchange Server is located. But if you need to send and receive messages from home or from a computer outside of your Exchange enterprise, you can work remotely.

Suppose that you are getting ready for a business trip and that you want to be able to use Exchange on your laptop computer while traveling. In this lesson, you will learn how to manage your incoming messages while away from the office, assign delegate privileges to a co-worker, set up your modem, and work offline.

IMPORTANT   Because this lesson explores the interactive aspects of Microsoft Exchange, you'll need to recruit some help from a co-worker on your network in order to complete the following exercises.

To complete the exercises in this lesson, you must be using Microsoft Exchange 5.0 Client with Microsoft Exchange Server. If you are not, skip this lesson.

Set up your Inbox for this lesson

For more detailed instructions on how to set up your Inbox, see Lesson 2.

1   Start Microsoft Exchange using the Chris Adams profile.

2   Copy the practice messages from the Exchange 5.0 SBS Practice\Lesson05 folder to your Inbox folder.

You are ready to start this lesson.

Managing Messages Using the Out Of Office Assistant

When you are away from your office for any length of time, you can process your messages automatically using the *Out Of Office Assistant*. The Out Of Office Assistant allows you to notify the people who send you messages that you are away by creating an automatic reply. As you've learned in Lesson 4 while using the Inbox Assistant, you can create rules that are applied automatically to incoming messages, even when you are not using your office computer. Rules allow you to move, copy, delete, or forward messages automatically.

Setting Up an Automatic Reply

Before you leave your office for an extended period of time, the first thing you'll probably do is create an AutoReply, a text message that is sent to each person who sends you mail while you're away. The Out Of Office Assistant sends only one response to each person who has sent you mail—regardless of the number of times the person sends you messages. When you return to the office and start Exchange to resume reviewing and replying to your messages, you are reminded that the Out Of Office Assistant is activated and you are given an opportunity to turn it off.

Because you will leave shortly on a business trip, you want to set up an automatic reply informing anyone who sends you e-mail that you're away from the office.

Set up an automatic reply

1 On the Tools menu, click Out Of Office Assistant.

The Out Of Office Assistant dialog box appears.

2 Click the I Am Currently Out Of The Office option button.

3 Click in the AutoReply Only Once To Each Sender With The Following Text box, and then type **I'm out of the office until Friday. Aaron Wells will be handling my accounts until then**.

Your dialog box should look similar to the following illustration.

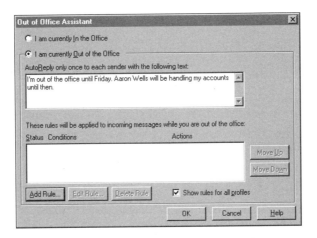

4 Click OK.

The AutoReply is set up for any incoming messages.

Test your AutoReply

In this exercise, you test the AutoReply you just created to see if you receive the automatic message.

New Message

1 On the Viewer toolbar, click the New Message button.

2 In the To box, type your name.

You are sending the message to yourself as a test message.

3 In the Subject box, type **AutoReply Test**

Send

4 Click the Send button.

After a moment, your message is sent and two messages are delivered to your Inbox: the "AutoReply Test" message and the "Out Of Office AutoReply" message.

5 Double-click the "Out Of Office AutoReply" message.

Your message should look similar to the following illustration.

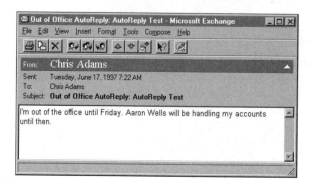

6 Close the "Out Of Office AutoReply" message.

 IMPORTANT All senders of incoming messages will now receive the AutoReply. If you want to disable the AutoReply until you leave on your trip, click Out Of Office Assistant on the Tools menu, and then click the I Am Currently In The Office option button.

Creating Out Of Office Rules

In Lesson 4, you learned how to create and use rules to process incoming messages when you are in the office. You can also create and use rules to process incoming messages while you are away from the office using the Out Of Office Assistant. For example, you can create a rule to forward incoming messages from your clients to another account executive while you are away. However, you cannot use the Out Of Office Assistant to forward your messages to someone outside of your Exchange enterprise. Because rules are processed in your mailbox on the Exchange Server, Exchange does not have to be open to use the Out Of Office Assistant.

 NOTE If you are using both the Inbox Assistant and the Out Of Office Assistant, and two rules conflict, the Out Of Office Assistant rule takes precedence over the Inbox Assistant rule.

Save an address to your personal address book

Because you will create a rule to forward messages from Joe Pecos to one of your co-workers, you must first save Joe Pecos' Internet address in your personal address book. In this exercise, you add Joe Pecos' Internet address to your personal address book.

1 In your Inbox folder, double-click the "Meeting" message from Joe Pecos.

2 In the From area, use the right mouse button to click the name "Joe Pecos."

A shortcut menu appears.

3 Click Add To Personal Address Book.

4 Close the "Meeting" message.

Set up a rule using the Out Of Office Assistant

In this exercise, you create a rule to forward the messages that you receive from Joe to one of your co-workers. This way, your co-worker can respond to any urgent messages while you are traveling.

1 On the Tools menu, click Out Of Office Assistant.

The Out Of Office Assistant dialog box appears.

2 Click Add Rule.

3 Under When A Message Arrives That Meets The Following Conditions, click From.

The Choose Sender dialog box appears.

4 Click the Show Names From The down arrow, and then click Personal Address Book.

5 Double-click Joe Pecos.

The name is added to the From box.

If you select more than one name in a rule, an "or" condition is created so that messages from either sender are searched for.

6 Click OK.

The Edit Rule dialog box reappears.

7 Under Perform These Actions, select the Forward check box, and then click To.

The Choose Recipient dialog box appears.

8 Double-click the name of the co-worker who is helping with this lesson.

Your co-worker will receive all messages from Joe Pecos while you are out of the office.

9 Click OK, and then click OK again.

The Out Of Office Assistant dialog box reappears. The rule that you created is selected.

10 Click OK.

Incoming messages from Joe Pecos will now be forwarded to your co-worker.

 IMPORTANT When you create an AutoReply, it is applied immediately. If you do not want the rule to be applied to your incoming messages yet, you can cancel it by clearing the check mark next to the rule in the Out Of Office Assistant dialog box.

Delegating Access to Another User

Now that you have created a rule so that messages from your clients are forwarded to one of your co-workers, you would also like that person to periodically check all the messages in your mailbox. In order for your co-worker to view the contents of your mailbox, you will need to specify him or her as a *delegate*.

By granting permission to a delegate, you can control which folders the delegate can view and what the delegate can do. For example, you can specify that your co-worker can work only in your Inbox, but not in other folders, depending on the role you assign. In addition, you can allow the delegate to send messages on your behalf. When your delegate addresses messages using your name in the From box, both your name and the delegate's name appear in the message header so that the recipients can easily see that the messages were sent on your behalf.

Exchange comes with several predefined roles for delegates with varying levels of permission. For example, you can assign your delegate permission to create and send messages, but not delete any messages. If you select a role, the associated permissions are automatically selected. The following table lists the roles and associated permissions that you can assign to a delegate.

Role	Permission to	Can edit or delete
None	No permissions	No items
Contributor	Create items	No items
Reviewer	Read items	No items
Non-editing Author	Create items, read items	Own items
Author	Create items, read items	Own items
Publishing Author	Create items, read items, create subfolders	Own items
Editor	Create items, read items	All items

Role	Permission to	Can edit or delete
Publishing editor	Create items, read items, create subfolders	All items
Owner	Create items, read items, create subfolders, folder owner	All items

NOTE Granting a delegate the authorization to read items (Reviewer) is the minimum permission required to allow that person to open your Inbox. Delegates cannot be assigned permission to access personal folders.

You are getting ready to leave for your business trip. Because you want your co-worker to be able to open your mailbox and reply to any of your messages, you decide to give that person access to your Inbox folder and permission to send mail on your behalf.

Grant permission to another user

In this exercise, you grant a co-worker permission as an author so that he or she can read messages in your mailbox and send messages on your behalf.

For a demonstration of how to grant permission to another user, double-click the Camcorder Files On The Internet shortcut on your Desktop or connect to the Internet address listed on p. xxx.

IMPORTANT To be able to assign permissions to a delegate, your computer must be connected to an Exchange Server. You can't assign permission while working offline.

1   In the folder list, click your Mailbox information store.

By selecting the mailbox information store, you specify where to grant permissions.

2   On the File menu, click Properties, and then click the Permissions tab.

The Mailbox Properties dialog box appears.

3   Click Add.

The Add Users dialog box appears.

4   In the upper-right corner of the Address Book dialog box, be sure that Global Address List appears in the Show Names From The box.

5   Double-click the name of the co-worker helping you with this lesson, and then click OK.

The Mailbox Properties dialog box reappears.

The None role is assigned by default.

6 Select your co-worker's name, and in the Permissions area, click the Roles down arrow, and then click Author.

Granting the predefined role of author allows the delegate to read and create messages. Your dialog box should look similar to the following illustration.

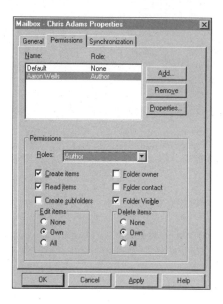

7 Click OK.

Your co-worker now has permission to read and create items in your mailbox.

8 In the folder list, click your Inbox folder.

9 In the folder list, click the Inbox folder, and then repeat steps 2 through 7 to assign permission to your Inbox.

You must also grant permission to your Inbox so that your delegate can access messages in your Inbox.

Grant your delegate permission to send messages on your behalf

Now that your co-worker has author permissions to your Inbox, you can grant that person permission to send messages on your behalf while you are away from the office.

1 On the Tools menu, click Options.

The Options dialog box appears.

2 Click the Exchange Server tab.

3 Click Add.

The Add Users dialog box appears.

4 Double-click the name of the co-worker who is helping you with this lesson, and then click OK.

5 Click OK.

Your co-worker now has permission to send messages on your behalf.

 IMPORTANT When you assign permission to a delegate, it takes effect immediately. If you do not want the delegate to be able to work in your mailbox or send messages on your behalf yet, on the File menu, click Properties, click the Permissions tab, click the delegate's name, and then click Remove.

Test delegate access

Now that your delegate has been assigned an author role, that person can access your mailbox. In this exercise, your delegate tests his or her access privileges.

 IMPORTANT Be sure that your delegate performs this exercise on his or her computer.

1 Start Microsoft Exchange.

2 On the Tools menu, click Services.

The Services dialog box appears.

3 Click Microsoft Exchange Server, and then click the Properties button.

4 Click the Advanced tab.

Options for the Microsoft Exchange Server information service appear.

5 Click Add.

The Add Mailbox dialog box appears.

6 Type the name of the mailbox to which you've been given access, and then click OK.

7 Click OK, and then click OK again.

Your co-worker's mailbox now appears under the Microsoft Exchange information store in the folder list.

8 In the folder list, click your co-worker's mailbox, and then double-click your co-worker's Inbox.

You can view the contents of your co-worker's Inbox.

Test sending messages on your behalf

In this exercise, your co-worker sends a message on your behalf.

IMPORTANT   Be sure that your delegate performs this exercise on his or her computer.

New Message

1   On the Viewer toolbar, click the New Message button.

2   On the View menu, click From Box.

   The From box is added to the message header.

3   In the From box, type the name of the person who gave you delegate access.

   By entering a name in the From box, the message header will indicate that the message was sent by you (the delegate) on behalf of your co-worker.

4   In the To box, type your name, and in the Subject box, type **Test**

5   Click the Send button.

Send

View the test message

Now that you have sent a test message on behalf of your co-worker, you view the "Delegate Test" message header.

1   In the folder list, click your Inbox folder.

2   Double-click the "Delegate Test" message.

   The message header indicates that the message was sent by you, on behalf of your co-worker.

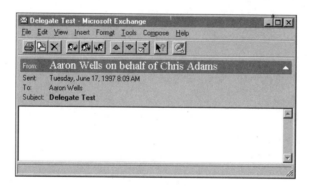

3   Close the "Delegate Test" message.

Working Offline

There are two ways to work with Exchange when you are offsite: you can work *offline* and occasionally use Remote Mail to transfer messages, or you can use a *continuous dial-up connection.*

When you work offline, your computer is not connected to the Exchange Server. So, when you want to send and receive messages, you need to use Remote Mail to quickly connect to your Exchange Server, send and receive your messages, and then disconnect from the server. This method is usually the fastest and the most economical because it minimizes long distance telephone charges.

Using a continuous dial-up connection provides continuous access to your office computer—as if you were working in the office. This method is more convenient because it provides you with easy access to your office, but it might be a less efficient use of telephone time and might also be slower, depending on the speed of your connection.

Preparing to Work Offline

You are preparing for a business trip and you want to be able to use your laptop computer to connect to your Microsoft Exchange Server at Fitch & Mather to check your new messages. Before you leave work, you make sure that your laptop computer is set up to work offline.

 IMPORTANT   Perform the following exercise on your offsite computer. Your offsite computer must be connected to an Exchange Server. To complete the exercises in the remainder of this lesson, your offsite computer must have Exchange installed as well as a modem, a telephone line, and dial-up networking software so that you can establish a dial-up connection.

In addition, to be able to work remotely with Exchange, your Windows NT Server account must have dial-up access rights. Contact your system administrator if you need more information or assistance.

Prepare to work offline

In this exercise, you set up Exchange on your offsite computer so that you can connect to your Exchange Server while away from the office.

 IMPORTANT   Perform the following exercise on your offsite computer.

1 Using your offsite computer, start Microsoft Exchange, making sure that you are connected to your Exchange Server.

If you're prompted to turn off the Out Of Office Assistant, click No because you will be working offline in the next section.

2 On the Tools menu, click Services.

The Services dialog box appears.

3 Be sure that Microsoft Exchange Server is selected, and then click Properties.

An underlined mailbox name indicates that it has been validated against the Exchange Server.

4 On the General tab, be sure that your Microsoft Exchange Server name and mailbox name appear, and that they are underlined.

If either or both of these names are not underlined, click the Check Names button to validate them or contact your Microsoft Exchange Server administrator.

5 Select the Choose The Connection Type When Starting check box.

The next time you start Exchange on your offsite computer, you will be prompted to choose between connecting to the server or working offline.

Offline folder files have an .OST extension.

6 Click the Advanced tab, click Offline Folder File Settings, be sure that the File box has a filename entry, and then click OK.

If you are prompted to create the file, click Yes.

7 Click OK, and then click OK again.

Your offline folder settings file is created.

 TIP If you work on an offsite computer on a regular basis, you might want to create a different profile that contains your offline folders configuration. To do this, on the Tools menu, click Options. Under When Starting Microsoft Exchange, click the Prompt For A Profile To Be Used option button, and then click OK. Exit and log off of Exchange, and then restart the program. For more information on creating a new profile, see "Installing and Using the Practice Files" earlier in this book.

If you use the same computer to work remotely and in your office, you can also create a separate profile that contains your remote configuration settings.

Download the Address Book

In this exercise, you download the Address Book for your Microsoft Exchange enterprise so that you can address and send messages while working offline.

IMPORTANT   Perform the following exercise on your offsite computer. Your computer must be connected to the Microsoft Exchange Server before you can download the Address Book.

1   On the Tools menu, point to Synchronize, and then click Download Address Book.

The Download Offline Address Book dialog box appears.

2   Be sure that the Download Offline Address Book option button is selected, and then click OK.

The Address Book is copied to your offsite computer hard disk and is now available on your offsite computer.

3   On the File menu, click Exit And Log Off.

You are logged off of Microsoft Exchange and ready to work offline.

Working Offline

When you work offline on your offsite computer, you need a place to store the messages that you send and receive because your Exchange mailbox is physically located on the Exchange Server. To store your messages, you use *offline folders*, which are representations of your server folders. The offline folders that are included by default on your offsite computer are the same as when you work online: Inbox, Outbox, Sent Items, and Deleted Items. You work with offline folders in the same way you work with your mailbox folders or any other folders.

When you are working offline, your server mailbox will still be receiving messages. Any messages you compose while working offline are stored in your offline Outbox until they are sent. Unsent messages are identified by italicized text in the message header. To transfer messages to and from the server, you need to connect to the Exchange Server using Remote Mail. During your Remote Mail session, any new message you want to read will be transferred, or copied, to your offline folders and any message that you want to send will be transferred from your offline folders to the server.

You are now on the road with your offsite computer, you want to check in at Fitch & Mather to keep up-to-date on the business at your office. Because you don't currently have access to a telephone line, you'll work offline and compose a message that will be stored in your Outbox. Later, you'll use Remote Mail to establish the dial-up connection to your server and transfer the message you've composed.

Work with offline folders

In this exercise, you compose a test message offline that will be stored in your Outbox until you can connect to the Exchange Server at Fitch & Mather.

 IMPORTANT Perform the following exercise on your offsite computer.

1 On your offsite computer, start Microsoft Exchange using the Chris Adams profile.

The Microsoft Exchange Server dialog box appears.

2 Click Work Offline.

The Viewer window with the offline folders appears.

3 In the folder list, click the Sent Items folder.

The folder contents list in the right half of the window should be empty because you have not yet sent any messages while working offline.

4 In the folder list, click the Outbox folder.

The folder contents list should be empty, because you have not sent any messages while working offline yet.

New Message

5 On the Viewer toolbar, click the New Message button.

6 In the To box, type your name.

7 In the Subject box, type **Offline Test**

Send

8 Click the Send button.

A copy of your message is created and stored in the Outbox folder until you connect to the Exchange Server. Your offline Outbox should look similar to the following illustration.

The "Offline Test" message you
sent appears in italicized text.

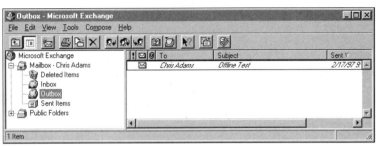

> **WARNING** If you open an italicized message in the offline
> Outbox, and then close it without clicking the Send button,
> the italic formatting is removed from the message, and it will
> not be sent when the offline folders are synchronized with the
> server folders. You will learn more about synchronizing folders
> in the following exercises.

Using Remote Mail to Transfer Message Headers

While working offline, you might want to periodically check your mailbox on
the Exchange Server for new messages. Or, you might want to send the messages you composed offline. You can establish a temporary connection using
Remote Mail to dial in to the server.

In the Remote Mail window, you view only the headers of the messages currently stored in your mailbox; this allows you to select the messages you want
to work with offline. If you have previously connected to your server, the message headers will be refreshed, or updated, to represent the current contents of
your mailbox. The Remote Mail window also includes a toolbar and buttons for
frequently performed tasks.

View message headers

You now have access to a telephone line, and are ready to send the message
you composed offline and check for new messages. In this exercise, you connect
to your Exchange Server, check for new messages, and send the "Offline Test"
message stored in the offline Outbox.

IMPORTANT Perform the following exercise on your offsite computer. Before you start this exercise, be sure you know your modem type, phone number to your Exchange server, and the domain server name so that you can log on to your network. If you need help, contact your system administrator.

1 On the Tools menu, click Remote Mail.

The Remote Mail window appears.

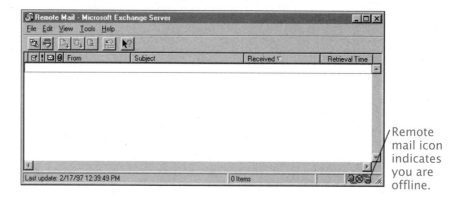

Remote mail icon indicates you are offline.

If Dial-Up Networking is not available in the My Computer window, you must install it first using Windows Setup.

2 On the Tools menu, click Options, and then click the Dial-Up Networking tab.

3 Be sure that the Dial Using The Following Connection option button is selected, and then click New.

The Make New Connection dialog box appears. If you have already created a dial-up connection for your Microsoft Exchange Server, skip to step 7.

4 In the Type A Name For The Computer You Are Dialing, type **Exchange Connection**, select your modem type, and then click Next.

If your connection requires a pause, before typing in an extension number for example, you can type a comma (,).

5 Type the phone number for your Microsoft Exchange Server, and then click Next.

You might have to precede the phone number with a 9 in order to establish an outside dial tone.

6 Click Finish.

Your dial-up connection, named Exchange Connection, is complete.

7 Type your username and password, and then type your Microsoft Exchange domain name.

8   Click the down arrow, and then click the dial-up connection you just created.

The Remote Mail tab should look similar to the following illustration.

9   Click OK.

Connect

You can also click Connect on the Tools menu.

10   On the Remote Mail Window toolbar, click the Connect button.

After a few moments, you are connected to your Exchange Server and the icon in the status bar changes to indicate that you are connected. Your message headers are transferred to the Remote Mail window. The "Offline Test" message that you sent to yourself and the message headers of any new incoming messages in your mailbox appear, and then you are automatically disconnected.

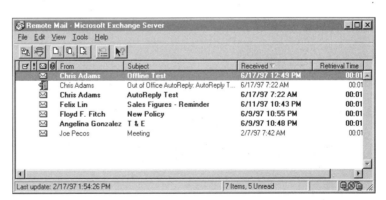

TIP You can choose to stay connected after downloading message headers instead of being automatically disconnected. To do this, on the Tools menu, click Options, click the Remote Mail tab, and then clear the Automatically Disconnect After check box.

Marking Messages in the Remote Mail Window

After your message headers have been transferred from the server to the Remote Mail window, you are disconnected and you can specify which message you want to work with. For example, if you want to *download* a message so that you can open it in your offline Inbox, you select the message in the Remote Mail window, and then click the Mark To Retrieve button. The next time you connect to your Exchange Server, your folders will be *synchronized* and the message will be downloaded from the server to your offsite computer. Then you can open the message and reply to it, just as you would if you were at the office.

When you connect to your Exchange Server using Remote Mail, any changes you made while working offline are synchronized with your mailbox folders on the server. Likewise, any changes in the Exchange Server folders are transferred to your offline folders. During the synchronization, Exchange compares the contents of the folders, and then performs the required actions to make them identical.

The following table lists the tasks you can perform when you mark messages while in the Remote Mail window.

To	Click this button
Delete messages on the server without downloading them.	
Download messages and delete them from the server.	
Copy messages without deleting them from the server.	
Unmark all messages.	

 WARNING When you mark a message for deletion in the Remote Mail window, the message will be permanently deleted when you synchronize your folders; it won't be moved to the Deleted Items folder.

If you have not read a message, the header appears in bold. If a message has been downloaded, but a copy also remains on the server, the header appears in plain text. Depending on the message type or action performed, each message will have an icon to the left of it to identify the action taken. In addition to the standard icons used in Exchange, the icons used in the Remote Mail window are listed in the following table.

Icon	Message description
	Message moved from the server to your offline Inbox.
	Message copied from the server to your offline Inbox.
	Message deleted from the server.

Mark to retrieve a message using Remote Mail

In this exercise, you copy a message from the server to your offline Inbox and delete another message on the server without downloading it.

IMPORTANT   Perform the following exercise on your offsite computer.

---

1   In the Remote Mail window, click the "Offline Test" message header.

You must select a message before marking it.

Mark To Retrieve

2   On the Remote Mail Window toolbar, click the Mark To Retrieve button.

An icon appears next to the message header to indicate that it is marked for retrieval. When the message is downloaded, it will be moved from your mailbox on the Microsoft Exchange Server to your offsite computer.

3   Click the "Sales Figures–Reminder" message header from Felix Lin.

4   On the Remote Mail Window toolbar, click the Mark To Delete button.

Mark To Delete

An icon appears next to the message header to indicate that it is marked for deletion. When you connect to the server, the message is moved from the Inbox folder into the Deleted Items folder on your server mailbox.

5   On the Tools menu, click Connect.

Your messages headers are updated.

6   Close the Remote Mail window.

The Viewer window with offline folders appears.

Synchronize a folder

Now that you have marked your message headers for action, you synchronize your offline folders, and then check the log file to verify that your folders were synchronized.

1 On the Tools menu, point to Synchronize, and then click All Folders.

Exchange starts to dial-up your connection. After a few moments, your offline folders are synchronized, and then you are automatically disconnected. All messages in your server folders are replicated in your offline folders, except for messages that you marked for deletion.

2 In the folder list, be sure the Outbox folder is selected.

The folder contents list should now be empty because the "Offline Test" message that you composed while working offline was sent.

3 In the folder list, click the Sent Items folder.

The "Offline Test" message appears.

4 In the folder list, click the Deleted Items folder.

A log file appears in the Deleted Items folder.

If you have several log files, open the most recent one.

5 Double-click the Synchronization Log file.

The log file appears and indicates the length of time you were connected, the names of the folders that were synchronized, and the number of items synchronized. Your log file should look similar to the following illustration.

6   Close the Synchronization window.

7   On the File menu, click Exit And Log Off.

You are logged off Microsoft Exchange.

TIP   You can schedule specific times to automatically establish a connection with your Exchange Server. For example, you can connect at night to save on long distance telephone charges or connect every two or three hours for convenience. To do this, leave your computer hooked up to a telephone line with Exchange running. In the Remote Mail window, click Options on the Tools menu, and then click the Remote Mail tab. Click Schedule, and then select times to connect.

Establishing a Continuous Dial-Up Connection

When you work offsite and still want to work with the Exchange Server as if you were using your office computer, you can dial in to your server to establish a continuous dial-up connection by using *Dial-Up Networking*. Although the server might respond more slowly, you can use features that are only available while connected to an Exchange Server. For example, if you want to use public folders or work with Schedule+, you must establish a continuous dial-up connection. When you use a dial-up connection, you won't have to use offline folders or establish a Remote Mail connection to transfer messages.

Establish a dial-up connection

Since you know how to work offline and download new messages, you can now establish a connection and work with your Exchange Server just as you would if you were in your office. In this exercise, you establish a continuous dial-up connection, send yourself another test message, and then disconnect from the server.

IMPORTANT   Perform the following exercise on your offsite computer.

To work with public folders or Schedule+, you must use a continuous dial-up connection. You will learn about public folders in Lesson 8 and about Schedule+ in Part 4.

1   On the Desktop on your offsite computer, double-click the My Computer icon.

The contents of your computer appear.

2 Double-click the Dial-Up Networking icon.

The Dial-Up Networking window appears. The connection that you created earlier, named Exchange Connection, is listed.

3 Double-click the Exchange Connection icon.

The Connect To window appears.

4 Type a password, if necessary, and then click Connect.

After a few moments, the dial-up connection is established.

5 Start Microsoft Exchange using the Chris Adams profile.

The Microsoft Exchange Server dialog box appears.

6 Click Connect.

The Viewer window appears, allowing you to work directly with the server. If you're prompted to turn off the Out Of Office Assistant, click No.

New Message

7 On the Viewer toolbar, click the New Message button, and then address the message to yourself.

You are sending the message to yourself as a test to verify that using a continuous dial-up connection is similar to using your office computer.

Send

8 In the Subject box, type **Another Test** and then click the Send button.

After a moment, your message appears in your Inbox because you are connected to the server.

9 On the File menu, click Exit And Log Off, and then disconnect the Exchange Connection dial-up.

NOTE If you'd like to build on the skills that you learned in this lesson, you can perform the exercises presented in the following section, One Step Further. Otherwise, skip to "Finish the lesson."

One Step Further: Signing and Sealing Messages

If you want to ensure that the recipients of your messages can verify that the messages actually did come from you, you can *sign* them. Signing your messages is a way to show that they were not tampered with after you sent them. A signed message is encrypted with a digital signature. You can't see a digital signature, but you can verify it by viewing the message properties. To sign a message, you need to have an advanced security password. You can sign each message you send individually, or you can sign them all. You can also *seal* a message, which ensures that only the recipients to whom you addressed your message can open it. In order to open sealed messages, the recipient must provide his or her own password and be registered in a Exchange security enterprise.

Before you can sign or seal messages, your Exchange Server administrator must first configure your mailbox for advanced security, and then give you a keyword created by the security software on the Exchange Server. The keyword is similar to a password, but is used only during the setup procedure. After advanced security has been set up for your mailbox, a security file (.EPF extension) is created for you and you must establish your security password. If you want to use this advanced security on your offsite computer, you can copy the EPF file to your offsite computer's Exchange folder. The icons used to identify advanced security messages in the folder contents list are listed in the following table.

Icon	Description
	Sealed encrypted e-mail.
	Digitally signed e-mail.

IMPORTANT   Before you can sign and seal messages, you must set up advanced security for your computer and obtain the keyword before you begin. Otherwise, the Digitally Sign Message button and the Seal Message With Encryption button will be dimmed. If you need help, contact your system administrator.

Set up advanced security

In this exercise, you set up your advanced security password so that you can sign your messages.

It is a good idea to make your advanced security password different from any of your other passwords.

1   On the Tools menu, click Options, and then click the Security tab.

2   Click Set Up Advanced Security.

The dialog box expands, and the security options appear.

3   In the Token box, type the keyword that your system administrator gave you.

Your advanced security password must have a minimum of six characters and is case-sensitive.

4   In the Password box, type an advanced security password, press TAB, and then type your advanced security password again.

5   Click OK.

A message appears, stating that your request has been sent to the server. After a few moments your request for advanced security is processed and you receive a message from the system attendant.

6   Click OK, and then click OK again.

7   Double-click the "Reply From Security Authority" message from the system attendant.

A message appears, prompting you to enter your advanced security password.

8   Type your advanced security password, and then click OK.

A message appears, stating that advanced security has successfully been enabled.

9   Click OK.

NOTE   You can change your advanced security password. To do this, on the Tools menu, click Options, and then click the Security tab. Click Change Password, and then type both your old and your new password.

Sign a message

1   Create a new message and address it to a co-worker.

2   In the Subject box, type **Sign Test**

3   In the message area, type **This is an encrypted message.**

4   On the New Message Form toolbar, click the Digitally Sign Message button.

5   Click the Send button.

The Microsoft Exchange Security Logon dialog box appears.

Digitally Sign Message

6 Type your advanced security password, and then click OK.

Your message is sent as an encrypted message.

 TIP If you want all your outgoing messages to be signed, on the Tools menu, click Options, and then click the Security tab. Under Options, select the Add Digital Signature To Message check box.

Seal a message

 TROUBLESHOOTING If the co-workers to whom you're trying to send the sealed message don't have the advanced security feature of Exchange enabled, they will not be able to open the sealed message or verify the digital signature.

1 Create a new message and address it to a co-worker.

2 In the Subject box, type **Sealed Test**

3 In the message area, type **This is a sealed message.**

*Seal Message
With Encryption*

4 On the New Message Form toolbar, click the Seal Message With Encryption button.

5 Click the Send button, enter your password, and then click OK.

Your message is sent as a sealed message.

Send

 TIP If you want all of your outgoing messages to be sealed, on the Tools menu, click Options, and then click the Security tab. Under Options, select the Encrypt Message Contents And Attachments check box.

View the messages

In this exercise, your co-worker opens the signed and sealed messages you sent in the previous exercises.

 IMPORTANT Be sure that the co-worker helping you with this lesson performs the following steps on his or her computer.

1 Open the "Sign Test" message.

A password is not necessary to open a message that has been digitally signed.

2 On the File menu, click Properties.

The Sign Test Properties dialog box appears.

3 Click the Security tab, and then click Verify Digital Signature.

4 Type your advanced security password.

The Verify Digital Signature dialog box appears, and the digital signature is verified.

5 Click OK, and then click OK again.

6 Close the "Sign Test" message, click No if prompted to save changes, and then double-click the "Sealed Test" message.

7 Type your password, and then click OK again.

A password is necessary to open a sealed message. The message opens.

8 Close the "Sealed Test" message.

 TIP You can encrypt and digitally sign messages you exchange with others outside your Exchange enterprise to ensure they are secure. However you must trade *public security keys* with a user outside your organization before you can sign and seal messages. To do this, on the Tools menu, click Options, click the Security tab, and then click Send Security Keys. Type the e-mail address of the person with whom you are exchanging security keys, fill out the rest of the required information, and then click Send.

Finish the lesson

Follow these steps to delete the practice messages you created in this lesson.

 NOTE Because you are logged on to Microsoft Exchange with your own username, be sure to delete only the practice files and messages you added or created during this lesson.

1 On the Tools menu, click Out Of Office Assistant, click the I Am Currently In The Office option button, and then delete the AutoReply text. Select the rule you created for Joe Pecos, and click Delete Rule. Click Yes when prompted to confirm the deletion, and then click OK.

2 In the folder list, click your mailbox. On the File menu, click Properties, click the Permissions tab, click the name of the co-worker who helped you with this lesson, click Remove, and then click OK. Repeat these steps to remove permissions for your Inbox folder.

Your co-worker no longer has permission to use your mailbox.

3   On the Tools menu, click Services, be sure that Microsoft Exchange Server is selected, and then click Properties. Clear the Choose The Connection Type When Starting check box, and then click OK.

4   On the Tools menu, click Options. Click theExchange Server tab, select the co-worker you assigned as a delegate, and then click Remove. Click OK.

5   In your Inbox and Sent Items folders, delete the practice messages you used in this lesson.

6   Close all open windows, except Microsoft Exchange.

7   If you want to continue to the next lesson, click the Inbox folder in the folder list.

8   If you are finished using Microsoft Exchange for now, on the File menu, click Exit And Log Off.

You are logged off Microsoft Exchange, and the Viewer window closes.

Lesson Summary

To	Do this	Button
Set up an AutoReply	On the Tools menu, click Out Of Office Assistant, click the I Am Currently Out Of The Office option button, and then type the message.	
Set up an Out Of Office Assistant Rule	On the Tools menu, click Out Of Office Assistant, click Add Rule, and then select the settings for the rule.	
Delegate access to your mailbox	In the folder list, click a mailbox folder. On the File menu, click Properties, click the Permissions tab, click Add, and then select the delegate's name and a role.	
Work offline	After you have set up your computer to work offline, log on to Microsoft Exchange, and then click Work Offline.	
Connect to a Microsoft Exchange Server	On the Remote Mail Window toolbar, click the Connect button.	
Disconnect from a Microsoft Exchange Server	On the Remote Mail Window toolbar, click the Disconnect button.	

To	Do this	Button
Use Remote Mail to view message headers	On the Tools menu, click Remote Mail, and then use the buttons on the Remote Mail Window toolbar to perform tasks.	
View a log file	After you are disconnected, click the Deleted Items folder, and then double-click a log file.	
Establish a dial-up connection	Log on to Microsoft Exchange. On the Tools menu, click Remote Mail, and then click Connect.	

For online information about	On the Help menu, click Microsoft Exchange Help Topics, click the Index tab, and then type
Creating an AutoReply	AutoReply
Using the Out Of Office Assistant	Out Of Office Assistant *or* rules
Delegating mailbox access	Delegates: choosing
Working offline	Working offline *or* remote computing
Downloading specific messages	Remote Mail
Establishing a dial-up connection	Remote computing: dial-up connections

Integrating with Microsoft Office

In this lesson you will learn how to:

Estimated time
35 min.

- Route a document to other Microsoft Office users.
- Link Microsoft Excel data to a Microsoft Word document.
- Distribute a document to multiple users.

Now that you are familiar with the basics of Microsoft Exchange, you can begin to explore ways to combine its capabilities with Microsoft Office programs. For example, you can create a document using Microsoft Word, link data from Microsoft Excel to your document, and then send the entire file to your co-workers using Exchange. In turn, your co-workers can make revisions to the document online, and then use Exchange to return the revised document to you. Using Word, you can also design an original message template on which to base your Exchange messages.

IMPORTANT You must have Microsoft Office 95 or Microsoft Office 97 installed on your computer to perform the exercises in this lesson. If you do not have Microsoft Office, skip this lesson. The following exercises were designed to be performed in Word 97. If you are using Word 95, differences will be stated in the margin.

Set up your Inbox for this lesson

For more detailed instructions on how to set up your Inbox, see Lesson 2.

1   Start Microsoft Exchange using the Chris Adams profile.

2   Copy the practice messages from the Exchange 5.0 SBS Practice\Lesson06 folder to your Inbox folder.

You are ready to start this lesson.

Sending a Document to Another User

Now that the Pecos Coffee Company project is in full swing, you and your team members are developing a variety of campaign materials, and you need to exchange documents and data quickly and efficiently. In Lesson 1, you learned how to send files to other users by attaching them to a message. But suppose you're working on a file in another program, such as Word, and want immediate feedback. Instead of starting Exchange, composing a new message, browsing for the file path, and then attaching the file, you can send a file to your co-workers without ever leaving the program you're in.

Open a document and start Microsoft Word

In this exercise, you open the Lesson 6 Letter practice file and start Word.

1   Click Start, and then click Open Office Document.

The Open Office Document dialog box appears.

2   In the Open dialog box, view the contents of Exchange 5.0 SBS Practice\ Lesson 06 folder.

3   Double-click the 06Letter file.

Microsoft Word starts, and the document opens. Be sure that the program window is maximized.

4   On the File menu, click Save As.

The Save As dialog box appears.

5   Click the Save In down arrow, and then click Desktop.

6   In the Save As Type box, be sure that Word Document appears.

If it does not, click the down arrow, and then select Word Document.

7   In the File Name box, type **Talent Letter** and then click Save.

The document is stored on your Desktop as Talent Letter.

Edit a document

You need to hire some vocalists for a series of Pecos Coffee Company radio ads. You have already drafted a letter to the local art school asking for recommendations. In this exercise, you add text to the Talent Letter.

1   Scroll downward until the second paragraph of the letter is visible.

2   Click after the "Thank you for your time and consideration" sentence.

3   Press the SPACEBAR, and then type **I look forward to your reply.**

4   On the Standard toolbar, click the Save button.

Your changes are saved in the document.

Save

Send a document to a co-worker

You want Lisa Ygarre, the media planner, to review your letter before you send it. In this exercise, you send the document to Lisa without leaving Word.

If you're using Word 95, on the File menu, click Send.

1   On the File menu, point to Send To, and then click Mail Recipient.

A new New Message form appears, containing an icon that represents your document.

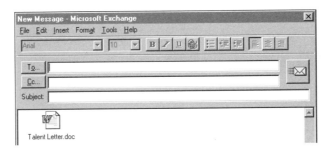

 TROUBLESHOOTING   If you see the text of your letter instead of an icon, the options used by Word need to be changed. Press ESC to close the dialog box. In Word, on the Tools menu, click Options. On the General tab, select the Mail As Attachment check box, click OK, and then repeat step 1.

2   In the To box, type **Lisa Ygarre**

3   In the Subject box, type **Talent Search**

4   In the message area, type **How does this sound to you?**

5   Click the Send button.

Your message containing the Word document is sent.

Send

6   On the File menu, click Close.

The Talent Letter document closes. Because the address you used in this exercise is fictitious, you will receive an undeliverable message notice from the system administrator.

Linking Microsoft Excel Data to a Microsoft Word Document

Suppose you are preparing a brief report summarizing the Pecos Coffee Company's corporate history. You want to include some sales data provided by the Pecos Coffee Company and stored in an Excel workbook. Because you want to be able to update both your report and the sales figures at the same time, you decide to create a link between the Word document and the Excel workbook.

Linking a file to another file in a different program is similar to copying information between programs: you use the Copy and Paste Special commands. The Paste Special command maintains an active link with the original, or source, file so that any changes made to the source file are automatically reflected in the destination file.

Open a Word document

In this exercise, you open the Pecos Coffee Sales Summary.

1   Click Start, and then click Open Office Document.

The Open Office Document dialog box appears.

2   Be sure that the Lesson06 folder appears in the Look In box.

3   Double-click the 06Doc file.

Microsoft Word starts, and the document opens.

4   On the File menu, click Save As.

The Save As dialog box appears.

5   Click the Save In down arrow, and then click Desktop.

6   Be sure that Word Document appears in the Save As Type box.

If it does not, click the down arrow, and then select Word Document.

7   In the File Name box, type **Sales Summary** and then click Save.

The document is stored on your Desktop.

Link Microsoft Excel data to a Microsoft Word document

In this exercise, you link sales figures from an Excel workbook to the Pecos Coffee Sales Summary.

1   Press CTRL+END, and then press ENTER.

The insertion point moves to a new line. The linked data will be inserted here.

2   Click Start, and then click Open Office Document.

The Open dialog box appears.

3   Be sure that the Lesson06 folder appears in the Look In box, and then double-click the 06Sheet file.

Microsoft Excel starts, and the workbook opens.

4   On the File menu, click Save As.

The Save As dialog box appears.

5   Click the Save In down arrow, and then click Desktop.

6   In the Save As Type box, be sure that Microsoft Excel Workbook appears.

If it does not, click the down arrow, and then select Microsoft Excel Workbook.

7   In the File Name box, type **Pecos Sales** and then click Save.

The document is stored on your Desktop.

Copy

8   Select cells B8 through E13, and then click the Copy button on the Standard toolbar.

The data is copied to the Clipboard.

9   On the taskbar, click the Microsoft Word–Sales Summary button.

The Sales Summary document appears.

10   On the Edit menu, click Paste Special.

The Paste Special dialog box appears.

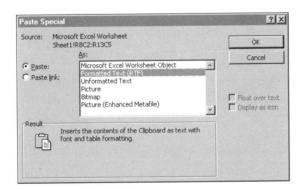

11   In the Paste Special dialog box, click the Paste Link option button.

12   In the As list, click Microsoft Excel Worksheet Object, and then click OK.

The information copied from the Excel workbook is inserted and linked to the Sales Summary. Your screen should look similar to the following illustration.

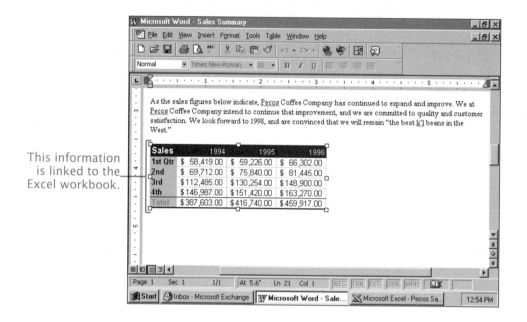

This information is linked to the Excel workbook.

Edit linked information

At your request, the Pecos Coffee Company just sent you updated sales data. In this exercise, you edit the information in the Excel workbook based on the newly received data, and then verify that the changes are reflected immediately in your Word document.

1   On the taskbar, click the Microsoft Excel–Pecos Sales button.

2   Click in cell E12, type **185000** and then press ENTER.

    The total for the fourth quarter in cell E13 changes.

3   On the taskbar, click the Microsoft Word–Sales Summary button.

    The changes you made in the Excel workbook are reflected in the linked object in the Word Sales Summary document.

4   On the Standard toolbar, click the Save button.

5   On the taskbar, use the right mouse button to click the Microsoft Excel–Pecos Sales button.

    A shortcut menu appears.

6   Click Close, and then, when prompted to save the changes, click Yes.

    The file closes, and Microsoft Excel closes.

Save

If you're using Office 97, click Yes when prompted to save in a New Excel format.

Distributing a Document to Multiple Users

Now that you've drafted the Sales Summary for the Pecos Coffee Company, you want to distribute it to several people on your team so that they can each make editorial suggestions. You could send a copy of the document to each reviewer using Exchange, but you would get several documents back and would have to compile them into one main document. Instead, you can attach a routing slip to your document. Each recipient can then make his or her own revisions online, and when he or she is finished, the document is automatically routed to the next person on the list.

If you want, you can set the options for the routing slip so that your document automatically opens in Revision mode. Any changes the recipient makes to the document are recorded as online revisions and are attributed to the recipient. When the recipient has finished making revisions, he or she can route the document to the next person on the list.

When each person on the routing list sends the document, you are sent a status message indicating who has the routed document. After each recipient has seen the document, it is automatically returned to the sender. This way, you can be sure that everyone has seen the document and has entered his or her revisions online, and you can review all the suggestions in one document.

Routing a document

In this exercise, you route the Pecos Coffee Company Sales Summary to Tammy Wu, the copywriter, and Nate Zostoc, the creative director, for their review.

 NOTE   Because you are using fictitious names in this exercise, you will receive an undeliverable message from the system administrator when you send this message. If you would like to use real names, you can ask two co-workers to assist you. Route the document to these two team members, ask each of them to make a few simple revisions, and then send the document on to the next recipient.

If you're using Word 95, on the File menu, point to Send To, and then click Add Routing Slip.

1   On the File menu, click Send To, and then click Routing Recipient.

The Routing Slip dialog box appears. Your name appears in the From area.

2   Click Address.

The Address Book dialog box appears.

3   In the personal address book, double-click Tammy Wu, double-click Nate Zostoc, and then click OK.

The document will be routed to Tammy, and then to Nate.

4   In the Subject box, select the text, and then type **Pecos Sales Summary**

5 In the Message Text box, type **Could you please submit your revisions to me by Friday?**

6 In the Route To Recipients area, be sure that the One After Another option button is selected.

7 Be sure that the Return When Done and Track Status check boxes are selected.

8 Be sure that Tracked Changes or Revisions appears in the Protect For box.

Any changes the recipients make will be marked as revisions.

9 Click Route.

The document is sent to the first recipient on your list.

10 Close the Sales Summary document.

Click Yes if prompted to save changes.

TIP If you want to continue working on your document before routing it, you can close the Routing Slip dialog box without sending the document. You can then send the document at a later time by clicking Send on the File menu. You can also make changes to the routing slip by clicking Edit Routing Slip on the File menu, pointing to Send To on the File menu, and then clicking Other Routing Recipient.

Reviewing Routed Documents

After your co-workers have seen and revised a routed document, it is sent back to you if you have selected the Return When Done option button. You can then open the document, review it, and accept or reject any changes.

Open a revised document

In this exercise, you open the routed document returned to you by your co-workers.

NOTE A document with simulated revisions by Tammy Wu and Nate Zostoc has been created for you in the Lesson06 folder. If you have not set up your Inbox for this lesson, refer to "Installing and Using the Practice Files" earlier in this book. If two of your co-workers helped with the previous exercise, you can use the messages they returned to you for this exercise.

1 In the folder list, click the Inbox folder.

2 Double-click the "Status: Routing" message from Tammy Wu.

Tammy was the first recipient on your routing slip. After she finished her revisions and sent the document, a tracking status message was automatically sent to you. Your screen should look similar to the following illustration.

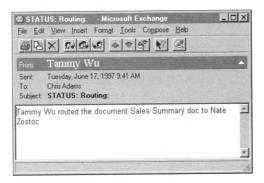

Previous

3 On the Read Message Form toolbar, click the Previous button until the "Routed" message from Nate Zostoc opens.

A note informs you that the routing has been completed. Your message should look similar to the following illustration.

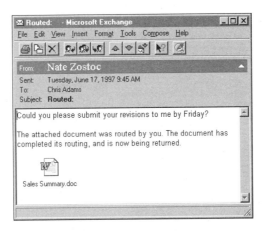

4 Double-click the Sales Summary document icon.

A copy of the document opens. A Route Document message appears, prompting you to merge any revision marks with the original version of the document.

5 Click Cancel.

The revised document appears.

Set up the document for review

In this exercise, you define the document review settings.

1 On the Tools menu, click Unprotect Document.

You are now able to view and accept or reject your co-workers' revisions.

If you're using Word 95, on the Tools menu, click Revisions, and then click Review.

2 On the Tools menu, point to Track Changes, and then click Accept Or Reject Changes.

The Accept Or Reject Changes dialog box appears.

Review revisions

In this exercise, you review the changes Tammy Wu and Nate Zostoc made to the document, and decide whether or not you want to accept the changes.

1 Click the Find button that has a right pointing arrow.

The first instance of revised text is selected. Your screen should look similar to the following illustration.

Indicates who made the change.

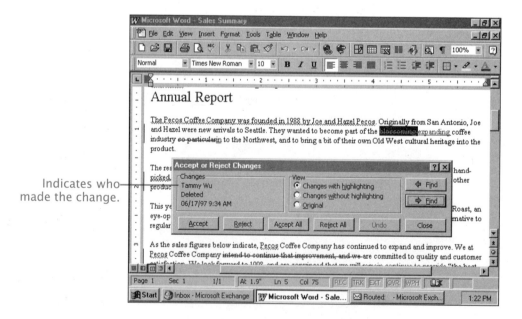

You can move the dialog box to show more of the document.

2 Click Accept, and then click Accept again.

Tammy's changes are made to the text. The next instance of revised text is selected.

3 Click Reject, and then click Reject again.

Nate's changes are not accepted, and the original text is restored. The next instance of revised text is selected.

4 Click Accept All, and when prompted to continue searching from the beginning of the document, click Yes.

You accept the rest of the revisions in the document.

5 Close the Accept Or Reject Changes dialog box.

6 On the File menu, click Save As.

The Save As dialog box appears.

7 Click the Save In down arrow, and then click Desktop.

8 In the Save As Type box, be sure that Word Document appears.

If it does not, click the down arrow, and then select Word Document.

9 Click the Sales Summary document, click Save, and when prompted to replace the existing document, click Yes.

The revised document is stored on your Desktop.

10 Close Word, and then close the "Routed:" message.

 NOTE If you'd like to build on the skills that you learned in this lesson, you can perform the exercises presented in the following section, One Step Further. Otherwise, skip to "Finish the lesson."

One Step Further: Modifying a Message Template Using Microsoft Word

If you're using Windows NT version 4.0, skip to "Finish the Lesson."

You can use the powerful word-processing capabilities in Word to edit your Exchange messages and modify their appearance. For example, suppose you want the members of your project team to update you on their progress weekly. You can create an original message template on which to base their reports. The easiest way to create a new message template is to modify an existing Exchange message template and save the changes with a new name.

IMPORTANT To complete the following exercises, you must have WordMail installed. To do this, run the Microsoft Office Setup program. In Setup, click Add/Remove, select the Microsoft Word check box, and then click Change Option. Select the WordMail check box.

To compose a message based on a WordMail template, you must have Word enabled as your e-mail editor. To do this, on the Compose menu, click WordMail Options, and then select the Enable Word As E-Mail Editor check box. To remove Word as your electronic mail editor, click WordMail Options on the Compose menu, and then clear the Enable Word As Email Editor check box.

Change a message template with Microsoft Word

In this exercise, you modify a message template in Word.

1 On the Compose menu, click WordMail Options.

The WordMail Options dialog box appears. A list of the available templates appears.

If you receive a warning that the template contains macros, click Yes to retain the macros.

2 Be sure that the Email template is selected, and then click Edit.

The Microsoft Word–Email window opens.

3 Type **Weekly Project Status Report** and then press ENTER twice.

4 Type **Please record your progress in the table below. Thank you!** and then press ENTER twice.

5 On the Table menu, click Insert Table.

The Insert Table dialog box appears.

6 In the Number Of Columns box, type **3** and then be sure that 2 appears in the Number Of Rows box.

7 Click OK.

A blank table appears in the document.

8 In the first row of the first column of the table, type **Account** and then press TAB.

The insertion point moves to the second column.

9 Type **Task**, press TAB, and then type **Date Completed**

10 Select the first row of the table, and then on the Formatting toolbar, click the Bold button.

The table column headings appear in bold type.

Bold

Save a document as an Exchange message template

In this exercise, you save the changes you made to the template as a new message template.

1 On the File menu, click Save As.

The Save As dialog box appears.

2 Switch to the \Microsoft Office\Office folder.

If you're using Word 95, save the template in the \Microsoft Office\Office \Wordmail folder.

3 In the file list box, double-click the Wordmail folder, and then double-click the Favorites folder.

The contents of the Wordmail folder appear.

4 In the File Name box, select the text, type **Status Report** and then click Save.

The file is saved as a new Wordmail template.

5 Close Word.

6 On the Compose menu, click WordMail Options.

The WordMail Options dialog box appears. The Status Report message template is included in the list of available templates.

7 Click Cancel.

TIP If you want to create a message based on the Status Report template, select it in the WordMail Options dialog box, be sure that the Enable Word As E-Mail Editor check box is selected, and then click Compose.

Finish the lesson

Follow these steps to delete the practice messages you created in this lesson.

NOTE Because you are logged on to Microsoft Exchange with your own username, be sure you delete only the practice files and messages you added or created during this lesson.

---

1 In your Inbox and Sent Items folders, delete the practice messages you used in this lesson.

If you're using Word 95, delete the template from the \Wordmail folder.

2 Delete the practice Word and Excel files on the Desktop.

3 On the Compose menu, click WordMail Options. Select the Status Report template, and then click Delete. Click Yes to confirm the deletion.

4 Close all open windows, except Microsoft Exchange.

5 If you want to continue to the next lesson, click the Inbox folder in the folder list.

6 If you are finished using Microsoft Exchange for now, on the File menu, click Exit And Log Off.

You are logged off Microsoft Exchange and the Viewer window closes.

Lesson Summary

To	Do this	Button
Open an Office document	Click Start, and then click Open Office Document. In the Look In box, select the appropriate folder, and then double-click the document you want to open.	
Send a document from an Office program	On the Office program File menu, click Send. Type the name of the recipient and the subject of the message. Type the message text, and then click Send.	
Link Microsoft Excel data to a Microsoft Word document	In the Microsoft Word document, position the insertion point. In Microsoft Excel, select the cells you want to link. On the Standard toolbar, click the Copy button. Switch to the Microsoft Word document, and click Paste Special on the Edit menu. Click Paste Link, click Microsoft Excel Worksheet Object, and then click OK.	
Edit linked information	Open the Office document you want to modify and edit the appropriate data. The linked data is automatically updated in the destination document.	

To	Do this
Route a document to multiple users	On the File menu, click Add Routing Slip. Click Address. In the Address Book, select recipients' names from the list, click To, and then click OK. Type a subject for your message. In the message area, add any necessary information. Select a routing order option, a return option, and a protection option. Click Route.
Review a revised document	Open the document in your Inbox. In the Revised Document message, click OK. In the Merge Revisions dialog box, be sure that the original document is selected, and then click Open. On the Tools menu, click Unprotect Document. On the Tools menu, click Revisions. Click Review, review the changes, and then accept or reject the modifications.

For online information about	On the Help menu, click Microsoft Exchange Help Topics, click the Index tab, and then type
Opening files	**Opening documents** in Microsoft Word
Sending documents	**Sharing information** in Microsoft Word
Linking data to a document	**Linked objects** in Microsoft Word *or* **Exchanging information** in Microsoft Excel
Routing documents	**Routing documents** in Microsoft Word
Reviewing revisions	**Revision marks** in Microsoft Word

Review & Practice

Estimated time
30 min.

You will review and practice how to:

- Group messages.
- Create a personal view.
- Route a document to others.
- Set up delegate access.
- Create an AutoReply and an AutoSignature.
- Work offline using Remote Mail and synchronize folders.

Before you move on to Part 3, which covers expanded features of Microsoft Exchange Client, you can practice the skills you learned in Part 2 by working through the steps in this Review & Practice section. You will group messages and create a personal view to organize your Inbox as well as create an AutoSignature and route a Microsoft Office document. You'll also set up delegate access and create an AutoReply before working with Exchange offline.

Scenario

You're getting ready to go on a business trip. Before leaving, you check for new messages and address the ones that need your immediate attention. You also assign one of your co-workers as a delegate to monitor your Inbox for important messages while you're away. Then, while on your business trip, you work offline.

Step 1: *Create a Personal View and Route a Document*

You first organize the messages in your Inbox by grouping them, and then create a personal view for later use based on these settings. You also route a draft document for review to the other account executives at Fitch & Mather.

1 Drag the messages from the R&P2 folder to your Inbox folder. (Hint: For detailed instructions on setting up your Inbox for this Review & Practice section, see the beginning of Lesson 2.)

2 Group the messages in your Inbox by Subject, then by Sender, and finally by Received Date. (Hint: On the View menu, click Group By.)

3 Define a folder view based on the current message grouping in your Inbox and name it "Subject And Sender."

4 Expand the messages under the Personnel Request category. Expand the Nate Zostoc category, and then open the message from Nate. Read and then close the message.

5 Open the Duties document in the Exchange 5.0 SBS Practice\R&P2 folder.

6 From Microsoft Word, add a routing slip to the Duties document including Aaron Wells, Chandra Shah, Debbie S. Abdul, and Keith Marowski as reviewers.

7 In the message area, type the text **Please revise the administrative assistant job description**. Route the document.

For more information on	See
Grouping messages	Lesson 4
Creating personal views	Lesson 4
Routing files	Lesson 6

Step 2: *Assign a Delegate and Set Up an AutoReply*

As an account executive, you frequently travel for business and need to let people know that you are out of the office. Therefore, you create an AutoReply message so that anyone who sends you a message will be informed that you are away. Also, because you want any urgent messages to be taken care of while you are away, you give one of your co-workers access to your mailbox and permission to read your messages.

1 Grant one of your co-workers permission as a Reviewer so that person can read your messages but cannot create messages on your behalf.

2 Using the Out Of Office Assistant, click the I Am Currently Out Of The Office option button, and then create an AutoReply by typing the following text:

I am traveling to the East Coast and will be back next Thursday. My co-worker will be handling any urgent matters until I return.

For more information on	See
Granting permission	Lesson 5
Creating an AutoReply	Lesson 5

Step 3: Create an AutoSignature and Communicate Remotely

You are now traveling. You have already downloaded the Address Book and configured your modem. Before you compose and send a message, you create a new AutoSignature including your offsite phone number.

 IMPORTANT Perform the following steps on your offsite computer.

1 Start Exchange on your offsite computer.

2 Create an AutoSignature named Offsite that includes your name and offsite phone number.

3 Create a new message titled "Thanks!" Type the following message to the co-worker who is your delegate: **Thanks for taking care of my messages while I'm gone!** Send the message.

4 Using Remote Mail, connect to the network so that you can view message headers. Mark to retrieve any new messages that you have received, and then close the Remote Mail window.

5 Synchronize your offline folders with your server folders.

6 Select the practice messages you used in this lesson in your Inbox and Sent Items folders, and then press DELETE. Delete the Offsite AutoSignature.

7 On the File menu, click Exit And Log Off.

For more information on	See
Working offline	Lesson 6
Using Remote Mail	Lesson 6
Synchronizing folders	Lesson 6

Finish the Review & Practice

Follow these steps to delete the practice messages you created and used in this Review & Practice.

 WARNING Because you are logged on to Microsoft Exchange with your own username, be sure you delete only the practice files and messages you added or created during this Review & Practice.

1 Reapply the Normal personal view to your Inbox. Delete the Subject And Sender personal view.

2 Remove the permissions you assigned to your co-worker.

3 Disable the AutoReply and delete the AutoReply text.

4 In your Inbox and Sent Items folders, delete the practice messages you used in this lesson.

5 Close all open windows, except Microsoft Exchange.

6 If you want to continue to the next lesson, click the Inbox folder in the folder list.

7 If you are finished using Microsoft Exchange for now, on the File menu, click Exit And Log Off.

You are logged off Microsoft Exchange and the Viewer window closes.

Part

3

Extending Your Messaging Capabilities

Lesson 7
Customizing Forms   129

Lesson 8
Using Public Folders   145

Lesson 9
Connecting to Exchange Through a Web
   Browser   167

Review & Practice   189

Lesson
7

Customizing Forms

Estimated time
30 min.

In this lesson you will learn how to:

- Use a sample form.
- Modify an existing form.
- Install a form in a library for later use.
- Use a new form.

You have probably used paper forms on many occasions for items like job applications, time sheets, or tax returns. Forms present information in a structure that helps you view and enter information. Using Microsoft Exchange Forms Designer, you can create and use electronic forms to keep track of information that is typically stored in a paper form. You can distribute electronic forms through e-mail or by posting them on your Microsoft Exchange Server.

You have worked extensively with the New Message form in the previous lessons. The New Message form is the standard form you use to create, send, respond to, and forward e-mail messages. In this lesson, you will create a form by modifying an existing form using the Forms Designer.

129

IMPORTANT To complete the exercises in this lesson, you must be using Microsoft Exchange 5.0 Client with Microsoft Exchange Server. If you are not, skip this lesson.

You must also have the Microsoft Exchange Forms Designer installed. To do this, run the setup program from the Efdsetup folder on the Exchange Client CD-ROM. If you need additional help, contact your system administrator.

Set up your Inbox for this lesson

Before you begin working through this lesson, you need to log on to Microsoft Exchange using the Chris Adams profile. You can also use your own profile, but it is recommended that you use the Chris Adams profile so that the exercises and illustrations in the book match more closely what you see on your screen.

IMPORTANT If you haven't imported the personal address book or created the Chris Adams profile yet, refer to "Installing and Using the Practice Files," earlier in this book. If you don't know your Microsoft Exchange username or password, contact your system administrator for further help.

 Start Microsoft Exchange using the Chris Adams profile.

Creating Forms by Using Sample Forms

The Forms Designer comes with a variety of predesigned forms that have been conceived for particular uses. For example, you can use the Schedule Time Away form to keep track of employee vacation time or the Charity Contribution form to record your company's charitable donations. The easiest way to create a form is to customize any of these sample forms to include any organization-specific information or requirements. If none of the sample form meets your needs, you can create your own.

You will learn more about public folders in Lesson 8.

Exchange provides two types of samples: *form applications* and *folder applications*. A form application creates forms that are used primarily to send information back and forth between people across a network. These types of forms are called *Send forms;* the basic New Message form is a Send form. A folder application creates a *Post form* that is placed in a specific folder. Post forms are typically sent to public folders on the network, where they can be viewed by multiple users.

Modifying an Existing Form

The easiest way to create a form is to modify an existing form. The sample forms (.EFP extension) provided with the Forms Designer can be used "as is," or can be customized and saved with another name—you use sample forms as you use templates.

Open a sample form

In addition to your duties as account executive, you perform other tasks related to the day-to-day operation of the agency. Recently, the Human Resources director asked you to design a form to track employee donations to local charities. You decide to use the Charity Donation sample form as a starting point, and then customize it to suit your company's needs.

If the Forms Designer command doesn't appear on the Tools menu, the Forms Designer is not currently installed.

1 On the Tools menu, point to Application Design, and then click Forms Designer.

The Microsoft Exchange Forms Designer wizard appears.

2 Click the A Form Template option button, and then click Next.

The Select Form Template dialog box appears.

3 Under Folders, double-click Efdforms, and then double-click Samples.

The sample forms provided with Forms Designer appear.

4 Double-click Donate.

The contents of the Donate folder appear in the file list.

You can view a description of the form at the bottom of the dialog box.

5 Under File Name, click Donate.efp, and then click OK.

A Charity Donation form appears in the Forms Designer main window. Your screen should look similar to the following illustration.

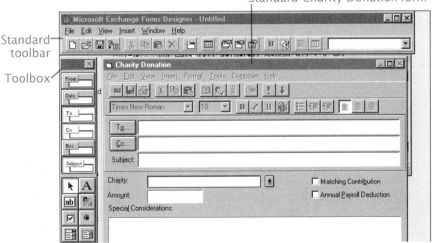

Standard Charity Donation form

Standard toolbar

Toolbox

Customize a field

In this exercise, you customize the existing Charity List field on the standard Charity Donation form by adding a new charity name to the list and formatting the field caption text to make it stand out.

1 In the Charity Donation form, click the Charity field.

Sizing handles appear around the caption and the field, indicating that they are selected.

Field Properties

2 On the Standard toolbar, click the Field Properties button.

The Field Properties dialog box appears.

3 Click the Initial Value tab.

The current list values for the field appear.

4 Click Insert New.

A blinking insertion point appears in a blank row at the top of the list.

5 Type **County Animal Shelter** and then click Sort.

The list is sorted in alphabetical order.

6 Click the Format tab.

7 In the Set Format Properties area, be sure that the Caption option button is selected, and then click Font.

The Font dialog box appears.

8 In the Font box, select Italic, and then, in the Size list, select 12.

9 In the Effects area, click the Color down arrow, and then select Navy.

10 Click OK to close the Font dialog box, and then close the Field Properties dialog box.

The formatting changes are applied to the field caption. Your form should look similar to the following illustration.

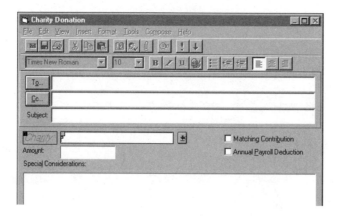

Resize a field

You will insert a picture field for the logo in a later exercise.

In this exercise, you resize the Special Considerations field to accommodate the Fitch & Mather logo.

1   Click the Special Considerations field.

You do not need to close the Field Properties dialog box to select a new field. The category names displayed on the Format tab vary depending on the selected field.

2   On the Standard toolbar, click the Field Properties button.

The Field Properties dialog box appears.

3   Click the General tab.

4   In the Size area, select the number in the Width box, and then type
5000

The dimensions are expressed in *twips*, a special unit of measure used to ensure that the placement and proportion of screen elements are the same on all different types of displays. There are about 1440 twips per inch.

5   Close the Field Properties dialog box.

The dimensions of the Special Considerations field are changed.

Delete a field

The resizing of the Special Considerations field caused another field to become visible. In this exercise, you delete the newly displayed field because you won't be needing it.

1   Click the newly displayed field behind the Special Considerations field.

The field is selected.

2   Be sure that the text "MAPI_Body_Custom" appears in the Field Reference Name box on the Standard toolbar.

3   On the Standard toolbar, click the Delete button.

The field is removed from the form.

Delete

Add a picture

In this exercise, you add the Fitch & Mather company logo to the form.

1   In the toolbox, click the PictureBox Field button.

The pointer changes to a plus sign (+) with a PictureBox Field icon.

PictureBox Field

2   Position the pointer to the right of the Special Considerations field, and then click.

A blank Picture field is added to the form, and the Insert Picture dialog box appears.

3   Switch to the Exchange 5.0 SBS Practice\Lesson07 folder.

The contents of the folder appear in the file list.

4   Select the fm1logo.bmp file, and then click OK.

The Fitch & Mather logo is inserted in the picture field.

5   Drag the Picture field to center it in the blank gray area to the right of the Special Considerations field.

Your form should look similar to the following illustration.

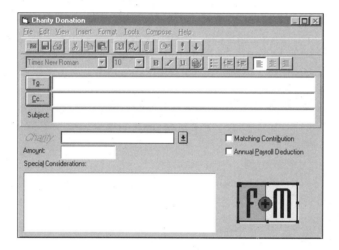

Insert a new field

In this exercise, you add a Date field to the standard Charity Donation form to help the Human Resources department keep better track of corporate donations.

Date Field

➤   In the toolbox, click the Date Field button.

A Date field is added to the top of the form, below the toolbar.

Change the form window caption

In this exercise, you customize the title bar to conform to the Fitch & Mather design guidelines.

Window Properties

1 On the Standard toolbar, click the Window Properties button.

The Window Properties dialog box appears.

2 In the Window Caption field, select the text, and then type **Fitch & Mather Gifts**

3 Close the Window Properties dialog box.

Saving a Form

When you save a form, it is by default saved as an EFP project file in the Forms Designer folder. It is recommended that you use the Save As command on the File menu to rename and save your modified forms. If you do not rename your form, the changes you make will be permanently incorporated in the original sample form.

TROUBLESHOOTING If you accidentally save changes to an original sample form, you can retrieve the original sample form by reinstalling the Microsoft Exchange Forms Designer.

Save a form

In this exercise, you save the changes you made to the Charity Donation sample form as a new form application.

1 On the File menu, click Save As.

The Save As dialog box appears.

2 Switch to the \Windows\Desktop folder.

If you are using Windows NT, save the form in the \Winnt.0\ Profiles\Alluse~1 \Desktop folder.

3 In the File Name box, type **fmgifts** and then click OK.

Your custom Fitch & Mather Gifts form is saved. Filenames used with the Form Designer must be composed of eight characters or less.

Installing a Form

Once a form has been created, it can be installed in a special folder, or *library*, so that it is easily accessible. When you install a form, the Forms Designer translates the form characteristics into Microsoft Visual Basic programming code. Microsoft Visual Basic converts the physical image of the form you have created into a format that can be read by Exchange. A form must be installed before it can be used.

Three types of libraries are available in Exchange.

Library type	Storage location	Access privileges required
Organization forms	Microsoft Exchange Server computer	Anyone with access to the server
Personal forms	The folder in which your e-mail messages are stored	Anyone to whom you grant access
Folder forms	A particular public folder	Anyone with access to the server and permission to use the public folder

 NOTE When you install a form, the conversion process can take several minutes. After the Visual Basic files are created, the Forms Designer prompts you to install the form in a library to make it available to a specific user or group of users. If you want to create more complex applications with forms, you can do so by using Microsoft Visual Basic version 4. If you would like step-by-step instructions on working in Visual Basic, refer to *Microsoft Visual Basic 4 for Windows 95 Step by Step*.

Install a form

In this exercise, you install the Fitch & Mather Gifts form in your personal forms library to test the form.

1 On the Standard toolbar, click the Install button.

Install

A message appears, informing you that Microsoft Exchange is generating Microsoft Visual Basic project code. After a few moments, the Set Library To dialog box appears.

2   Be sure that the Forms Library option button is selected and that Personal Forms appears in the Forms Library box, and then click OK.

The Form Properties dialog box appears.

3   In the Display Name box, type **Fitch & Mather Gifts**

4   In the Contact box, type **Chris Adams**

Chris Adams will be listed as the contact person for any questions about the form.

5   In the Comments box, type **Fitch and Mather Donation form**

If a form is hidden, it will not be visible in the folders list contents.

6   Be sure that the Hidden check box is cleared, and then click OK.

The form is installed in your mailbox. The Viewer window appears.

7   In Microsoft Exchange Forms Designer, on the File menu, click Exit.

The Microsoft Exchange Forms Designer closes.

Send a form

In this exercise, you use the Fitch & Mather Gifts form you just created to make a donation to a local charity, and then send the form to Karen Quan, the donations coordinator.

1   On the Compose menu, click New Form.

The New Form dialog box appears.

2   Be sure that Personal Forms is listed and that the Fitch & Mather Gifts form is selected, and then click OK.

A message appears, indicating that the form is being installed on your computer. After a few moments, the Fitch & Mather Gifts form appears. Your name automatically appears in the Cc box.

3   Click To.

The Address Book dialog box appears.

4   In the Personal Address Book, double-click Karen Quan, and then click OK.

5   Click the Charity field down arrow, and then click County Animal Shelter.

6   In the Amount field, type **100**

7   Select the Annual Payroll Deduction check box.

8   Click the Send button.

The Fitch & Mather Gifts form is sent to Karen Quan.

Send

View the form

Because you were listed in the Cc box, you also received a copy of the form you sent to Karen Quan. In this exercise, you view the Charitable Donations form.

1   Double-click the "Charitable Donations" form in your Inbox.

The form appears. Your form should look similar to the following illustration.

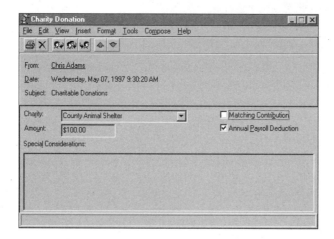

2   Close the "Charity Donation" form.

   NOTE   If you'd like to build on the skills that you learned in this lesson, you can perform the exercises presented in the following section, One Step Further. Otherwise, skip to "Finish the lesson."

One Step Further: Creating New Forms

While the sample forms can be put to many uses, you might find that none of the predesigned forms meets your specific needs. In that case, you can use the Microsoft Exchange Forms Designer to create an original custom form.

Create a new form

In this exercise, you use the Form Template Wizard in the Forms Designer to start designing a phone message form for your company.

1   Start the Microsoft Exchange Forms Designer.

The Microsoft Exchange Forms Designer dialog box appears.

2   Be sure that the Form Template Wizard option button is selected, and then click Next.

The form destination options appear.

3   Be sure that the To Another User (Send) option button is selected, and then click Next.

The form use options appear.

4   Be sure that the To Send Information option button is selected, and then click Next.

Your form will be used to send information to other users. The number of window options appear.

5   Be sure that the One Window option button is selected, and then click Next.

Your form will consist of a single window where users can enter or read information. The form name and description areas appear.

6   In the Form Name field, type **Telephone Message** and then press TAB.

7   In the Description field, type **To record telephone messages in Exchange** and then click Next.

The final screen of the Forms Designer–Form Template Wizard appears, with instructions on using the toolbox and toolbar buttons to complete and install the form.

8   Click Finish.

After a moment, a blank form appears. Your form should look similar to the following illustration.

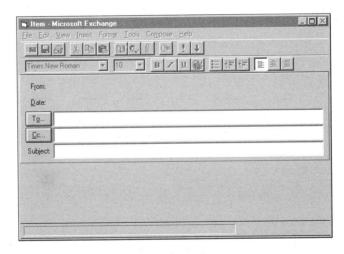

Add custom fields to your original form

Now that you have a new blank form, you want to customize it. In this exercise, you add several check box fields and a field for the caller's name.

Entry Field

1 In the toolbox, click the Entry Field button.

The pointer changes to a plus sign (+) with an Entry Field icon.

2 Position the pointer in the message area of the form below the Subject field, and then click.

A new caption area and a blank field appear.

3 Be sure that the text in the caption area is selected, and then type **Caller:**

The caption text is replaced as you type.

CheckBox Field

4 In the toolbox, click the CheckBox Field button.

The pointer changes to a plus sign (+) with a CheckBox Field icon.

5 Position the pointer to the right of the Caller field, and then click.

A new check box and label appear. The check box label text is selected.

To align a field on a form, select the field, click the Field Properties button, and then enter precise field coordinates on the General tab.

6 Type **Will call again** and then click outside the check box area.

A new check box is added to the form. Users can select this check box to inform the message recipient that the caller will call back later.

7 Repeat steps 5 through 7 to add a new check box below the first one, labeled **Please call back**

Users can select this check box if the message recipient should return the call. Your form should look similar to the following illustration.

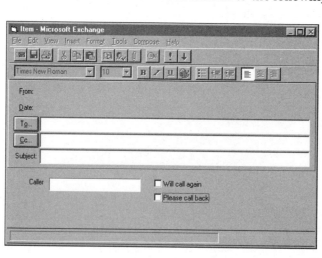

If you are using Windows NT, save the form in the \Winnt.0\ Profiles\Alluse~1 \Desktop folder.

8 Save the form as **Phone** in the \Windows\Desktop folder.

If you want to install the form for later use, follow the steps listed in the "Install a form" exercise, earlier in this lesson.

9 On the File menu, click Exit.

The Microsoft Exchange Forms Designer closes.

Finish the lesson

Follow these steps to delete the practice message you created in the lesson.

1 In your Inbox and Sent Items folders, delete the practice messages you used in this lesson.

2 On the Tools menu, click Options.

The Options dialog box appears.

If you do not want to delete the forms you worked on, skip to step 6.

3 Click the Exchange Server tab, and then click Manage Forms.

The Forms Manager dialog box appears. The personal forms list appears on the right.

4 Be sure that the Fitch & Mather Gifts form is selected, and then click Delete. When prompted to confirm the deletion, click Yes. Click Close, and then click OK.

5 Delete the forms and folders you created in this lesson from your Desktop.

6 If you want to continue to the next lesson, click the Inbox folder in the folder contents list.

7 If you are finished using Microsoft Exchange for now, on the File menu, click Exit And Log Off.

You are logged off Microsoft Exchange and the Viewer window closes.

Lesson Summary

To	Do this	Button
Start Microsoft Exchange Forms Designer	On the Tools menu, point to Application Design, and then click Forms Designer.	
Open a sample form	On the Forms Designer Standard toolbar, click the Open button. In the folders list, double-click the Samples folder, and then double-click the folder and the file you want.	

To	Do this	Button
Customize a field	Select the field you want to customize. On the Standard toolbar, click the Field Properties button, and then make your changes. Click Close.	
Resize a field	Select the field you want to resize. On the Standard toolbar, click the Field Properties button. Click the General tab. In the Size area, type the new dimensions. Click Close.	
Delete a field	Select the field you want to delete. On the Standard toolbar, click the Delete button. *or* Select the field and press DELETE.	
Add a picture to a form	In the toolbox, click the PictureBox Field button. Click where you want to insert the picture on the form. In the Insert Picture dialog box, select the picture file to insert, and then click OK.	
Insert a field	In the toolbox, click the appropriate field button.	
Change the form window caption	Select the form. On the Standard toolbar, click the Window Properties button. In the Window Caption field, type the caption text you want. Click Close.	
Save a form	On the File menu, click Save As. In the File Name box, type a new name for the file, and then click Save.	
Install a form	On the Standard toolbar, click the Install button. In the Set Library To dialog box, select a location for the form, and then click OK. In the Form Properties dialog box, add a display name and any other information, and then click OK.	

For online information about	On the Help menu in Microsoft Exchange Forms Designer, click Search for Help On, and then type
Using sample forms	Sample applications
Modifying existing forms	Forms: Overview
Installing forms	Install button

Lesson

8

Using Public Folders

Estimated time
40 min.

In this lesson you will learn how to:

- View a public folder.
- Create a public folder.
- Post public information.
- Reply to public items.
- Create a shortcut to a public folder.

In the previous lessons, you used Microsoft Exchange as a messaging tool. In this lesson, you will use Exchange as a company-wide information service to create and maintain public folders on your network. Public folders provide the most current information on topics of mutual interest to an entire organization or to select groups within an organization.

IMPORTANT   To complete the exercises in this lesson, you must be authorized to view and create public folders on your network. To find out more about access permissions, contact your Microsoft Exchange Server administrator. If you do not have access to public folders on your network, skip this lesson.

For detailed instructions on how to set up your Inbox, see Lesson 2.

Set up your Inbox for this lesson

> Start Microsoft Exchange using the Chris Adams profile.
>
> You are ready to start this lesson.

Viewing a Public Folder

You have learned how to use the folders in your own mailbox as well as how to organize your personal messages and other documents within folders. You can also create and use *public folders*. The contents of public folders are accessible to everyone in a particular group. By storing and updating information in a public folder, you can ensure that the most current information is available to each person on your team or in your company at any time. Additionally, you can restrict access to a particular public folder by setting up and granting access permissions.

Public folders are stored on Microsoft Exchange Server computers. Various types of Exchange-compatible information can be stored in a public folder. For example, you can design public folders to post job openings, track progress on projects, display employees' classified ads, or compile local restaurant reviews. Public folders can also contain information in a variety of formats, from ordinary messages to slide presentations or video clips. Microsoft Office documents can also be stored in a public folder. In addition, public folders can can be used for Internet newsgroups.

To create a public folder, you must either be a Microsoft Exchange Server administrator or have been granted access permission to create a public folder. Administrators and other folder owners can in turn set different access permissions for other individual users. These permissions determine how much control each person on the network has over the contents of a public folder. For example, someone might be able to read items in a folder, but not be allowed to post any new items. By setting specific access permissions for each public folder, you can make some folders available only to members of a single project team, and others available to everyone in your company. A folder owner may assign more than one person to serve as a folder contact.

IMPORTANT To complete the following three exercises, you must have access to an existing public folder on your network. If you do not have access to a public folder or if there are no public folders currently on your network, skip these exercises.

The illustrations in this lesson will be different than what you see on your screen—the public folders you see will vary depending on how your system administrator has set up Exchange in your organization.

Open a public folder

In this exercise, you open an existing public folder on your network.

1   In the folder list, click the plus sign (+) next to the Public Folders information store.

    Two default subfolders, the Favorites folder and the All Public Folders folder, appear in the folder list.

2   Click the plus sign (+) next to the All Public Folders folder.

Your organization's public folders will look different from this illustration.

The public folders available to members of your organization appear. Your screen should look similar to the following illustration.

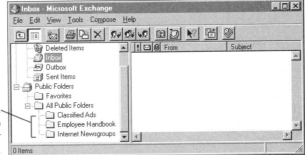

Public folders available to Fitch & Mather employees.

Check folder access permissions

To view the contents of a public folder in detail or to post information of your own to a public folder, you must have the appropriate access permissions for that folder. In this exercise, you check your access permissions for a particular folder.

1   Use the right mouse button to click a public folder, and then, on the shortcut menu, click Properties.

    The Properties dialog box for the selected folder appears.

If you are the owner of the folder, the Properties dialog box will look different from what others see; for example, it will not contain a Summary tab.

2   Click the Summary tab.

    The summary information about the folder appears. Your screen should look similar to the following illustration.

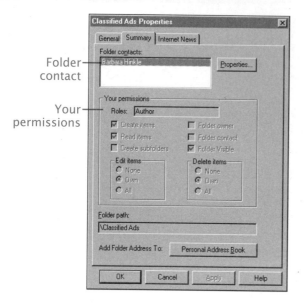

Folder contact

Your permissions

3 Close the Properties dialog box.

TIP You can add the address of the public folder to your personal address book to quickly address a message that you want to post. To do this, use the right mouse button to click the appropriate folder, click Properties on the shortcut menu, click the Summary tab, and then click Personal Address Book.

View the contents of a public folder

In this exercise, you display the contents of a public folder.

1 In the folder list, click a public folder.

The contents of the folder appear in the folder contents list.

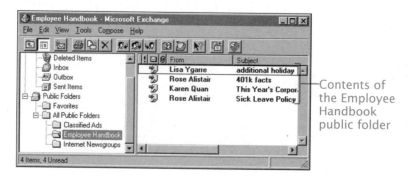

Contents of the Employee Handbook public folder

2 In the folder contents list, double-click the item you want to open. Your screen should look similar to the following illustration.

Use the navigation buttons
to browse through posts.

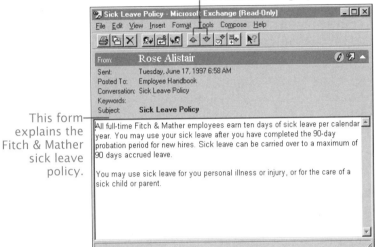

This form explains the Fitch & Mather sick leave policy.

3 Close the post.

TIP You can use the Previous, Next, Next Unread, and Next Group buttons to browse through posted messages in public folders.

Creating a Public Folder

If you want to share information with other users on your network, you can create and design your own public folder. When you design a public folder, you set the folder properties depending on the purpose of the folder. For example, you must decide what types of forms can be posted to the folder, and then define views and rules for organizing its contents. As owner of a public folder, you also establish access permissions for the other users on your network. Additionally, you can designate one or more people as folder contacts to maintain the folder.

One type of public folder is a *discussion folder*. Messages posted in a discussion folder in response to another post are automatically sorted based on their topic, or conversational thread, with the most recent posts first.

You and your Fitch & Mather co-workers have decided to create a public folder to keep track of all the current advertising campaigns. This folder will store forms containing the names of each account, the account executive responsible for it, and the type of campaign. By making this information available to everyone, you can quickly determine what your colleagues are working on and advise each other on new accounts. You have volunteered to design a Current Accounts folder for the network and install a form for recording information about new accounts.

TIP You can get additional help and detailed step-by-step instructions on how to create a public folder by using the Folder Design Cue Cards. To do this, on the Tools menu, point to Application Design, and then click Folder Design Cue Cards.

Create a public folder

In this exercise, you create a new public folder on your network.

1 In the folder list, click the All Public Folders folder.

2 On the File menu, click New Folder.

   The New Folder dialog box appears.

3 In the Folder Name box, type **Current Accounts** and then click OK.

   The new Current Accounts folder appears in the folder contents list. Your screen should look similar to the following illustration.

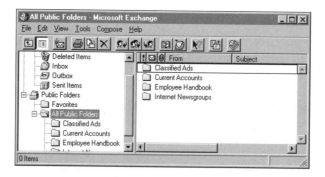

TIP You can quickly find a public folder. To do this, on the Tools menu, click Find Public Folders, and then type the name of the folder you are looking for. If you are not sure of its name, you can search for the path or for text in the folder description.

Installing Forms in a Public Folder

For additional information on using Exchange forms or creating your own custom forms, see Lesson 7.

Now that you have created a public folder, you must decide how its contents should be entered and how information will appear. Most information in a public folder is presented using one or more forms. Forms provide a structure for users to post, view, and respond to information in a folder.

Install a custom form in a folder

In this exercise, you install an existing custom Account Profile form that Fitch & Mather account executives can use to keep track of client information.

1   In the folder list, click the Current Accounts folder.

You can also use the right mouse button to click the folder, and then click Properties.

2   On the Tools menu, point to Application Design, and then click Folder Designer.

The Current Accounts Properties dialog box appears.

3   Click the Forms tab, and then click Manage.

The Forms Manager dialog box appears.

4   Click Install.

The Open dialog box appears.

5   Click the Look In down arrow, and then open the \Exchange 5.0 SBS Practice\Lesson08\Client.vb folder.

The contents of the folder appear.

6   Click the Clients.cfg file, and then click Open.

The Form Properties dialog box appears. Your dialog box should look similar to the following illustration.

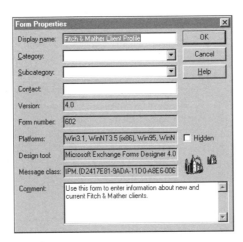

7 Click the Contact field, type your name, and then click OK.

A message appears, informing you that the form is being installed in the Current Accounts folder. The Forms Manager dialog box appears.

8 Close the Forms Manager dialog box.

The Fitch & Mather Client Profile form now appears in the Current Accounts Properties dialog box.

Designate specific forms to use in a folder

You have just installed the Fitch & Mather Client Profile form in your Current Accounts folder. Now you need to define in which formats the users of the Current Accounts folder can post information. In this exercise, you set up the folder so that users can send or post regular electronic messages as well as files from other programs.

1 In the Allow These Forms In This Folder area, click the Forms Listed Above And The Standard Forms option button.

Users will be able to post Fitch & Mather Client Profile forms and standard message forms in the Current Accounts folder as well as files from other programs.

2 Click Apply.

The allowable forms for the Current Accounts folder are set.

Setting Folder Access for Other Users

When you create a public folder, you are considered the owner of that folder. As the owner, you decide who has access to the folder and who can modify or add to its contents. For example, you can make a folder available to everyone on your network or just to the members of a particular project team.

For a detailed description of each role and related permissions, see Lesson 5.

You can also decide what kind of access each individual on your network has to your public folder. Different levels of access based on different roles are assigned using the Permissions tab. By default, each person who is granted access to the folder is assigned the Author role, allowing that person to read the items currently posted, as well as create, edit, and delete their own items. The person listed as the folder contact is assigned the Owner role—the contact can be someone other than the person who created the folder. An Anonymous permission is also provided for non-Exchange users, such as a person accessing public folders from the Internet.

Set folder access permissions

In this exercise, you assign the Editor role to one of your co-workers.

1 Be sure that the Current Accounts Properties dialog box is open.

2   Click the Permissions tab.

Your name is listed as the folder owner.

3   Click Add.

The Add Users dialog box appears.

4   In the address list, select the name of one of your co-workers, click Add, and then click OK.

The name is added to the list of users on the Permissions tab.

5   Select your co-worker's name, click the Roles down arrow in the Permissions area, and then click Editor.

The selected options in the Permissions area change to reflect the privileges associated with the role of Editor.

6   Click OK.

The Current Accounts Properties dialog box closes.

 TIP   There might be times when you don't want other users to have access a public folder, such as when you are creating or editing a folder design. You can make the folder accessible only to users with the Owner role so that you don't have to change the access permissions for everyone. To do this, use the right mouse button to click the appropriate folder, and then click Properties on the shortcut menu. Click the Administration tab, and then click the Owners Only option button.

Posting Information in a Public Folder

A public folder is similar to an office bulletin board: it is a central location where you and your co-workers can post and exchange information. Just as you can display articles or messages by tacking them up on a bulletin board, you can post, or *attach,* items to a public folder so that they're available to every user with the appropriate access privileges.

Earlier in this lesson, you set the formats allowed in your public folder. The Account Profile form that you installed is a custom form designed specifically for use in the Current Accounts folder. Each time Fitch & Mather obtains a new account, a user can fill out a blank Account Profile form and post it to the Current Accounts folder.

In addition to the custom form, you can designate other standard forms to be used in the Current Accounts folder. If users want to reply to an item in a public folder with a comment or a question, they can do so in several ways. They can use the New Post form to add items to the folder, and even carry on a conversation with other folder users. They can also use the New Message form to send a message to be posted in the folder without actually opening the folder. Finally, users can reply to an item by sending a message to the person who originally created a public folder item.

By default, any file format is allowed in a public folder, in addition to the standard forms. For example, a user could post a Microsoft Word document describing the product line for an account or a Microsoft Excel worksheet containing recent sales figures to the Current Accounts folder. A public folder might contain custom forms for responding to a particular item. If a folder allows custom forms, they are added to the bottom of the Compose menu. If the folder allows standard forms, you can respond to an item using the New Post form. The New Post form is much like the New Message form you use when sending electronic mail, but it's designed for posting to public folders rather than for sending e-mail messages.

Post a custom form to a public folder

In this exercise, you test the Fitch & Mather Client Profile form in the Current Accounts folder by posting the information about the Pecos Coffee Company account.

1 In the folder list, click the Current Accounts folder.

Custom forms installed in a folder appear at the bottom of the Compose menu.

2 On the Compose menu, click New Client Profile.

If this is the first time you've used the form, a message appears informing you that the form is being installed on your computer. After a few moments, the Client Profile form appears. Your screen should look similar to the following illustration.

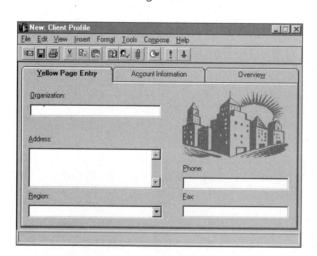

3 In the Organization field, type **Pecos Coffee Company**

4 In the Phone field, type **206-555-1957**

5 Click the Account Information tab, click the Account Executive down arrow, and then click Chris Adams.

6 Click the Status down arrow, and then click Medium Priority.

7 On the New Post Form toolbar, click the Post button.

The Fitch & Mather Client Profile form is posted to the Current Accounts folder.

Post

The Post button is identical in appearance to the Send button in forms.

 TROUBLESHOOTING If you receive an error message when using a newly installed form to post a message in a folder, try restarting Exchange. To do this, on the File menu, click Exit And Log Off in Exchange, restart Exchange, and then post the message again.

View a custom form

In this exercise, you open the custom form you just posted to the Current Accounts folder to see if the information is displayed correctly.

1 In the folder contents list, double-click the "Pecos Coffee Company" form you just posted.

After a moment, the Client Profile form for the Pecos Coffee Company appears. Your form should look similar to the following illustration.

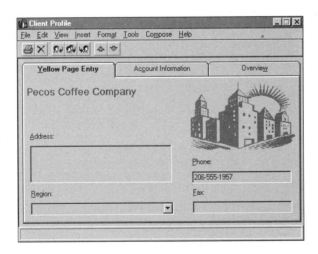

2 Close the "Pecos Coffee Company" form.

Designing Folder Views

To help you organize and locate the information in a public folder, you can create different views that display the contents of the folder according to different criteria. When you create a view, you can choose which columns of information appear, group items by category, sort items so that they appear in a particular order, and apply a filter to display only certain items in each column. For example, you can choose to display the contents of the Current Accounts folder and organize the information based on the account executive assigned to each account.

When a user opens a folder for the first time, items appear in Normal view. Normal view displays items based on the item type and the name of the sender, and sorts the items by time and date received. You can create custom views for a public folder, but only the owner of the public folder can designate what the default view is and what views are available.

Select columns for your custom view

In this exercise, you specify the columns you want to appear in a new custom view for the Current Accounts folder.

1 Use the right mouse button to click the Current Accounts folder.

A shortcut menu appears.

You can also click Properties on the File menu.

2 Click Properties.

The Current Accounts Properties dialog box appears.

3 Click the Views tab.

4 Be sure that the Folder Views option button is selected, and then click New.

The New View dialog box appears.

5 In the View Name box, type **By Executive** and then click Columns.

The Columns dialog box appears.

You can change the order in which the columns appear by using the Move Up and Move Down buttons.

6 In the Available Columns list, click Account Executive, and then click Add.

The Account Executive column is added to the Show The Following list.

7 Repeat step 6 to add the Account Status column to the Show The Following list.

8 In the Show The Following list, select Importance, and then click Remove.

The Importance column is removed from the list.

9 Repeat step 8 to remove the Attachment, From, and Size columns from the Show The Following list.

Your dialog box should look similar to the following illustration.

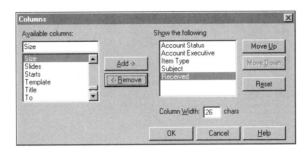

10 Click OK.

Group columns

In this exercise, you group the columns in the view by Account Executive.

1 Be sure that the New View dialog box is open.

2 Click Group By.

The Group By dialog box appears.

3 In the Group Items By area, click the down arrow, and then click Account Executive.

The data will be organized based on the name of the account executive in charge of each account.

4 In the Then Sort Items By area at the bottom of the dialog box, click the down arrow, and then click Account Status.

The account status information for each account executive will be sorted in alphabetical order.

5 Click OK, and then click OK again.

The new By Executive view is created.

6 In the Current Accounts Properties dialog box, be sure that By Executive is selected in the Folder Views list, and then click OK.

The By Executive view is applied to the contents of the Current Accounts folder.

7 In the folder contents list, click the plus sign (+) next to Chris Adams.

The Chris Adams category expands. Your screen should look similar to the following illustration.

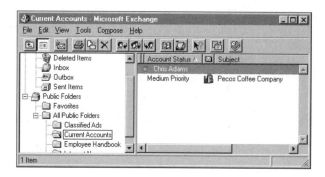

TIP If you have Owner access privileges to a folder, you can change the default view. To do this, use the right mouse button to click the appropriate folder, and then click Properties on the shortcut menu. Click the Administration tab, click the Initial View On Folder down arrow, and then select a different view.

Add new items to the folder

To test the new By Executive view you just created, the folder contents list needs to contain more than one item. In this exercise, you insert some practice Fitch & Mather Client Profile forms that have already been created in the Current Accounts folder.

For detailed instructions on how to set up your Inbox, see Lesson 2. Do not copy the Client.vb folder.

1 In Windows Explorer or Windows NT Explorer, copy the three messages in the Exchange 5.0 SBS Practice\Lesson08 folder to the Current Accounts folder.

The view specifications are applied to the copied items, and the contents are grouped by account executive.

2 Click the plus sign next to Chandra Shah.

The details of each category appear. Your screen should look similar to the following illustration.

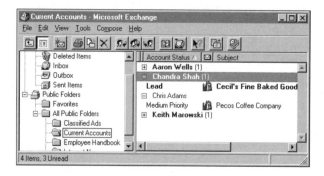

Replying to Public Items

You can reply directly to the person who posted a public item by clicking the Reply button on a form. A shortcut to the original post is automatically attached to your message so that the recipient of your reply can open the original item if necessary.

Reply to a public item

In this exercise, you reply to one of the forms posted in the folder.

Reply

1 In the Chandra Shah category, double-click the "Cecil's Fine Baked Goods" item.

After a few moments, a form appears with the data on the Cecil's Fine Baked Goods account.

2 On the Standard toolbar, click the Reply button.

After a moment, a New Message form addressed to Chandra Shah appears. A shortcut to the original Cecil's Fine Baked Goods post form is attached.

3 In the message area, type **This is similar to my new account. Can we discuss campaign strategies?**

Your screen should look similar to the following illustration.

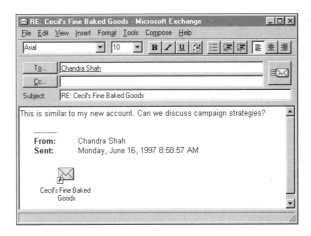

Send

4 Click the Send button.

The response is sent.

NOTE Because the e-mail address used in this exercise is fictitious, you will receive an undeliverable message from the system administrator.

Opening a Public Folder Quickly

Suppose your organization has a long list of public folders available on the network and you want to be able to quickly locate a specific public folder that you use often. You can create a shortcut to that folder by adding it to your Favorites folder.

Add a public folder to the Favorites folder

As an account executive, you frequently use the Current Accounts public folder. In this exercise, you create a shortcut to that folder.

1   Be sure that the Current Accounts folder is selected in the folder list, and then click Add To Favorites on the File menu.

    The Add To Favorites dialog box appears.

2   Click Add.

    A shortcut to the Current Accounts folder is added to your Favorites folder.

 TIP   You can add subfolders of a top-level public folder to a public folder shortcut. To do this, select the appropriate folder, and then click Add To Favorites on the File menu. Click Options, and then select the Add Subfolders Of This Folder check box.

Use a shortcut

In this exercise, you use the shortcut to open the Current Accounts folder.

1   In the folder list, click the Favorites folder.

    The contents of the Favorites folder appear in the folder contents list. Your screen should look similar to the following illustration.

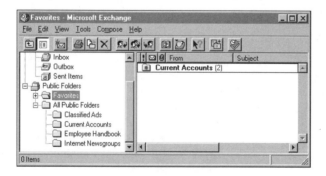

2 In the folder contents list, double-click the shortcut to Current Accounts.

The contents of the Current Accounts folder appear in Normal view.

Different views can be applied to public folder shortcuts.

3 On the View menu, point to Folder Views, and then click By Executive.

The By Executive view is applied to the contents of the Current Accounts folder.

 NOTE If you'd like to build on the skills that you learned in this lesson, you can perform the exercises presented in the following section, One Step Further. Otherwise, skip to "Finish the lesson."

One Step Further: Creating a Moderated Folder

Suppose you want to review the contents of a message in a particular public folder before it gets posted. You can do so if you are designated as the moderator of a *moderated folder.* Incoming posts are automatically placed in the moderator's Inbox or in another folder to which only the moderator has access. The messages can then be reviewed and approved by the moderator. If the moderator decides not to post the message, it can be deleted or returned to the sender.

Moderated folders are common on the Internet because their contents have to be reviewed for appropriateness and certain policies must be enforced. Any folder can be set up as a moderated folder and can have more than one moderator.

As the folder contact, you are now responsible for maintaining the Current Accounts folder. Because the content of this folder will be used by all the account executives, you want to make sure the content is accurate and approved before it is posted. As the owner of the Current Accounts folder, you designate it as a moderated folder so that all messages will initially be forwarded to you.

Create a moderated folder

In this exercise, you make the Current Accounts folder a moderated folder.

1 In the folder list, use the right mouse button to click the Current Accounts folder, and then click Properties.

The Current Accounts Properties dialog box appears.

2 Click the Administration tab, and then click Moderated Folder.

The Moderated Folder dialog box appears.

3 Select the Set Folder Up As A Moderated Folder check box.

4 In the Forward New Items To box, type your name, and then click Check Names.

All incoming postings will be sent to you for approval.

5 Under Moderators, click Add, double-click your name, and then click OK.

You are now designated as the moderator for this public folder.

6 Click OK, and then click OK again.

All messages posted to this folder by others will be forwarded to you, the moderator.

Messages can also be forwarded to another folder.

 TIP The moderator of a public folder can automatically send a standard response when items are submitted to the folder for review. To do this, use the right mouse button to click the appropriate public folder, and then click Properties on the shortcut menu. Click the Administration tab, and then select the Reply To New Items With check box. You can draft a custom response or use the standard response provided with Exchange.

Test the moderated folder

 IMPORTANT You'll need to recruit some help from a co-worker to complete the following exercise and demonstrate how moderated folders work. Choose a co-worker who is on your network and has not been granted specific permissions for the Current Accounts folder. Be sure your co-worker performs the following steps on his or her computer.

1 In the folder list, click the Current Accounts folder.

2 On the Compose menu, click New Post In This Folder.

A new Post form appears.

3 In the Subject box, type **Moderated Folder Test** and then click the Post button.

The post is sent to the moderator.

Post

Review the post

Your co-worker posted an item to the Current Accounts folder. Because this folder is moderated, you receive the post to review the contents.

IMPORTANT   Be sure that you, the folder moderator, perform the following steps on your computer.

1   In your Inbox, double-click the item from your co-worker.

The form opens.

2   Review the contents, and then close the form.

3   Drag the Moderated Folder Test item in your Inbox to the Current Accounts public folder.

The item is now posted to the Current Accounts public folder.

Finish the lesson

Follow these steps to delete the practice messages you created in the lesson.

1   In the Favorites folder, delete the Current Accounts shortcut.

2   In the All Public Folders folder, delete the Current Accounts folder.

3   In the Inbox and Sent Items folders, delete the messages created in this lesson.

4   Close all open windows except Microsoft Exchange.

5   If you want to continue to the next lesson, click the Inbox folder in the folder list.

6   If you are finished using Microsoft Exchange for now, on the File menu, click Exit And Log Off.

You are logged off Microsoft Exchange, and the Viewer window closes.

Lesson Summary

To	Do this
View the contents of a public folder	In the Viewer window, double-click Public Folders in the folder list. Double-click the All Public Folders folder, and then double-click the appropriate public folder. In the folder contents list, double-click an item to view it in detail.

To	Do this	Button
Create a public folder	In the folder list under Public Folders, click All Public Folders. On the File menu, click New Folder. Type a name for the new folder, and then click OK.	
Install forms in a public folder	Select the folder you want. Use the right mouse button to click folder, and then click Properties. Click the Forms tab, click Manage. Click Install. Select a form file, and then click Open. Click OK. Click Close.	
Designate a specific form to use in a folder	If you are the owner, use the right mouse button to click the appropriate folder, and then click Properties. Click the Forms tab. In the Allow These Forms In This Folder area, select the option you want, and then click Apply.	
Set folder access for other users	If you are the owner, use the right mouse button to click the appropriate folder, and then click Properties. Click the Permissions tab. Click Add, double-click the name of the person to whom you want to grant access in the address list, and then click OK. Click the Roles down arrow, select a role, and then click Apply.	
Post public information	In the folder list, select the appropriate public folder. On the Compose menu, click a form. Enter text in the form fields, and then click the Post button.	
Design a folder view	In the folder list, use the right mouse button to click the appropriate public folder. Click the Views tab. Be sure Folder Views is selected, and then click New. Choose the columns you want to view. Apply any group, sort, or filter options. Click OK. Click Apply.	

To	Do this	Button
Reply to a public item	In the folder contents list, double-click the item you want to open. On the Standard toolbar, click the Reply button. Type your message, and then click Send. *Or* On the Compose menu, click a new form. Enter text in the form fields, and then click Post.	
Create a shortcut to a public folder	Select the folder for which you want to create a shortcut. On the File menu, click Add To Favorites, and then click Add.	

For online information about	**On the Help menu, click Microsoft Exchange Help Topics, click the Index tab, and then type**
Using public folders	**Creating: public folders**
Installing forms in public folders	**Forms: creating** *or* **Public folders: forms**
Posting information	**Post forms**
Responding to public items	**Replying: to posted items**
Creating public folder shortcut	**Public folders: adding to Favorites**

Connecting to Exchange Through a Web Browser

Estimated time
35 min.

In this lesson you will learn how to:

- Send and receive messages through your Web browser.
- View the Address Book through your Web browser.
- View public folders through your Web browser.

You use the Viewer window in Microsoft Exchange to perform tasks such as reading and sending messages. But what if you are out of the office working on a computer that doesn't have Exchange and you need to check your mail? Or you are viewing documents on the Internet and you want to quickly check your mail? Using Exchange 5.0, you can send and check for new messages without opening the Exchange program—instead you use your Web *browser*, a program that interprets and displays documents formatted for the World Wide Web, to work in the Viewer window.

More and more people have discovered and now rely on the *Internet* as a source of information. The Internet contains millions of text-based documents located on servers around the globe. The *World Wide Web* (WWW), which is a part of the Internet, presents information in a multimedia format, using text, pictures, sounds, video, and animation.

The World Wide Web is a client/server-based system; each computer that connects to a *server,* or main computer, is referred to as a *client.* The client software allows you to view the information located on a server. Microsoft Exchange is also a client/server–based system. A computer on which the

Exchange 5.0 Client software has been installed can connect to an Exchange 5.0 Server and view public folders, create rules, and perform other server-based functions.

For more information, see the Microsoft Internet Explorer 3.0 Step by Step book.

When you browse through the Web, you move from Web page to Web page by clicking *hyperlinks*. These links are words or graphics that are underlined or highlighted in a unique color, for example. When you click a link, you automatically go, or *jump*, to another Web page. When you use a Web browser to view and manipulate your e-mail messages, you use links to navigate between messages and perform tasks. Having Internet connectivity integrated into Exchange Server means that you can use your Web browser to perform basic messaging tasks as well as work with forms and public folders without opening the Exchange Client program. The *WebView* feature of Microsoft Exchange allows you to view the contents of your mailbox through a browser. There are two main viewer areas in WebView—the Mailbox Viewer and the Public Folders Viewer.

You're getting ready for a week-long vacation and want to be able to check your messages at the office periodically. You want your clients and co-workers to be able to reach you if needed. In the following exercises, you will view and manage your new messages as well as work with public folders using a Web browser.

 IMPORTANT   To complete the exercises in this lesson, you must have an account and a mailbox on an Exchange Server. In addition, your Exchange server must be configured to allow Internet access. You must also have a current Web browser and know the IP address or URL (Uniform Resource Locator) of your Microsoft Exchange Server. An example of an IP address is http://207.14.42.113/Exchange. An example of a URL is www.fitch&mather.com/exchange. Contact your system administrator to obtain your organization's Internet address or for further assistance. If your system doesn't meet the above requirements, skip this lesson.

The following exercises were designed to be performed in a current Web browser that supports frames and JavaScript. Microsoft Internet Explorer 3.0 was the Web browser used to complete the exercises in this lesson.

Set up your Inbox for this lesson

For more detailed instructions on how to set up your Inbox, see Lesson 2.

1   Start Microsoft Exchange using the Chris Adams profile.

2   Copy the practice files from the Exchange 5.0 SBS Practice\Lesson09 folder to your Inbox folder.

3   On the File menu, click Exit And Log Off.

   You are logged off of Microsoft Exchange. You are ready to start this lesson.

Accessing Your Exchange Mailbox on the World Wide Web

For a demonstration of how to view a mailbox in a web browser, double-click the Camcorder Files On The Internet shortcut on your Desktop or connect to the Internet address listed on p. xxx.

When you first use your Web browser to open your mailbox, the Mailbox Viewer is displayed by default. To change views or select other messaging options, you use the Navigation Bar located on the left side of the window. Depending on what task you are performing, relevant links are displayed. For example, the Reply and Forward links appear only while you are reading a message.

Many similarities exist between viewing your mailbox contents through a Web browser and viewing them through the standard Exchange Client. For example, in both cases, unread messages appear in bold type; messages are sorted according to column headings; and you can read, delete, reply, forward, move, and copy messages.

Log on to Exchange

In this exercise, you open your Web browser, connect to your Exchange mailbox to check for new messages, and then send a test message.

1 Open your Web browser and maximize the window.

2 Type the IP address or URL of your Exchange Server followed by /**Exchange** and then press ENTER.

   The home page appears. Your screen should look similar to the following illustration.

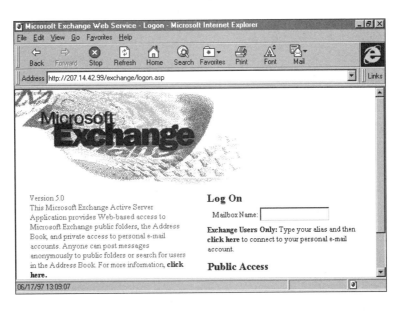

You can also click the Click Here link.

3 In the Mailbox Name box, type your mailbox name, and then press ENTER.

If a security warning message appears, click Yes. Be sure to type your exact mailbox name. A dialog box appears, prompting you for authentication information. If you are not sure what your mailbox name is or need additional help, contact your system administrator. If no security message appears, skip step 4.

Your username is the network name you use to log on to your domain.

4 Type your username, press TAB, type your mailbox password, and then click OK.

If you are logged onto a network, you won't have to enter your username and password. After a few moments, the Mailbox Viewer is displayed. Your screen should look similar to the following illustration.

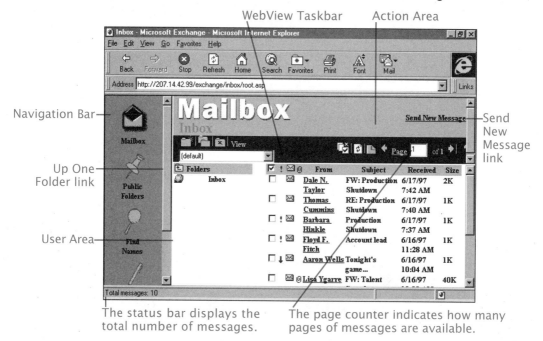

The status bar displays the total number of messages.

The page counter indicates how many pages of messages are available.

TROUBLESHOOTING Anytime a page doesn't load or you don't get the results you expected, try refreshing the Web page. Most browsers have a Refresh command that you can use to quickly reload your current Web page.

Explore the Mailbox Viewer

In this exercise, you explore the various WebView areas.

You can position your pointer over a link to view a ToolTip.

1   In the User Area, click the Up One Folder link.

Your mailbox folders appear. The four built-in folders—Deleted Items, Inbox, Outbox, and Sent Items—are displayed. Your screen should look similar to the following illustration.

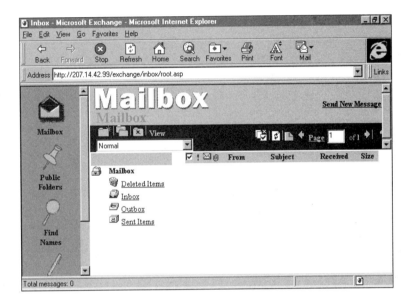

2   In the User Area, click the Sent Items link.

The contents of your Sent Items folder appear.

3   In the User Area, click the Up One Folder link.

Your mailbox folders appear.

4   In the User Area, click the Deleted Items link.

The contents of your Deleted Items folder appear.

5   In the User Area, click the Up One Folder link.

Your mailbox folders appear.

6   In the User Area, click the Inbox link.

The contents of your Inbox folder reappear.

TIP   If the page counter on the WebView Taskbar indicates that you have another page of messages, you can easily view the contents of that page. To do this, click the Go To The Next Page Of Messages link.

Organizing Messages by Using Your Web Browser

You can organize your mailbox by grouping messages, deleting messages, and applying views—similar to working in the standard Exchange Client view, except that you use links to accomplish these tasks. In addition, you might have to refresh your mailbox to see the results of some actions, such as deleting messages. The view applied by default is the Normal view.

Read messages

In this exercise, you view messages through your Web browser.

1   Click the Barbara Hinkle link for the "Production Shutdown" message.

The message opens. Your screen should look similar to the following illustration.

Click the Next and Previous buttons to browse through messages.

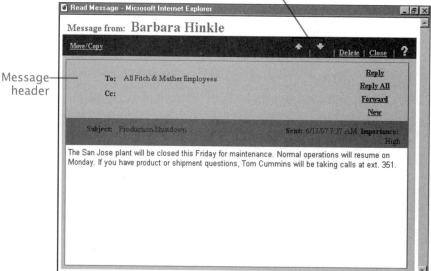

Message header

172

2   Click the Previous link.

The "RE: Production Shutdown" message from Thomas Cummins opens.

3   Scroll down to view the entire message, and then click the Close link.

Delete a message

1   Click the Dale N. Taylor link for the "FW: Production Shutdown" message.

The message opens.

2   Click the Delete link.

The message is deleted from your mailbox.

 IMPORTANT   Messages that have been altered might not reflect those changes until you update your mailbox by either checking for new messages or refreshing your current Web page. For example, even though you opened a message, it still appears in bold type, as though it is unread. Or if you deleted a message, it might not appear in the Deleted Items folder.

Refresh your mailbox

In this exercise, you refresh the contents of your current Web page by checking for new messages.

You can also use your browser Refresh command.

 On the WebView Taskbar, click the Check For New Messages link.

After a few moments, the two messages that you read appear in regular text and Dale's message is moved to the Deleted Items folder.

Group messages

In this exercise, you reorganize your messages using different group options.

1   On the WebView Taskbar, click the View down arrow, and then click Group By Subject.

The messages in your Inbox are listed alphabetically by subject. The Subject column is now the first column header. Your screen should look similar to the following illustration.

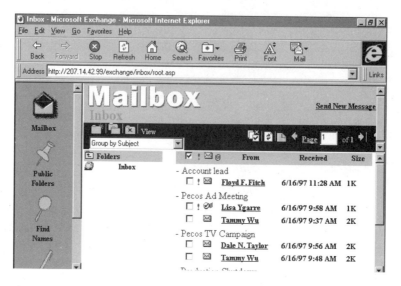

2 On the WebView Taskbar, click the View down arrow, and then click Unread By Conversation Topic.

The unread messages in your Inbox are listed alphabetically by conversation topic. The Conversation Topic column is now the first column header.

3 On the WebView Taskbar, click the View down arrow, and then click Normal.

The default sort order is applied.

Move messages

In this exercise, you create a folder for new account leads, make a copy of an important message, and then clean your mailbox by deleting a few messages.

1 On the WebView Taskbar, click the Create A New Folder link.

A dialog box appears.

2 In the Name box, select the text, type **Leads** and then click OK.

A subfolder named Leads is created in your Inbox.

3 Click the Floyd F. Fitch link for the "Account Lead" message.

After a few moments, the message opens.

4 Click the Move/Copy link.

After a few moments, the Move Copy Folder Dialog page appears.

5 Click the Mailbox link.

The Leads subfolder appears.

6 Click the Leads link.

7 Click the Move link, and then click the Close link.

The message is copied to the Leads folder. The Viewer window opens.

8 Close the Move Copy Folder Dialog page, if necessary.

9 Click the Leads link.

The contents of the Lead subfolder, the "Account Lead" message from Floyd F. Fitch, appear.

10 Click the Up One Folder link.

The Mailbox Viewer window reappears.

Viewing the Address Book

You can look up names of others in your organization using the Address Book stored on the Exchange Server computer. Other information, such as department or phone number, can also be viewed by looking up names in the Address Book.

Find names in the Address Book

In this exercise, you search for your name in the Address Book.

 NOTE Only names in your organization's global address list can be searched for or viewed through your Web browser—you cannot look up names in your personal address book.

1 On the Navigation Bar, click the Find Names link.

The Find Names page appears.

2 In the Display Name box, type your first name.

3 Click the Find link.

If a security warning message appears, click Yes. After a few moments, your entry in the Address Book appears. If there are several people in the Address Book with the same first name, they are also listed.

4 Click the link labeled with your name.

A page with more detailed information appears.

5 Close the Detailed Information window.

The Find Names page reappears.

6 Click the Close link.

The Mailbox Viewer page reappears.

TIP You can view the members of a distribution list in your Address Book. For example, you can quickly see the names of all the employees included in the Accounting Department distribution list. To do this, type the distribution list name in the Display Name box, and then click Find.

Sending Messages Through Your Internet Browser

Using the Mailbox Viewer in your Web browser, you can manage your mailbox contents just as you can in Exchange. The main difference between working through a Web browser and working in Exchange is that you perform messaging tasks by clicking links rather than toolbar buttons or commands.

Send a test message

In this exercise, you send yourself a test message.

1 In the Action Area, click the Send New Message link.

   The Compose New Message page appears.

2 In the To box, type your name.

3 In the Subject box, type **WebView Test**

4 In the message area, type **Just testing.**

5 Click the Importance down arrow, and then click Low.

6 Select the Delivery Receipt check box.

   You will receive a Delivery Receipt when the message is successfully delivered.

7 Click the Send Button link.

   If a security warning message appears, click Yes. After a moment, a notification message appears informing you that your message was sent.

8 Click OK.

   The Compose New Message page closes, and the Mailbox Viewer page reappears.

TIP You can attach files to messages you send through a Web browser.

Check for new messages

In this exercise, you view the test message you sent yourself in the previous exercise.

1 On the WebView Taskbar, click the Check For New Messages link.

After a few moments, your "WebView Test" message and a Delivery Receipt from the system administrator are displayed.

2 Click the link labeled with your name for the "WebView Test" message.

Your screen should look similar to the following illustration.

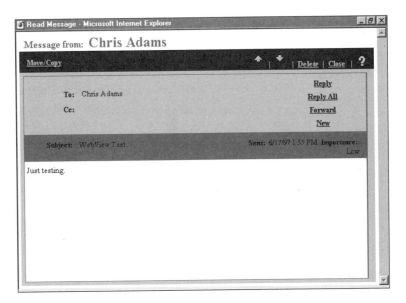

3 Click the Close link.

The message closes.

Respond to messages

In this exercise, you reply to a message, and then verify that your reply was sent.

1 Click the Lisa Ygarre link for the "FW: Talent Search" message.

The message opens.

2 Click the Reply link.

The Compose New Message page appears.

3 In the message area, type **Thanks for your feedback!**

4 Click the Send Button link.

If a security warning message appears, click Yes. After a few moments, a message notifies you that your message was sent.

5 Click OK.

6 Click the Up One Folder link.

Your mailbox folders appear.

7 Click the Sent Items link.

After a few moments, the contents of the Sent Items folder appear, including the "WebView Test" message and the reply to Lisa's message. Your screen should look similar to the following illustration.

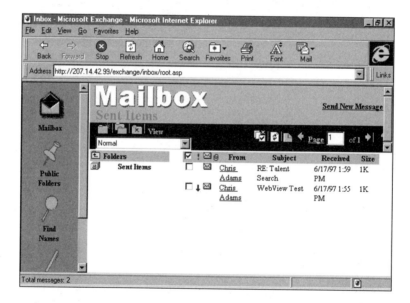

Delete multiple messages

1 Select the checkbox next to both messages in your Sent Items folder.

2 On the WebView Taskbar, click the Delete Marked Messages link.

The messages are deleted.

3 Click the Up One Folder link.

Your mailbox folders appear.

Working with Public Folders on the World Wide Web

If your organization has set up public folders, you can also open those folders by using your Web browser. Public folders are stored on Exchange Servers and are used to share a wide variety of information between co-workers. Forms can be associated with a particular folder, as can access permissions that define who can view and post items to the folder.

Using the Public Folders Viewer, you display and view the contents of public folders just as you would using the Mailbox Viewer. You use links to see the contents of each folder and check for new posts by refreshing the view.

 IMPORTANT To complete the following exercises, you must be authorized to view and create public folders on your network. To find out more about access permissions, contact your Microsoft Exchange Server administrator. If you do not have access to public folders on your network, skip the following exercises.

The illustrations in this lesson will be different from what you see on your screen—the public folders you see will vary depending on how your system administrator has set up Exchange for your organization.

View the contents of a public folder

In this exercise, you explore the Public Folders Viewer and display the contents of a public folder.

1   In the Navigation Bar, click the Public Folders link.

All public folders for your organization appear in the User Area. Your screen should look similar to the following illustration.

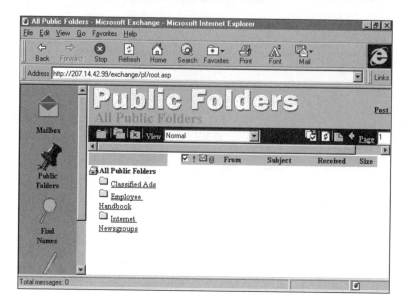

2   In the User Area, click a link to a public folder.

The contents of the folder appear in the folder contents list.

3   Click a link to a post.

The post appears.

4   Click the Close link.

The post closes.

5   Click the Up One Folder link.

All public folders reappear.

> **TIP**   You can reply to a folder, reply to a sender, or forward a post while viewing it. To do this, click the appropriate link in the Action Area.

Create a public folder

In this exercise, you create a new public folder on your network.

1   On the WebView Taskbar, click the Create A New Folder link.

A dialog box appears.

2   In the Name box, select the text, type **Test** and then click OK.

A public folder named Test is created.

3   Click the Test link.

180

Create a new post

In this exercise, you post a new item to the Test public folder you created in the previous exercise.

1   In the Action Area, click the Post link.

A blank Compose New Post form appears. Your screen should look similar to the following illustration.

Your organization's public folders will look different from this illustration.

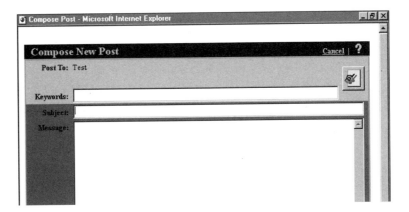

2   In the Subject box, type **Post Test**

3   Click the Post Button link.

If a security warning message appears, click Yes. After a few moments, a message notifies you that your message was posted.

4   Click OK.

The Compose New Post page closes, and the Public Folders Viewer page reappears.

 TIP   You can set a priority level for your post. To do this, create a new post, click the Importance down arrow, and then click the appropriate level (Low, Normal, or High).

Check for new posts

In this exercise, you check for new posts to view the post you sent in the previous exercise.

1   On the WebView Taskbar, click the Check For New Posts link.

After a few moments, your "Post Test" message is displayed.

2 Click the link labeled with your name for the "Post Test" message. Your screen should look similar to the following illustration.

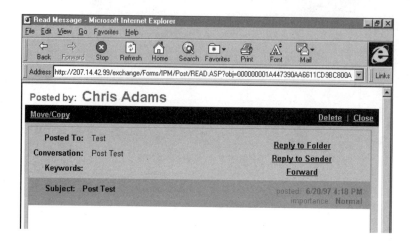

3 Click the Close link.

 NOTE If you'd like to build on the skills that you learned in this lesson, you can perform the exercises presented in the following section, One Step Further. Otherwise, skip to "Finish the lesson."

One Step Further: Using the Out Of Office Assistant

You can create an AutoReply using the Out Of Office Assistant so that anyone who sends you a message will receive an automated response notifying them that you are unavailable. Creating an AutoReply in your Web browser is similar to creating an AutoReply in Exchange.

Create an AutoReply

To learn more about creating an AutoReply, see Lesson 4.

Because you will be away from your office for the upcoming week, you want to let people know that you have received their messages and that you will reply to them when you return. In this exercise, you set up your AutoReply.

1 On the Navigation Bar, click the Options link.

The Options page appears.

2 Click the Out Of The Office option button.

3 In the Reply To Each Sender With The Following Text box, type **I am on vacation until July 6th. Feel free to call me on my cell phone for urgent matters.**

Your screen should look similar to the following illustration.

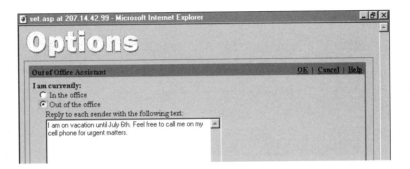

4 Click the OK link.

If a security warning message appears, click Yes. Your AutoReply is now in effect.

IMPORTANT All senders of incoming messages will now receive the AutoReply. If you want to disable the AutoReply until you leave on your trip, click the Options link on the Navigation Bar, and then click the In The Office option button.

Send a test message

In this exercise, you send yourself a test message to make sure that the AutoReply is working.

1 Switch to your Inbox.

2 Send a new message addressed to yourself titled **AutoReply Test**

3 Click the Send Button link.

If a security warning message appears, click Yes. After a few moments, a message notifies you that your message was sent.

4 Click OK.

The Compose New Message page closes, and the Viewer page reappears.

Check for new messages

In this exercise, you check for new messages to view the test message you sent to yourself in the previous exercise and make sure that you also received an AutoReply message.

1 On the WebView Taskbar, click the Check For New Messages link.

   After a few moments, your "AutoReply Test" message and an AutoReply to that message are displayed in the folder contents list.

2 Click the link labeled with your name for the "AutoReply Test" message.

3 Click the Close link.

   The message closes.

Disable the AutoReply

1 On the Navigation Bar, click the Options link.

   The Options page appears.

2 Under I Am Currently, click the In The Office option button, delete the AutoReply text, and then click the OK link.

   If a security warning message appears, click Yes. Your AutoReply is now disabled.

Finish the lesson

Follow these steps to delete the practice messages you created in the lesson.

1 Switch to the Inbox, click the Leads link, and then click the Delete The Current Folder link. Click OK when prompted to confirm the deletion.

2 In the Inbox folder, select the check box next to each practice message, and then click the Delete Marked Messages Button link.

3 Switch to the Sent Items folder, delete each practice message by opening the message, and then clicking the Delete link.

4 Switch to the Deleted Items folder, delete each practice message by opening the message, and then clicking the Delete link.

5 Switch to your organization's public folders. Delete the Test folder by clicking the Test link and then clicking the Delete The Current Folder link. Click Yes when prompted to confirm the deletion.

6 If you are finished using your Web browser, on the Navigation Bar, click the Log Off link.

7 Close the browser window.

⚡ WARNING For security reasons, it is highly recommended that you log off of your mailbox, and then close your Web browser window. This method of quitting ensures that your session with the Exchange Server is terminated.

Lesson Summary

To	Do this
Read a message	Click the link for the message you want to read, read the message, and then click the Close link.
Delete a message	Click the link for the message you want to delete, and then click the Delete link.
Group messages	On the Taskbar, click the View down arrow, and then click a group name.
Move or copy messages	Click the link for the message you want to move or copy, click the Move/Copy link, and then click the appropriate link.
Find names in the Address Book	On the Navigation Bar, click the Find Names link, in the Display Name box, type your first name or other information, and then click the Find link.
Send a message	In the Action Area, click the Send New Message link, fill in the recipient information and set any delivery options, and then click the Send Button link.
Check for new messages or refresh the mailbox	On the Taskbar, click the Check For New Messages link.
Reply to a message	Click the link for the message you want to reply to, click the Reply link, type your reply message, and then click the Send Button link.

To	Do this
Forward a message	Click the link for the message you want to forward, and then click the Forward link. Fill in the recipient information, type your reply message, and then click the Send Button link.
View contents of a public folder	On the Navigation Bar, click the Public Folders link, and then click a link to a public folder.
Create a public folder	Be sure that you are viewing all public folders, and on the WebView Taskbar, click the Create A New Folder link. Type a name, and then click OK.
Create a new post	In the Action Area, click the Post link, type keywords and a subject, and then click the Post link.
Check for new posts	On the WebView Taskbar, click the Check For New Posts link.

For online information about	Click the Get Help Information On The Current Window link, click the Table of Contents link, and then click the following link
Logging on and exploring messages using a Web browser	Web Access Overview
Browsing through messages	Reading Messages
Organizing messages	Web Access Overview
Setting message options	Viewing and Setting Message Options *or* Requesting Message Receipts
Viewing the Address Book	Finding Names
Sending messages	Creating New Messages
Setting up Out of Office Assistant	Setting User Options
Working with public folder	Public Folders Overview
Creating a post	Creating New Messages for Posting

Review & Practice

Estimated time
25 min.

You will review and practice how to:

- Create a custom form using the Microsoft Exchange Forms Designer.
- Design a public folder and use a custom form.
- Send and post messages through a Web browser.

Before you move on to Part 4, which covers using Microsoft Schedule+, you can practice the skills you learned in Part 3 by working through the steps in this Review & Practice section.

Scenario

The Human Resources director has approved the head count for the Administrative Assistant position you requested. In addition to recruiting outside applicants, you want to advertise the job internally. You want to create a custom form using the Microsoft Exchange Forms Designer, and then create a public folder in which to post your job listing. You're also getting ready for a short business trip, and use your Web browser to connect to your Exchange Server and set up an AutoReply message.

Step 1: Create a Custom Form

You want to make the Administrative Assistant job listing available to current Fitch & Mather employees before the position is advertised in the local newspaper. In this step, you create a Job Posting form to use for this purpose.

1. Start the Microsoft Exchange Forms Designer. Using the Form Template wizard, open the Miscactv.efp file in the C:\Exchange\Efdforms\Samples\Custrack folder.

2. Change the window caption to Job Posting.

3. Add a From field and a Date field to the form.

4. Select the Summary field. Change the caption to "Title:" and format the caption text as bold and 12 points. Change the text color to teal. (Hint: In the Field Properties dialog box, click the Format tab, and then select the Caption option button.)

5. Save the form as Fmjobs on your Desktop. (Hint: Use the Save As command, and locate the C:\Windows\Desktop folder.)

6. Install the Job Posting form in the Personal Forms library. In the Form Properties dialog box, clear the Hidden check box.

7. Exit the Microsoft Exchange Forms Designer.

For more information on	See
Microsoft Exchange Forms Designer	Lesson 7
Viewing sample forms	Lesson 7
Modifying forms	Lesson 7
Installing forms	Lesson 7

Step 2: Design a Public Folder and Use a Custom Form

Now that you have created a Job Posting form, you want to design a public folder in which to store your form on the network, and then post the Administrative Assistant position information to make it available to everyone at Fitch & Mather. In this step, you design a public folder, add a form to the newly created folder, and then use the form.

1. Create a public folder called Employment Opportunities on the network.

2. Install the Job Posting form you created earlier in the Employment Opportunities folder. (Hint: Use the Forms Manager dialog box to open the \Fmjobs.vb\Fmjobs.cfg file stored on your Desktop.)

3. In the Form Properties dialog box, change the display name to "Job Postings," and then type **Use this form to list job opportunities at Fitch & Mather.** in the Comment area. (Hint: Be sure that the Hidden check box is cleared.)

4. In the new public folder, create a new job post. In the Summary field, type **Administrative Assistant**. In the Details area, type **See me or Rose Alistair for a formal job description or if you have any additional questions.**

5 Post the form to the Employment Opportunities folder.

6 Log off of Exchange.

For more information on	See
Creating public folders	Lesson 8
Installing forms in folders	Lesson 8
Posting information in public folders	Lesson 8

Step 3: *Work in Exchange Through Your Web Browser*

You are now at home preparing for a short business trip. Before leaving, you want to check your mailbox to see if there are any new posts in the Employment Opportunities public folder. You also want to make sure that people who send you e-mail messages during your absence are notified that you're away from the office. In this step, you check your mail through your Web browser and set up an AutoReply message.

 IMPORTANT Perform the following steps on your offsite computer.

1 Open your Web browser.

2 Enter the IP address or URL of your Exchange Server followed by **/Exchange**.

3 Enter your mailbox name and username, if necessary, to view your Mailbox Viewer.

4 View the contents of your Inbox folder, and group posts in your Inbox folder by subject.

5 Create an AutoReply by typing **I will be away from the office until Monday. The Administrative Assistant position is still available, and I will answer any inquiries regarding the position when I return.** (Hint: Enable the AutoReply by clicking Options on the Navigation Bar, and then selecting the Out Of The Office option button.)

6 Send yourself a test message titled "Out of Office Test" to verify that the AutoReply is working, and then check for new messages.

7 In WebView, disable the AutoReply, and then delete the AutoReply text.

8 If you are finished using your Web browser, on the Navigation Bar, click Log Off, and then close the browser window.

WARNING For security reasons, it is highly recommended that you first log off of your mailbox, and then close your Web browser window. This method of quitting ensures that your session with the Exchange Server is terminated.

For more information on	See
Logging on to WebView	Lesson 9
Grouping messages in WebView	Lesson 9
Sending messages in WebView	Lesson 9
Checking for new messages in WebView	Lesson 9
Setting up an AutoReply in WebView	Lesson 9
Posting messages in WebView	Lesson 9
Logging off WebView	Lesson 9

Finish the Review & Practice

Follow these steps to delete the practice messages you created and used in this Review & Practice.

NOTE Because you are logged on to Microsoft Exchange with your own username, be sure you delete only the practice files and messages you added or created during this Review & Practice.

1 Delete the Fmjobs.vb folder and Fmjobs.epf file from your Desktop.

2 In your Inbox and Sent Items folders, delete the practice messages you used in this lesson.

3 Delete the Employment Opportunities public folder.

4 Close all open windows, except Microsoft Exchange.

5 If you want to continue to the next lesson, click the Inbox folder in the folder list.

6 If you are finished using Microsoft Exchange for now, on the File menu, click Exit And Log Off.

You are logged off Microsoft Exchange, and the Viewer window closes.

Working
with Microsoft
Schedule+

Part

4

Lesson 10
Organizing Your Personal Calendar   193

Lesson 11
Managing Tasks   213

Lesson 12
Planning Meetings   233

Review & Practice   249

Organizing Your Personal Calendar

Estimated time
40 min.

In this lesson you will learn how to:

- Create and modify appointments.
- Schedule events.
- Print schedules.
- Customize the appearance of your schedule.

Keeping track of all your appointments can be difficult. Is the planning meeting on Thursday or Friday? Ten o'clock or twelve? Many people use an appointment book, a desk calendar, or a daily planner to keep track of their schedules. Microsoft Schedule+ is an electronic appointment book that you can use to record appointments and plan daily tasks. You can also set reminders for upcoming appointments and events, and even coordinate meetings electronically.

Using Schedule+, you can view your appointments for a single day, for a week, or for a month at a time. You can create a task list to help you monitor your progress on various projects; in the task list, you can schedule tasks for specific times, and you can cross off the tasks as you complete them. You can also print a copy of your schedule to carry with you or tack to your bulletin board.

You are working on the new Pecos Coffee Company account. In this lesson, you'll learn how to create a Schedule+ file and use that file to record all your business and personal appointments.

NOTE To preserve your own schedule data, you'll use your own logon name and Schedule+ file for Part 4 of this book, but change the year to 1999 to avoid confusion with your real appointments if you've already been working in Schedule+. The illustrations in the next three lessons use the Chris Adams profile.

Creating and Editing Appointments

To manage your appointments by using Schedule+, you need to create your own Schedule+ file. When you start Schedule+ for the first time, you are prompted to create a new file or select an existing file.

Start Schedule+

1   Click the Start button. On the Start menu, point to Programs, and then click Microsoft Schedule+.

If you don't see the Choose Profile dialog box, skip to step 3.

2   In the Choose Profile dialog box, select the Chris Adams profile, and then click OK.

The Microsoft Schedule+ dialog box appears. If you don't see the Microsoft Schedule+ dialog box, skip to step 5.

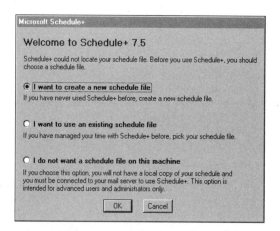

3   Be sure that the I Want To Create A New Schedule File option button is selected, and then click OK.

The Select Local Schedule dialog box appears.

*If you are using
Microsoft Office,
you might need
to move the
Office toolbar.*

4   In the File Name box, type your full name, and then click Save.

A Schedule+ file (.SCD) is created with your name and is saved in
the MSOffice\Schedule folder. If you are using Windows NT, the file
is saved in the \Microsoft Office\Office folder. The program opens, and
today's date appears in Daily view.

5   Maximize the Schedule+ window.

Your screen should look similar to the following illustration.

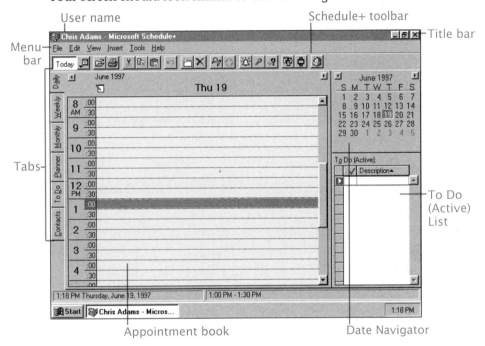

Creating Appointments

When you create a Schedule+ file, by default the file is displayed in the Daily
view of the Appointment Book. A Daily view, a Weekly view, and a Monthly
view are available to help you track appointments. In the Daily view and the
Weekly view, the Appointment Book resembles a standard daily planner. The
date and the day of the week appear at the top of the page, and each day is
divided into 30-minute time slots in which you can enter appointments. By
default, the workday starts at 8 A.M. and ends at 5 P.M.

*You will learn
more about the
To Do List in
Lesson 11.*

In the Daily view, the Date Navigator shows the current calendar date and
month. It can be used to scroll to a different date so that you can add future
appointments or refer to past ones. Bold dates in the Date Navigator indicate
at least one appointment on that day. The To Do (Active) list, which is below
the Date Navigator, displays tasks assigned to the current date, organized by
project.

195

Using the tabs on the left side of the screen, you can switch between six views. The Schedule+ toolbar and the menu bar appear below the title bar in all Schedule+ views. The status bar, at the bottom of the Schedule+ window, displays the current date and the duration of the selected time slot.

You want to add the upcoming Pecos Coffee meetings to your personal schedule. You also want to schedule some personal appointments and make sure that they do not interfere with your work on the Pecos Coffee Company campaign.

Change the date

In this exercise, you change the year to 1999 to avoid confusion with your real appointments.

You can also press CTRL+G.

1   On the Edit menu, click Go To.

The Go To dialog box appears.

2   In the Date box, click the current month.

The month is highlighted to indicate that it is selected.

3   Type **2/15/99** and then click OK.

The Appointment Book and the Date Navigator display the date Monday, February 15, 1999.

Add an appointment

In this exercise, you add an appointment to your schedule by typing the appointment description directly into the appropriate time slot.

1   In the Appointment Book, drag the pointer over the time slots from 11:00 A.M. to 12:30 P.M.

As you drag, the selected start time and end time appear in a ToolTip, and the time slots are highlighted. Your screen should look similar to the following illustration.

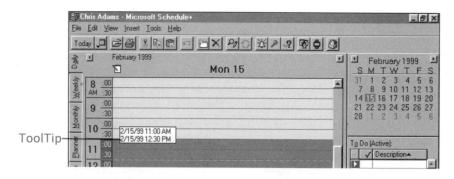

2   Type **Pecos ad meeting**

The new appointment appears as you type.

196

Modifying Appointments

To verify the date, time, and duration of an appointment, you can simply click on it to view a ToolTip. To make detailed changes to an appointment, you have to use the Appointment dialog box.

You can modify the appointment in the Appointment Book in several ways. For example, you can move an appointment to a new date or time, change its duration, or delete the appointment. You can schedule several similar appointments by copying an appointment to the Clipboard, and then pasting it to the appropriate dates. You can also set appointments to recur over months and even years.

Schedule+ uses several symbols to indicate additional information about cerain appointments. For example, a private appointment is identified by a key symbol. The following table illustrates and explains the different Schedule+ symbols.

Symbol	Explanation
☼	A reminder is set for the appointment.
🔑	The appointment is private.
🏠	The appointment has a specific location.
↻	The appointment is recurring.
👥	The appointment is a meeting scheduled with other Schedule+ users.

As an account executive, you have many different responsibilities, and you need to make frequent changes to your schedule to accommodate the needs of both your clients and your co-workers at Fitch & Mather.

Create a detailed appointment

In this exercise, you create an appointment and add detailed information.

Insert New Appointment

You can also enter a new time by typing the number in the Start box.

1 In the Appointment Book, drag to select the 2:30 P.M. to 4:00 P.M time period.

2 On the Schedule+ toolbar, click the Insert New Appointment button.

   The Appointment dialog box appears.

3 On the General tab, select 30 in the Start box.

4 Click the Start up arrow once.

   The meeting is now set to start at 2:45 P.M.

5 In the Description box, type **Team strategy meeting** and then click OK.

   The new appointment appears in the Appointment Book.

Change an appointment

In this exercise, you modify an existing appointment.

You can click an appointment to activate it.

1 Be sure that the "Team strategy meeting" appointment is active.

A dark top border and a gray bottom border identify an active appointment.

2 Drag to select the word "Team," type **Campaign** and then press the SPACEBAR.

3 Point to the top border of the "Campaign strategy meeting" appointment.

The pointer changes to a four-headed arrow.

4 Drag the top border downward one time slot to 3:15 P.M.

The appointment is now set to start at 3:15 P.M. and end at 4:30 P.M.

5 Point to the bottom border.

The pointer changes to a two-headed arrow.

6 Drag the bottom border downward one time slot to 5:00 P.M.

The meeting is now set to end at 5:00 P.M. Your screen should look similar to the following illustration.

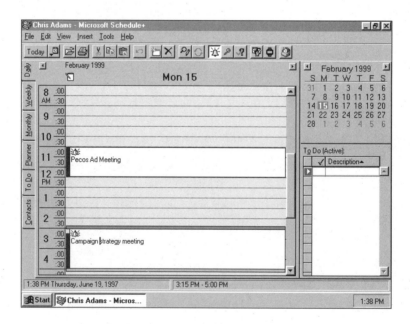

TIP Dragging the top border of an appointment changes both the start time and the end time, but dragging the bottom border of an appointment changes only the duration. You can also drag appointments sideways to add them to the To Do (Active) list, or to move them to a new day if you have more than one day visible in the Appointment Book. For example, you can select an appointment in Weekly view, point to the top border until the four-headed arrow pointer appears, and then drag the appointment to a different day and time.

Edit an appointment

In this exercise, you modify the start time of an appointment and add a location.

Edit

The hour section advances in 1-hour increments while the minute section advances in 15-minute increments.

1 Click the "Pecos ad meeting" appointment.

2 On the Schedule+ toolbar, click the Edit button.

The Appointment dialog box appears.

3 In the Start box, select 11, and then click the Start up arrow once.

The meeting is now set to start at 12:00 P.M.

4 In the End box, select 30, and then click the End up arrow twice.

The meeting is now set to end at 1:00 P.M.

5 In the Where box, type **Convention Hall** and then click OK.

A location, indicated by the location symbol, is added to the appointment, and the name of the location is displayed. Your screen should look like the following illustration.

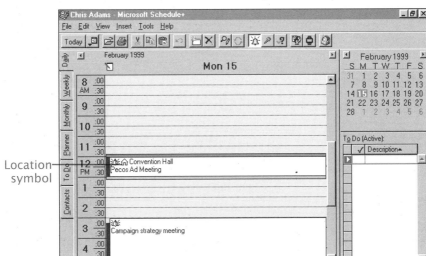

Location symbol

Move an appointment

In this exercise, you use a command to quickly move an appointment to a different day.

You can also press CTRL+M.

1 Click the "Campaign strategy meeting" appointment.

2 On the Edit menu, click Move Appt.

The Move Appointment dialog box appears.

3 Under New Time, be sure that 3:15 P.M. appears in the left-most box, and then click the down arrow next to the right-most text box.

A calendar appears.

4 In the calendar, select February 12, and then click OK.

The appointment is now set to start at 3:15 P.M on Friday, February 12, 1999.

Setting Recurring Appointments

Suppose you have an appointment that occurs at regular intervals, such as a weekly meeting with your team members. Instead of entering the meeting information every week, you can use Schedule+ to set up recurring appointments. To convert an existing appointment to a recurring appointment, you simply enter how often the appointment occurs (such as weekly) and specify until when the meeting will be needed.

As your team continues its work on the Pecos Coffee Company account, you want to monitor everyone's progress and make sure that each team member is kept up to date on the project's status.

Set a recurring appointment

In this exercise, you set an appointment to recur twice a week with the Pecos Coffee Company account team.

1 In the Date Navigator, click February 15.

The date changes to Monday, February 15, 1999.

2 Select the 9:00 A.M. to 10:00 A.M time period.

3 Type **Project team update**

The appointment is added to your Appointment Book.

4 On the Schedule+ toolbar, click the Recurring button.

The Appointment Series dialog box appears.

Recurring

5 Under This Occurs, be sure that the Weekly option button is selected.

6 In the text box between Every and Week(s) On, be sure that 1 is selected.

7   Under Weekly, be sure that the Monday check box is selected, and then select the Wednesday check box.

The "Project team update" appointment is set to recur twice a week, on Monday and Wednesday mornings from 9:00 A.M. to 10:00 A.M.

 If the Until check box is not selected, the appointment will recur indefinitely.

8   Under Duration, select the Until check box.

An end date box appears. The default end date for recurring appointments is one year from the start date.

9   In the end date box, select 2, and then type **6/16/99,** and then click OK.

The appointment and a recurring appointment symbol appear on your schedule until Wednesday, June 16, 1999. The selected dates appear bold in the Date Navigator. Your screen should look like the following illustration.

Bold dates in the Date Navigator indicate appointments on those dates.

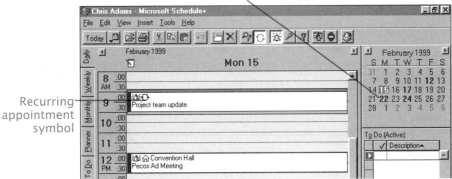

Recurring appointment symbol

Using Reminders

You can set a reminder for any appointment. When you have set a reminder, a message appears on your screen to remind you of the upcoming appointment. By default, you are reminded of each appointment 15 minutes before the start time, but you can also customize how far in advance of the appointment the reminder should appear by choosing increments of minutes, hours, days, weeks, or months.

Modify a reminder

In this exercise, you change the timing of the reminder for the "Pecos ad meeting" so that you will get the reminder earlier and have enough time to get to the Convention Hall.

1   Click the "Pecos Ad Meeting" appointment.

2   On the Schedule+ toolbar, click the Edit button.

The Appointment dialog box appears.

Edit

3   Be sure that Minute(s) appears in the Beforehand box.

4   In the Set Reminder For box, select 15, type **30** and then click OK.

You will be reminded of the meeting 30 minutes before its start time.

NOTE The time setting for a reminder does not appear in the Appointment Book, but you can easily check it. To do so, double-click the left border of the appointment for which you want to verify the time settings, and then make the appropriate modifications using the Set Reminder check box and the associated text boxes.

You can also quickly cancel a reminder. To do this, clear the Set Reminder check box or click the Reminder button on the Schedule+ toolbar. The Reminder button is a toggle switch, which means that you click the same button to turn reminders on or off.

Creating Other Appointment Types

You'll learn more about setting access permissions and using Schedule+ over a network in Lesson 12.

Not only can you use Schedule+ to set and maintain your own appointments, you can also view your co-workers' Appointment Books, and coordinate meetings and appointments with them. You can set or change user access permissions to your Appointment Book at any time, which gives you complete control over who has access to your schedule. The different access permission levels control how your co-workers can view or work with parts of your schedule.

Customizing your appointments also limits how much of your Schedule+ information can be viewed by others. For example, you can designate personal appointments as *private* so that they cannot be read by other Schedule+ users. Private appointments appear as busy time when others view your Appointment Book, but the details of the appointment are not visible.

You can also schedule *tentative appointments* that do not appear when others use the Planner. You can finalize a tentative appointment in your Appointment Book or move it to another time if a colleague schedules a conflicting appointment with a higher priority.

Schedule a private appointment

In this exercise, you schedule an appointment with Rose Alistair, Fitch & Mather's Human Resources director, because you want to discuss a change in your retirement fund. Because this appointment is personal, you want to designate it as private.

1   In the Date Navigator, click February 12.

The date changes to Monday, February 12, 1999.

2   Drag to select the 10:30 A.M. to 11:30 A.M. time period.

3   Type **Discuss retirement fund with Rose Alistair**

Your appointment is added to the Appointment Book.

Private

You can also select the Private check box in the Appointment dialog box.

4 On the Schedule+ toolbar, click the Private button.

A key symbol appears, indicating that the appointment is private. Your screen should look similar to the following illustration.

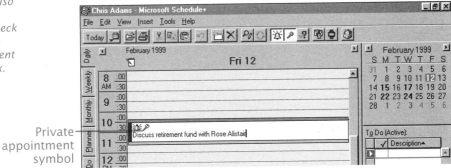

Private appointment symbol

Make an appointment tentative

In this exercise, you make the "Campaign strategy meeting" tentative because you are not sure whether everyone will be able to attend. When others view your schedule, this appointment will appear in your Appointment Book, but not in the Planner.

1 Click the "Campaign strategy meeting" appointment.

2 On the Schedule+ toolbar, click the Tentative button.

The appointment is dimmed, indicating that it is tentative.

Tentative

You can also select the Tentative check box in the Appointment dialog box.

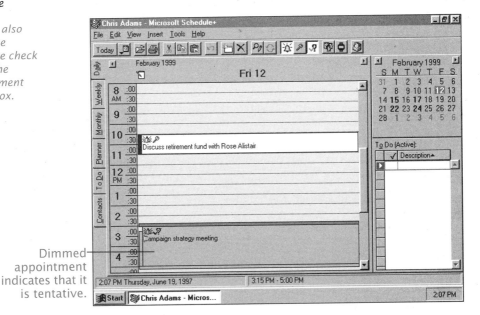

Dimmed appointment indicates that it is tentative.

203

Cancel an appointment

In this exercise, you cancel one of the recurring "Project team update" appointments, because you will be out of the office that day.

1 In the Date Navigator, click February 17.

The date changes to Wednesday, February 17.

2 Click the "Project team update" appointment.

3 On the Schedule+ toolbar, click the Delete button.

A message appears, asking if you want to delete all instances of the recurring appointment.

Delete

You can also press CTRL+D.

4 Click No.

The "Project team update" appointment on February 17 is canceled. The rest of the recurring appointments stay unchanged and the dates on which they are scheduled remain bold in the Date Navigator.

> **NOTE** You cannot delete a Schedule+ appointment by pressing the DELETE key on your keyboard.

Adding Events

Events do not appear in the Planner.

You can add an *event*, such as a trade show or a vacation, to your schedule. When an event is entered for a particular day, a message appears in the Appointment Book on the date of the event, but the event is not scheduled for a particular time. You can, however, set reminders for events. You can also insert annual events, such as holidays or birthdays, in your schedule. An annual event automatically recurs in your Schedule+ file each year.

Add an event

In this exercise, you add an all-day convention to your schedule as an event.

1 Be sure that February 17, 1999, appears in the Appointment Book.

Events

2 At the top of the Appointment Book page, click the Events icon.

A shortcut menu opens.

3 Click Insert Event.

The Event dialog box appears.

4 Be sure that Wed 2/17/99 appears in the Event Starts box and in the And Ends box.

Event dates do not appear bold in the Date Navigator.

5 In the Description box, type **Northwest Beverage Industry Convention**

6 Clear the Set Reminder check box, and then click OK.

Because the convention is an all-day event, you don't need to be reminded of it at a specific time. "Northwest Beverage Industry Convention" appears in an Event box at the top of the Appointment Book.

Lines appear on the Events icon to indicate an event.

Printing Schedules

You can print a copy of any portion of your Schedule+ file, including your To Do List or your Contact List, so that you can carry the information with you or distribute it to others. You can determine how the printed copy appears on the page by choosing from a variety of print layouts and modifying the attributes of the printed text, such as the font size. Additionally, you can choose to display your private items or keep them hidden.

While you are attending the Northwest Beverage Industry Convention as a representative of Fitch & Mather, you want to have a printed copy of your schedule so that you can refer to it and write down any new appointments immediately, instead of waiting until you return to the office.

Print a schedule

In this exercise, you print one week of your schedule.

NOTE There is no substantial difference between the Daily–Dynamic layout and the Daily–Fixed layout. The Daily–Dynamic layout prints events above the To Do List on the right side of the page. The Daily–Fixed layout prints events at the top of the page, and displays a task list and a space for other appointments on the right side of the page.

Print

You can also press CTRL+P.

1 On the Schedule+ toolbar, click the Print button.

The Print dialog box appears.

2 In the Print Layout box, select Daily–Dynamic.

3 In the Private Items box, be sure that Show is selected.

4 In the Paper Format box, be sure that Full Page is selected.

5 In the Schedule Range area, click the Starting down arrow.

A calendar appears.

6 Click February 15.

The date changes to February 15, 1999.

7 In the Schedule Range area, be sure that 1 appears in the first For box, click the the second For down arrow, and then click Week(s).

8 Click Preview.

The Print Preview window opens.

9 Click Close, and then click OK.

A copy of your schedule for Monday, February 15, 1999, through Wednesday, February 17, 1999, is printed. Because you have no appointments or events scheduled for Thursday or Friday, the pages for those days are not printed. However, you can choose to print blank pages by selecting the Include Blank Pages check box in the Print dialog box.

Customizing Schedule+ Options

You can customize most of the Schedule+ options. For example, you can set the default the workday to start at 9:00 A.M. instead of 8:00 A.M. or have the work week start on Tuesday. You change the Weekly view to display a seven-day week or add a tab to the Appointment Book so that you can view your schedule for the year at a glance. You can also change the display colors to match your Windows Desktop color scheme.

As an account executive in a busy advertising agency, you need to manage your time efficiently; even on weekends. So, you decide to customize your Schedule+ options by displaying more than five days on the Weekly view tab, changing the Schedule+ default settings to reflect your workday, and changing the background color of your Appointment Book.

Add days to the Weekly view

In this exercise, you change the number of days displayed on the Weekly view tab.

1 Click the Weekly tab.

The Weekly view appears.

2 On the View menu, point to Number Of Days, and then click 7.

The view changes to display a seven-day week.

Change Schedule+ default options

In this exercise, you change the start and end times of your workday.

1 On the Tools menu, click Options.

The Options dialog box appears.

2 Be sure that the General tab is active, select the minutes section of the Day Starts At box, and then click the up arrow twice.

Your Schedule+ work day now scheduled starts at 8:30 A.M.

3 In the Day Ends At box, select the minutes section, and then click the up arrow twice.

Your Schedule+ work day now ends at 5:30 P.M.

The time slots for active workday hours appear lighter than other time slots.

4 Click OK.

Your screen should look similar to the following illustration.

Change display colors

In this exercise, you change the background color of your Appointment Book.

1 On the Tools menu, click Options.

The Options dialog box appears.

2 Click the Display tab.

3 Under Backgrounds, click the Appointment Book down arrow.

A list of colors appears.

4 Select light blue, and then click OK.

The Appointment Book color changes.

5 Click the Daily tab.

The Daily view appears.

NOTE If you'd like to build on the skills that you learned in this lesson, you can perform the exercises presented in the following section, One Step Further. Otherwise, skip to "Finish the lesson."

One Step Further: Preparing a Schedule for Viewing on the World Wide Web

For more information, see the Microsoft Internet Explorer 3.0 Step by Step book.

You can take advantage of the Internet connectivity in Schedule+ by publishing your schedule on the Web. You can use the Microsoft Internet Assistant to help create a hypertext markup language (HTML) file, which can then be viewed through a Web browser.

You can control how your schedule is published—whether private appointments will appear or how many weeks will be displayed, for example. In addition, you can include your e-mail address so that others can send you messages over the Internet using a link on your Web page. You can also preview your schedule before publishing it by using your Web browser.

IMPORTANT To complete this exercise, you must have a current Web browser installed. Microsoft Internet Explorer 3.0 was used in the following illustration.

For a demonstration of how to create and preview a web schedule, double-click the Camcorder Files On The Internet shortcut on your Desktop or connect to the Internet address listed on p. xxx.

Create and preview your Web schedule

In this exercise, you create a schedule HTML file so that your clients with Internet access will be able to view your schedule when you publish it.

1 On the File menu, click Internet Assistant.

The Microsoft Schedule+ Internet Assistant dialog box appears.

2 In the For The Next Weeks box, type **4**

Others will be able to view four weeks of your schedule on the Internet.

3 Select the Include An E-mail Address check box.

4 In the Include An E-mail Address box, type your Internet email address.

5 Be sure that the Include Private Appointments check box is cleared.

Appointments that you have designated as private will not appear in your published schedule.

6 Click Preview.

Your Web browser window opens, and your schedule is displayed.

7 Close the Web browser window.

8 Close the Microsoft Schedule+ Internet Assistant dialog box.

NOTE By default, the schedule is saved as Schedule.htm in the Temp folder. To save your schedule under another filename or in another location, click Save As in the Microsoft Schedule+ Internet Assistant dialog box.

Finish the lesson

Follow these steps to delete the practice appointments you created in this lesson.

1 On the Tools menu, click Options, click the General tab, change Day Starts At to 8:00 AM and Day Ends At to 5:00 PM. Click the Display tab, click the Appointment Book down arrow, click light yellow, and then click OK.

2 On the View menu, point to Number Of Days, and then click 1.

3 Switch to Daily view, and then click February 15 in the Date Navigator.

Delete

4 Click the "Project team update" appointment, click the Delete button, and then click Yes when prompted to confirm the deletion.

5 Repeat step 3 to delete the remaining practice appointments you scheduled in this lesson.

6 On Wednesday, February 17, 1999, double-click the Northwest Beverage Industry Convention event, and then click Delete.

7 If you want to continue to the next lesson, click the Select Today button on the Schedule+ toolbar to display the current date.

8 If you are finished using Schedule+ for now, on the File menu, click Exit.

The Schedule+ file closes.

NOTE The Exit command on the File menu closes only the Schedule+ program. The Exit And Log Off command closes Schedule+ and Microsoft Exchange, if Microsoft Exchange is running, as well as any other systems that are using the underlying Windows Messaging system.

Lesson Summary

To	Do this	Button
Start Schedule+	On the Start menu, point to Programs, and then click Microsoft Schedule+. If the Choose Profile dialog box appears, select a profile.	
Create a new schedule file	Start Schedule+. In the Microsoft Schedule+ dialog box, choose the I Want To Create A New Schedule File option button, and then click OK. Type a name for the new schedule file in the File Name box, and then click Save.	
Change the date	On the Edit menu, click Go To. In the Date box, type the new date, and then click OK. *or* In the Date Navigator, select the new date.	
Add an appointment to the Appointment Book	On the Schedule+ toolbar, click the Insert New Appointment button, and then fill in the appointment information.	
Edit an appointment	Click the appointment you want to edit. To change the start time of the appointment without modifying its length, drag the top border to a new start time. To change the duration and the end time of an appointment, drag the bottom border to a different time. To change the description of an appointment, select the text, and then type the new description.	
Add information to an appointment	On the Schedule+ toolbar, click the Edit button. In the Appointment dialog box, type the new information.	

To	Do this	Button
Move an appointment	Click the appointment. On the Edit menu, click Move Appt. Change the time and the date, and then click OK.	
Schedule a recurring appointment	Click the appointment. On the Schedule+ toolbar, click the Recurring button. Enter the appointment frequency and an end date, if desired, and then click OK.	
Change a reminder	Double-click the left border. Be sure that the Set Reminder check box is selected. In the For box, select the number and type the new time. Be sure that the Beforehand boxes are set to the correct increment. Click OK.	
Schedule a private appointment	Click the appointment. On the Schedule+ toolbar, click the Private button.	
Schedule a tentative appointment	Click the appointment. On the Schedule+ toolbar, click the Tentative button.	
Cancel an appointment	Click the appointment. On the Schedule+ toolbar, click the Delete button.	
Add an event	Click the Events icon. Select Insert Event or Insert Annual Event. Type the start and end date as well as a description, and then click OK.	
Print a schedule	On the Schedule+ toolbar, click the Print button. Specify the appropriate parameters, and then click OK.	
Change the number of days in Weekly view	On the View menu, point to Number Of Days, and then click 7.	

To	Do this
Change the start and end times of your workday	On the Tools menu, click Options, and then click the General tab. Select appropriate options, and then click OK.
Change display options	On the Tools menu, click Options, and then click the Display tab. Select appropriate options, and then click OK.

For more information about	On the Help menu, click Microsoft Schedule+ Help Topics, click the Index tab, and then type
Starting Schedule+	**Starting Schedule+**
Creating appointments	**Appointments**
Editing appointments	**Appointments: editing** *or* **Editing: Appointments**
Making appointments private	**Private**
Making appointments tentative	**Tentative**
Setting reminders	**Reminders: setting**
Creating recurring appointments	**Recurring appointments**
Adding events	**Events: adding**
Printing a schedule	**Printing**
Changing default options	**Options**

Lesson

11

Managing Tasks

Estimated time
40 min.

In this lesson you will learn how to:

- Create a To Do List.
- Set task priorities.
- Organize tasks.
- Create and maintain a Contact List.

Microsoft Schedule+ is invaluable for organizing your daily appointments, but what about managing the various duties and projects that you work on each day? Schedule+ includes a separate To Do List that you can use to keep track of all your daily tasks. You can use it to record tasks, assign tasks to specific projects, and set priorities and end dates for each task. You can also sort your tasks into different categories and view them in the order that is most useful to you.

Using Schedule+, you can also maintain a record of all your important business and personal contacts through a Contact List. Contacts can be added or updated at any time to ensure that you are working with the most current names, addresses, and phone numbers. Like tasks, contacts can be organized into different groups so that you can quickly find the information you need.

In this lesson, you will add the Pecos Coffee Company project to your To Do List, as well as create and organize a list of tasks to help monitor your progress on the project. You will also edit your Contact List to add information about your new clients and update existing entries.

213

Start Schedule+

1   Click the Start button. On the Start menu, point to Programs, and then click Microsoft Schedule+.

2   In the Choose Profile dialog box, select the Chris Adams profile, and then click OK.

The Microsoft Schedule+ window opens.

3   Maximize the window.

4   In the Appointment Book, click the To Do tab.

The To Do List becomes active.

Creating a To Do List

For a demonstration of how to create and add to a To Do List, double-click the Camcorder Files On The Internet shortcut on your Desktop or connect to the Internet address listed on p. xxx.

When the To Do tab is active, you can view the entire To Do List. In addition, an abridged version of the To Do List, containing only active tasks, appears below the Date Navigator in the Daily view. Tasks with a specified end date or due date appear as active tasks on the day they are supposed to be completed. Tasks without a specified end date are also active tasks and appear in the To Do (Active) List daily until you complete or delete them. The column headings, such as Description, Duration, and End Date, identify information about each task and corresponding project.

Add a project

In this exercise, you create a Pecos Coffee Company account project in your To Do List.

1   On the Insert menu, click Project.

The Project dialog box appears.

2   In the Name box, type **Pecos Coffee Company** and then click OK.

The new project heading is added to the To Do List. Your screen should look similar to the following illustration.

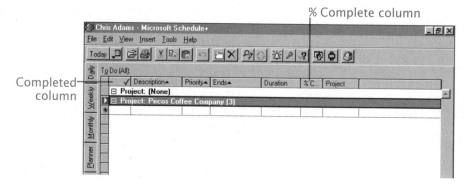

Add tasks

Tasks can, but don't have to, be assigned to a project. In this exercise, you add tasks to the Pecos Coffee Company project.

If you enter a task in a blank row on the To Do List, the task is added under the None project heading.

1 Be sure that the Pecos Coffee Company project heading is selected.

This will ensure that the task you create is added under the Pecos Coffee Company heading. When a project heading is selected, tasks are added under that project heading.

2 Type **Review storyboards with Nate**

As you type, the task is added to the Pecos Coffee Company project.

3 Click the Pecos Coffee Company project heading, and then type **Prepare monthly expense report**

The task is added to the Pecos Coffee Company project.

Insert detailed tasks

In this exercise, you add tasks to the To Do List and enter detailed information, such as the end date of the task.

Insert New Task

The Insert New Appointment button in the Appointment Book view becomes the Insert New Task button in To Do List view.

You can also click any section of the date, and then use the arrow keys to move between sections.

1 On the Schedule+ toolbar, click the Insert New Task button.

The Task dialog box appears. The General tab is active.

2 Under Active Range, select the Ends check box.

The date in the Ends box becomes available. The current date appears.

3 In the Ends box, select the month, and then type **2/19/99**

February 19, 1999 is assigned as the end date for the task.

4 In the Description box, type **Submit logo design to printers** and then click OK.

The task is added to the Pecos Coffee Company project. Your screen should look similar to the following illustration.

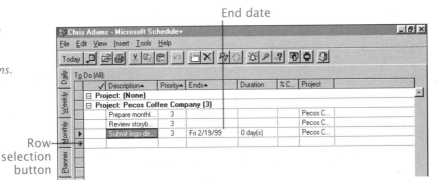

End date

Row selection button

> **NOTE** If you enter a task using the Task dialog box and do not specify an end date, the current date appears in the Ends column by default. If you enter a task directly in the To Do List, it is not assigned an end date by default.

Editing Tasks

If a task changes, you can easily edit it to update the information. You can modify tasks in several ways—end date, priority, project, or description. In addition, you can reassign a task to another project, delete a task, or delete a project and its tasks. When you have finished a task, you select the Completed column to check off the task, and a line through the task indicates that the task is complete.

Edit tasks

In this exercise, you adjust the duration of several tasks.

1   Click the row selection button next to the "Review storyboards with Nate" task.

The entire row is selected.

Edit

2   On the Schedule+ toolbar, click the Edit button.

The Task dialog box appears.

3   Under Active Range, select the Ends check box, and then change the date to 2/23/99.

You can also use the Starts up or down arrow to change the duration. Click the Before End Date down arrow to change the Starts increment to Week(s) or Month(s).

4   In the Starts box, select the number, and then type **2**

A duration of 2 days is assigned to the task.

5   Be sure that the Starts increment is set to Day(s), and then click OK.

6   In the "Prepare monthly expense report" task, click the Ends field.

The current date appears as the end date. Your screen should look similar to the following illustration.

Check box —

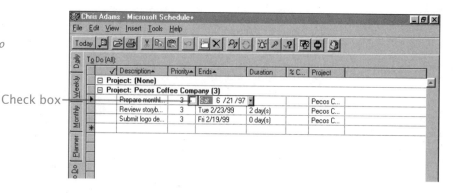

7 Select the check box in the Priority column, and then press ENTER.

The current date is assigned to the task as an end date.

Assign an existing task to a different project

In this exercise, you reassign a task to a different project.

1 Click the row selection button next to the "Prepare monthly expense report" task.

The entire row is selected.

2 Drag the task above the Pecos Coffee Company project heading.

The task is placed under the "Project: (None)" heading. The text in the Project column changes to (None). Your screen should look similar to the following illustration.

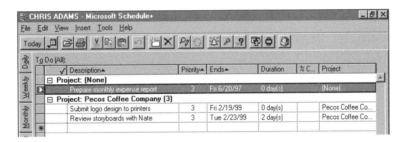

Mark a task as completed

In this exercise, you mark a task as completed, and then make it active again.

You can also mark tasks as completed in the To Do (Active) List in the Daily view.

1 In the "Review storyboards with Nate" task, click the Completed field.

A check mark appears in the Completed column. A line through the task indicates that the task is completed. Your screen should look similar to the following.

100 % appears in the % Complete column, indicating that the task is finished.

A checkmark appears in the Completed column.

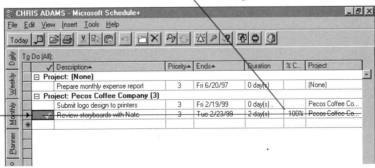

2   Be sure that the "Review storyboards with Nate" task is still selected, and then click the Completed field again.

The strikethrough line and the check mark in the Completed column are removed. The task is active again.

Organizing Tasks

After you create your To Do List, you can organize it to make sure that all the tasks are completed on time. You can set priorities for each task and project to help you focus on your tasks in order of importance. You can further organize your tasks by grouping, sorting, or filtering them. You can also add a task to the Appointment Book and schedule it for a specific time of day.

Setting Priorities

Using Schedule+, you can assign different priorities to your tasks to help you easily identify which one requires your attention first. You can assign each task a single-number priority (from 1 to 9), a single-letter priority (from A to Z), or a letter-number combination priority (such as A1 through A9). Numbered priorities take precedence over lettered priorities. For example, a priority 4 task is of higher priority than a priority D task. If you do not assign a priority to a task, it is assigned a 3 priority by default. When you create a new task, you can assign your own priorities or accept the default; you can modify a priority at any time.

Modify task priorities

In this exercise, you edit priorities of tasks contained in your To Do List.

You can also select a task, click the Edit button, and then change priorities in the Task dialog box.

1   In the "Submit logo design to printers" task, click the Priority field, and then type **1**

The priority increases to the highest priority.

2   In the "Prepare monthly expense report" task, click the Priority field, type **2** and then press ENTER.

The priority is set to 2.

Arranging Tasks

You can display tasks in ways that are most useful to you by arranging them by priority, by end date, by duration, or by project. For example, you can *group* tasks by up to three specific categories, *sort* tasks alphabetically by task names, or *filter* tasks by applying specific criteria so that only certain tasks appear in your To Do List.

Group tasks

In this exercise, you group the tasks in the To Do List into different categories.

By default, tasks are grouped by project.

1 On the View menu, click Group By.

The Group By dialog box appears.

2 Click the Group Tasks By down arrow, select Priority, and then click OK.

The tasks appear in order of priority. Your screen should look similar to the following illustration.

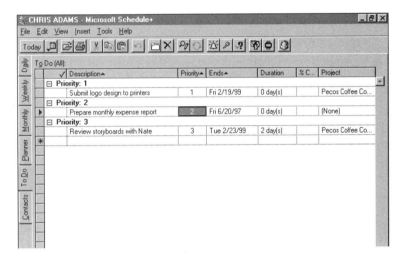

3 On the View menu, click Group By.

The Group By dialog box appears.

4 Be sure that Priority is selected under Group Tasks By, click the first Then By down arrow, click End Date, and then click OK.

The tasks appear in order of priority, and the end date for each task appears above the task.

Filter tasks

In this exercise, you filter your To Do List so that only those tasks that match the criteria appear.

If you have active tasks on your schedule, they also appear.

➤ On the View menu, point to Filter, and then click Upcoming.

Only active tasks and tasks with end dates in the future appear. Your screen should look similar to the following illustration.

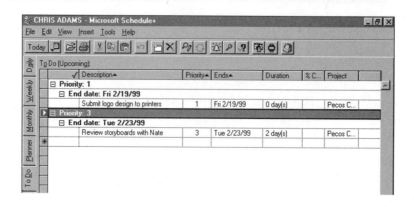

Scheduling Tasks

You can easily add tasks to the Appointment Book and assign them to specific times so that they appear in your daily schedule. This is a good way to make sure you have enough time to complete a task during a particular day.

Change the date

In this exercise, you switch to February 22, 1999, in the Daily view of the Appointment Book so that you can view active tasks for that date.

1 Click the Daily tab.

The Appointment Book appears in Daily view.

You can also press CTRL+G.

2 On the Edit menu, click Go To.

The Go To dialog box appears.

3 In the Date box, select the month, type **2/22/99** and then click OK.

The Appointment Book and the Date Navigator display the date Monday, February 22, 1999. Your active tasks appear in the To Do (Active) List below the Date Navigator.

Schedule tasks

In this exercise, you schedule your tasks in the Appointment Book.

1 In the To Do (Active) List, click the row selection button for the "Prepare monthly expense report" task.

The task is highlighted.

2 Drag the "Prepare monthly expense report" task to the 10:30 A.M. time slot.

As you drag the task, the pointer changes to an arrow with a selection box and a plus sign, indicating that the task is being copied. Your screen should look similar to the following illustration.

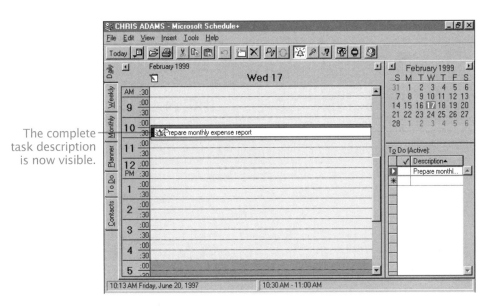

The complete task description is now visible.

3 Drag the bottom border of the task downward to 12:00 P.M.

The duration of the task is changed.

Creating Your Contact List

To communicate efficiently with your business associates and personal friends, you probably keep track of important phone numbers, addresses, and other relevant information in an address book or a business card holder. Using Schedule+, you can create and maintain a directory of professional colleagues and personal friends in a Contact List.

In Schedule+, contacts are presented in a list format. When you select a contact in the contact grid area on the left side of the tab, the details about the contact are displayed in the business card on the right. You can sort, filter, and group your contacts in the grid to display only the information you need, just as you can in the To Do List.

Add a contact

In this exercise, you add Joe Pecos, the contact for your new account, to your Contact List.

If you haven't imported the practice Schedule+ Contact List yet, see "Installing and Using the Practice Files," earlier in this book.

1 Click the Contacts tab.

The Contacts tab becomes active. A list of contacts appears in the grid on the left, and the current contact information appears in the business card on the right. Your screen should look similar to the following illustration.

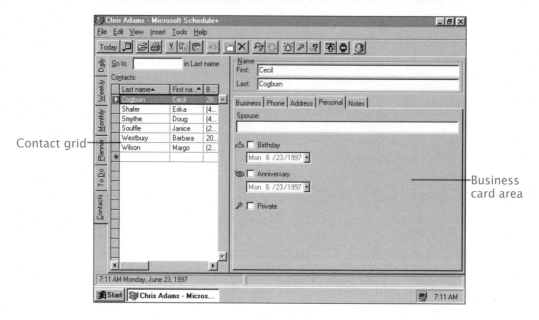

Contact grid

Business card area

Insert New Contact

You can also press the SPACEBAR *to move the insertion point to the Last box.*

2 On the Schedule+ toolbar, click the Insert New Contact button.

The Contact dialog box appears. The Business tab is active.

3 Be sure that the insertion point is in the First box under Name, type **Joe** and then press TAB.

The insertion point moves to the Last box.

4 Complete the contact information as follows, pressing TAB after each entry.

In this box	Type
Last	**Pecos**
Address	**916 Yale Street**
City	**Seattle**
State	**WA**
Postal Code	**98109**
Country	**USA**
Title	**Founder**
Company	**Pecos Coffee Company**
Phone Number	**206-555-5154**

5   Click OK.

The new contact is added to the contact grid. The information you entered is displayed in the business card on the right.

Editing Your Contact List

Names, titles, addresses, and phone numbers change frequently in the business world. Using Schedule+, you can easily edit contact information in the contact grid or in the appropriate contact record to keep your entries up to date.

Edit contacts

In this exercise, you update your Contact List.

1   In the contact grid, click the row selection button next to Janice Souffle.

The information for Janice Souffle is displayed in the business card.

2   In the business card, click the Address tab.

3   In the Address box, select "220 Monahan Plaza."

The text is highlighted.

4   Type **15 Bistro Drive**

5   In the business card, click the Phone tab.

A list of phone number types is displayed.

6   In the Fax box, type **206-555-1530**

The fax number is added to the business card for Janice Souffle.

7   In the business card, click the Notes tab.

8   In the Notes box, type **30% discount for business catering**

The note is added to the business card.

Personalizing Your Contact List

By default, when you enter a contact name and related information, this information is available to anyone who has access to your schedule. You can make specific contacts private, just as you can make an appointment private. If you make a contact private, the information about that particular person is not available to other Schedule+ users on your network.

You can also add personal information in the business card. For example, the Personal tab contains fields for birthdays and anniversary dates. If you select the Birthday or Anniversary check boxes on the Personal tab, an annual event is inserted in your Appointment Book by default on the date you specified.

Make a contact private

In this exercise, you prevent other Schedule+ users from viewing information about a personal contact.

Private

1   In the contact grid, select Barbara Westbury.

2   On the Schedule+ toolbar, click the Private button.

A key symbol appears next to Barbara Westbury's name in the contact grid, indicating that the contact is private and the contact information cannot be viewed by other Schedule+ users.

Add personal information

In this exercise, you add a birthday and an anniversary to your Contact List.

1   In the contact grid, select Cecil Cogburn.

2   In the business card, click the Personal tab.

3   Select the Birthday check box.

The date box becomes available.

4   In the date box, select the current month, and then type **12/10/1920**

5   In the contact grid, select Joe Pecos.

The birthday symbol appears next to Cogburn in the contact grid, and the selected name is highlighted.

6   In the business card, click in the Spouse box, and then type **Hazel Pecos**

7   Select the Anniversary check box, and change the date to **2/14/1988**

8   In the contact grid, select Joe Pecos again to display the anniversary symbol.

Your screen should look similar to the following illustration.

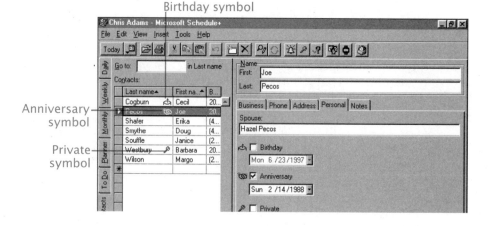

View personal information

In this exercise, you view personal information for a particular date in the Appointment Book.

1 Click the Daily tab.

The Daily tab becomes active.

2 In the Date Navigator, click February 14.

The date switches to Sunday, February 14, 1999. The text "Joe Pecos: Anniversary" appears at the top of the Appointment Book. Your screen should look similar to the following illustration.

Personal information appears here.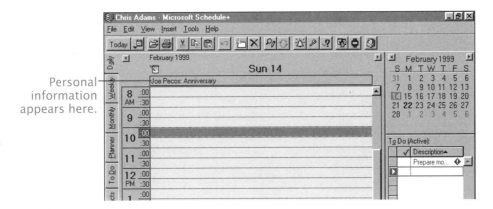

Organizing Your Contact List

You can group and sort contacts in the Contact List, just as you can group and sort tasks in the To Do List. You can use up to three category levels–such as company, city, and title–to group and display your contacts. Grouping allows you to view only the specific sections of your Contact List that you need at a particular time. For example, if you want to call each of your colleagues in California, you can group your Contact List by company and state, and display all your California contacts in one category. Additionally, you can sort your contacts alphabetically in any category.

Group contacts

In this exercise, you group your contacts by company.

1 Click the Contacts tab.

The Contacts tab becomes active.

2 On the View menu, click Group By.

The Group By dialog box appears.

3 Click the Group Contacts By down arrow, click Company, and then click OK.

The contacts in the contact grid are grouped by company. Your screen should look similar to the following illustration.

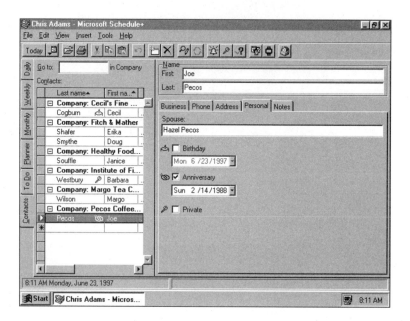

Collapse categories

1 In the contact grid, click the minus sign (-) next to the "Company: Fitch & Mather" heading.

The category collapses, and the minus sign changes to a plus sign. The names of your contacts at Fitch & Mather are hidden.

2 In the contact grid, click the plus sign (+) next to the "Company: Fitch & Mather" heading.

The category expands, the plus sign changes to a minus sign, and all of your contacts' names are displayed.

NOTE If you'd like to build on the skills that you learned in this lesson, you can perform the exercises presented in the following section, One Step Further. Otherwise, skip to "Finish the lesson."

One Step Further: Creating a Recurring Task

Suppose you have a task that you perform regularly, such as compiling a monthly expense report or generating a quarterly budget proposal. You can create a recurring task that appears in your Daily view To Do (Active) List at the appropriate intervals.

As an account executive, you are responsible for managing your own schedule and for monitoring the schedules of your project team. At the end of each month, you collect each person's job costing sheet, compile the information, and then submit a cost report to the Accounting department. You want to add this task to your To Do List as a recurring task.

Create a recurring task

Insert New Task

1   Click the To Do tab.

   The To Do List tab becomes active.

2   On the Schedule+ toolbar, click the Insert New Task button.

   The Task dialog box appears.

3   In the Description box, type **Compile project time sheets**

4   Click the Project down arrow, and then click Pecos Coffee Company.

5   Click Make Recurring.

   The Task Series dialog box appears. The When tab is active.

6   Under This Occurs, select Monthly.

7   Under Monthly, be sure that the second frequency option is selected, and then click the first down arrow.

   A list of intervals appears.

8   Select Last, click the second down arrow, and then select Weekday.

   The task is set to recur on the last weekday of each month.

9   Click OK.

   The task is added to the To Do List. A reminder symbol and a recurring symbol appear next to the task description.

View the recurring task in the Appointment Book

In this exercise, you view the recurring task in the To Do (Active) List.

1   Click the Daily tab.

   The Daily tab becomes active.

2 In the Date Navigator, click the last weekday of the current month.

The "Compile project time sheets" task appears in the To Do (Active) List. Your screen should look similar to the following illustration.

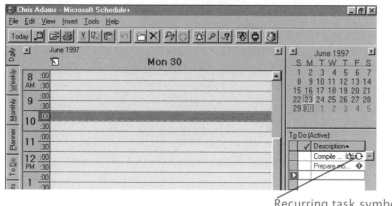

Recurring task symbol

Finish the lesson

Follow these steps to delete the tasks and contacts, and remove the groupings you created in this lesson.

1 Click the To Do tab. On the View menu, point to Filter, and then click All.

2 On the View menu, click Group By. Click the Group Tasks By down arrow, and then click Project. Click the first Then By down arrow, click (None), and then click OK.

Delete

3 Click the first row selection button, hold down CTRL, click each row selection button to select all practice tasks, and then click the Delete button on the Schedule+ toolbar. Click Yes To All when prompted to confirm the deletion.

4 Switch to the Contacts List. On the View menu, click Group By. Click the Group Contacts By down arrow, click (None), and then click OK.

5 In the contact grid, select the first contact in the list, hold down CTRL, click each row selection button to select all practice contacts, and then click the Delete button on the Schedule+ toolbar. Click Yes To All when prompted to confirm the deletion.

6 In the Daily view, delete the practice appointment on February 22, 1999.

7 If you want to continue to the next lesson, click the Select Today button on the Schedule+ toolbar to display the current date.

8 If you are finished using Schedule+ for now, on the File menu, click Exit.

The Schedule+ file closes.

Lesson Summary

To	Do this	Button
Add a project	Click the To Do tab. On the Insert menu, click Project. Type a name in the Project box, and then click OK.	
Add a task	Select a project heading. Type the task description. *or* On the Schedule+ toolbar, click the Insert New Task button. Enter the task information in the Task dialog box, and then click OK.	
Edit a task	Select the task. On the Schedule+ toolbar, click the Edit button. Make the changes you want in the Task dialog box, and then click OK.	
Assign an existing task to a different project	Select the task, and then drag it to place it under a different project heading.	
Mark a task as completed	In the task row, click the Completed field.	
Set a priority for a task	In the task row, click the Priority field. Type the new priority, and then press ENTER.	
Group tasks	On the View menu, click Group By. Select the categories you want to group your tasks by, and then click OK.	
Filter tasks	On the View menu, point to Filter, and then click the filter you want.	
Schedule a task	In the Appointment Book, select the date when you want to schedule the task. In the To Do (Active) list, select the task, and then drag it to the appropriate time slot.	

To	Do this	Button
Add a contact	Click the Contacts tab. On the Schedule+ toolbar, click the Insert New Contact button. In the Contact dialog box, enter the contact information in the appropriate boxes, and then click OK.	
Edit a contact	In the contact grid, select the contact name. In the business card, type changes in the appropriate boxes. *or* In the contact grid, select the contact name. On the Schedule+ toolbar, click the Edit button. Make changes in the Contact dialog box, and then click OK.	
Make a contact private	In the contact grid, select the contact name. On the Schedule+ toolbar, click the Private button.	
Add a personal date to the Contact List	In the contact grid, select the contact name. In the business card, click the Personal tab. Select the appropriate check box, and then enter the date.	
Group contacts	On the View menu, click Group By. Select the categories you want to group your contacts by, and then click OK.	
Collapse categories	In the contact grid, click the minus sign (-) next to the category heading.	

For more information about	On the Help menu, click Microsoft Schedule+ Help Topics, click the Index tab, and then type
Creating and editing a task list	**Tasks**
Prioritizing tasks	**Priority**
Grouping tasks and contacts	**Grouping**
Filtering tasks	**Filters**
Sorting tasks	**Sorting tasks**
Scheduling tasks	**Tasks**
Adding and editing contacts	**Contacts**
Making contacts private	**Private: setting as**
Collapsing and expanding categories	**Minus sign** *or* **Plus sign**

Planning Meetings

Estimated time
40 min.

In this lesson you will learn how to:

- View your schedule in the Planner.
- Set permissions for others to access your schedule.
- Set up meetings using the Meeting Wizard.
- Schedule meetings using the Planner.

The Microsoft Schedule+ Appointment Book, the To Do List, and the Contact List help you organize your schedule. In addition, you can use Schedule+ over a network to coordinate meetings with other people in your office. You can use the Planner to first look at your own schedule and the schedules of your co-workers, and to then set up meetings at mutually available times. You can also use the *Meeting Wizard* to quickly determine an acceptable meeting time and location. You can send out meeting requests and receive responses through Microsoft Exchange while you are working in Schedule+. You can also reschedule meetings and notify attendees of the changes.

Everyone assigned to the Pecos Coffee Company account is hard at work on his or her piece of the project. As the account executive, your job is to ensure that everyone is aware of the current project status and of any new developments. In this lesson, you'll learn how to set access permissions in Schedule+ so that your team members can view your schedule in the Planner. You'll also learn how to use Schedule+ to request and add meetings to your schedule.

IMPORTANT   Because this lesson explores the interactive aspects of Schedule+, you'll need to recruit some help from one or two other people on your network to complete the exercises. Find at least one person on your network who will give you access to his or her personal schedule and will cooperate with your practice meeting requests.

Start Schedule+

1   Click the Start button. On the Start menu, point to Programs, and then click Microsoft Schedule+.

2   In the Choose Profile dialog box, select the Chris Adams profile, and then click OK.

The Microsoft Schedule+ window opens.

3   Maximize the window.

Viewing Your Schedule in the Planner

In the Appointment Book, you can see all your appointments in some detail. In the To Do List, you can see all your tasks. But what if you want a longer-range view of your time commitments at a glance? In the Planner, you can see one or two weeks of scheduled time on a page, depending on the size of your Schedule+ window. The Planner displays schedules in a grid format. The Date Navigator and Attendees list are also displayed. Using the Planner, you can easily see the times that are blocked off on your schedule for existing appointments and the times that are available for new meetings or appointments.

View your own schedule

In this exercise, you display the Planner, examine your schedule, and then check specific details for an appointment.

IMPORTANT   The exercises in this lesson will be more useful and interesting if you and your co-workers have other appointments scheduled. If you don't have any appointments on the current page, you can add some, or you can select a day on which you and your co-workers have appointments. You can use the Date Navigator or the left and right arrows at the top of the Planner page to switch to a different week.

1   Click the Planner tab.

The Planner is active. The time periods during which you have an appointment or a meeting scheduled are marked, but no details are shown. Your screen should look similar to the following illustration.

Your Planner schedule will look different from this illustration.

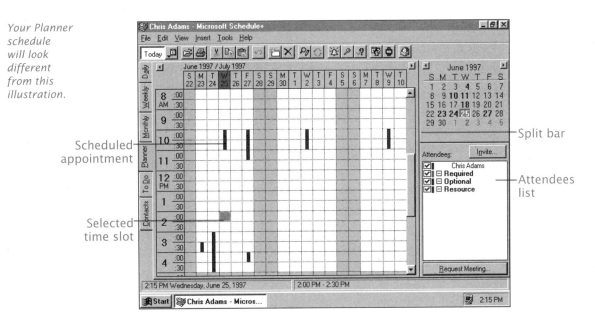

Scheduled appointment

Split bar

Attendees list

Selected time slot

To see more days in the Planner, you can enlarge the window by dragging the split bar.

2 Use the right mouse button to click a busy time slot.

Your name appears as the name of the person busy at that time.

3 Select your name.

The appointment time and description appear. Your screen should look similar to the following illustration.

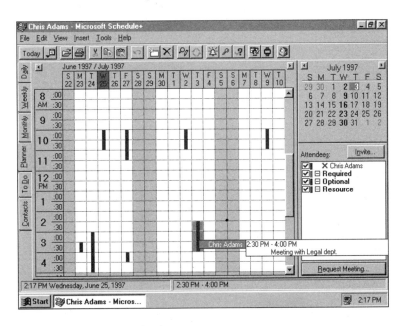

235

Setting Up Meetings

In the Planner, you can see at a glance when your schedule is open for new appointments. But how can you find out when other people are available so you can set the time and date for a meeting? Using Schedule+ and your network, you can open your co-workers' schedules and determine the best time for a meeting.

To use Schedule+ effectively over a network, you must ask your co-workers to give you access to their schedules and you must give them access to your schedule.

Setting Access Permissions

In Schedule+, you can grant eight different levels of schedule *access permission* to your co-workers. These access permissions allow your co-workers to view only certain parts of your schedule or view your schedule in its entirety. Some levels of access permission even allow selected co-workers to make changes to your schedule. For example, a company president could grant an administrative assistant full access.

The default access permission level is "None," which means your co-workers can view your free and busy times, but cannot read the details of your appointments and tasks. However, your manager and co-workers will probably request "Read" access so that they can see appointment details and coordinate meetings easily. It is advisable to be careful about granting other users permission to create, modify, or delete your appointments. The following table describes the eight levels of access permission that you can assign in Schedule+ and the privileges associated with each of them.

Access permission	User privileges
None	Denies access to the details of your schedule.
Read	Grants read-only access to view the details of your schedule, except for items designated as private.
Create	Grants access to create new entries and to view the details of existing entries, except for items designated as private.
Modify	Grants access to create, delete, and modify any entries in your schedule, except for items designated as private.
Delegate	Grants access to read and modify entries in selected areas of your schedule, including items designated as private.
Owner	Grants access to modify your schedule, including items designated as private, and to change the schedule access permission level of other users.

Access permission	User privileges
Delegate Owner	Grants access to modify your schedule, including items designated as private; to change the access permission levels of other users; and to send and receive messages on your behalf.
Custom	Grants access to a specific type of entry, such as Appointments, Events, Tasks, or Contacts.

Set access permissions

In this exercise, you set access permissions for someone else on your network.

 IMPORTANT If the co-workers helping you with this lesson have not granted you access permission to their schedules, they should do so by following the steps in this exercise.

1   On the Tools menu, click Set Access Permissions.

The Set Access Permissions dialog box appears.

2   Be sure that the Users tab is active, and then click Add.

The Add Users dialog box appears.

3   Hold down CTRL, select the name or names of the people helping you with this lesson, and then click Users.

The names appear in the Users list in the right half of the dialog box.

4   Click OK.

The name is added to the list of users in the Set Access Permissions dialog box.

5   Be sure that the new username is selected, and then click the User Role down arrow in the Permission Details area.

A list of access permissions is displayed.

6   Click Read.

7   Click OK.

Your co-workers with Read access permission can now read the descriptions of your appointments and tasks, and your contact information, except for any items you have marked as private.

 TIP You can easily grant everyone on your network the same access to your schedule. To do this, select the Default username in the Set Access Permissions dialog box, click the User Role down arrow, and then select the access permission you want.

IMPORTANT When you assign permission to your schedule, it takes effect immediately. If you do not want your co-workers to be able to view the details of your schedule yet, on the Tools menu, click Set Access Permissions, click the Permissions tab, click their names, and then click Remove.

Setting Up Meetings Using the Meeting Wizard

For a demonstration of how to schedule a meeting with the Meeting Wizard, double-click the Camcorder Files On The Internet shortcut on your Desktop or connect to the Internet address listed on p. xxx.

Using the Meeting Wizard is the easiest way to schedule a meeting with several of your co-workers. It allows you to determine each person's busy and free times without having to look at individual schedules. The Meeting Wizard lets you specify meeting attendees, location, and any equipment you need. It also prompts you for approximate meeting duration, day, and times so that it can search the schedules of attendees for the first available time that meets all the requirements.

When you select attendees for a meeting, you can define whether their presence is required or optional. Optional attendees are informed of the meeting, but not required to attend. If you name any optional attendees, the Meeting Wizard gives you the option of checking their schedules for available times, but the date and time that will be chosen by the Wizard will only take into account the required attendees' schedules. Optional attendees do however, receive a carbon copy of the meeting request message so they can choose to attend if they wish.

If schedules for locations and resources are maintained on your network, you can also use Schedule+ to select a meeting location and request specific equipment. If you select a location or a resource, this information will be included at the top of the meeting request form.

After you select a meeting time using the Meeting Wizard, you can send a message to the attendees, asking whether or not they are available. The attendees can accept or decline the invitation; if they accept, the meeting is added to their Appointment Book.

Schedule a meeting using the Meeting Wizard

In this exercise, you use the Meeting Wizard to find a convenient time and schedule a meeting with required attendees. For the purposes of this exercise, you will not select any optional attendees, locations, or resources.

Meeting Wizard

1 On the Schedule+ toolbar, click the Meeting Wizard button.

The Meeting Wizard appears.

2 Clear the A Location Such As A Conference Room check box, be sure that the Required Attendees Who Must Attend check box is the only check box selected, and then click Next.

A blank text box appears for you to list your required attendees.

3 Click Pick Attendees.

Your company's global address list appears.

4 Select the names of the people helping you with this lesson, and then click Required.

The names are added to the Required Attendees list.

5 Click OK, and then click Next.

The meeting duration options appear.

6 In the first Duration box, change the time to 2 hours.

7 Be sure that the To Meeting travel time is set to 5 minutes and that the From Meeting travel time is set to 0, and then click Next.

The meeting time and day options appear. You use these options to give the Meeting Wizard additional information that will help it choose the optimum time for the meeting.

8 Change the Meeting Starts After time to 9:00 A.M. and the And Ends Before time to 11:00 A.M.

9 Select the Mon, Tue, and Wed check boxes as acceptable meeting days.

10 Be sure that the Thu, Fri, Sat, and Sun check boxes are cleared, and then click Next.

The Meeting Wizard checks your co-workers' schedules and selects the next available meeting time for all attendees. Your screen should look similar to the following illustration.

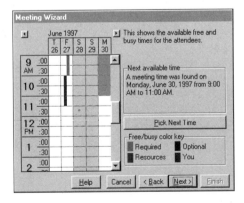

11   Click Next.

The last Meeting Wizard screen appears.

12   Click Finish.

A meeting request form appears. The time and date of the proposed meeting appear in the When field, and your co-workers' names appear in the To field. Your screen should look similar to the following illustration.

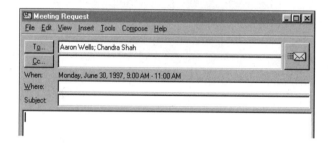

Requesting a Meeting

Although you can switch to Microsoft Exchange and send out messages inviting people to a meeting, Schedule+ provides a faster way. When you use the Meeting Wizard or request a meeting using the Planner, Schedule+ creates a meeting request form that you can send without leaving the program.

Send a meeting request

In this exercise, you fill out and send a meeting request form.

1   In the Subject box, type **Pecos ad development**

2   In the message area, type **Now that we have some feedback from Hazel and Joe, let's meet to discuss our project schedule.**

3   Click the Send button.

The meeting request is sent to your co-workers and the meeting is added to your schedule.

Send

You can send meeting requests from Microsoft Schedule+ version 7.0 to co-workers who are using Microsoft Schedule+ version 3.x.

    IMPORTANT   Be sure to ask the co-workers helping you with this lesson to send responses to your meeting request so that you can complete later exercises in this lesson.

Verify meeting details

1   Click the Planner tab.

The Planner tab becomes active.

2   Use the right mouse button to click the meeting time slot.

Your name appears as the name of the person busy at that time.

3   Select your name.

The "Pecos ad development" meeting time and description appear.

Viewing Responses to Meeting Requests

When you send out meeting requests, you can view the responses from other attendees without leaving Schedule+. In the Appointment dialog box, you can view the list of meeting invitees and find out their responses to your request by looking at the symbol next to their names. The following table explains the different response symbols.

Symbol	Indicates that the attendee has
✓	Accepted
☑	Accepted with a response
?	Tentatively accepted
☑	Tentatively accepted with a response
✗	Declined
☒	Declined with a response
☒	Not yet responded

For more information about viewing your mail from Schedule+, see the One Step Further section later in this lesson.

When you send a meeting request, the invitees can respond in three ways: accept, decline, and tentatively accept. When they receive a meeting request, the invitees choose one of these reply options. They can also choose to add a message to their response. You can view these messages in your Inbox in Microsoft Exchange.

View responses to a meeting request

In this exercise, you view responses to your meeting request.

1   Click the Daily tab.

The Daily tab becomes active.

2   In the Appointment Book, double-click the left border of the "Pecos ad development" meeting.

The Appointment dialog box appears.

3 Click the Attendees tab.

The list of invitees' responses appears. Your screen should look similar to the following illustration.

Accepted meeting

Tentatively accepted
meeting

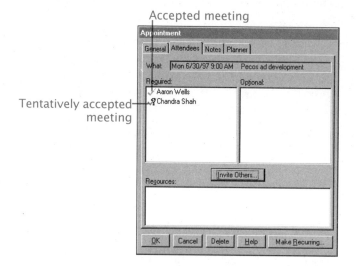

4 Click OK.

The Appointment dialog box closes.

Scheduling Meetings Using the Planner

Although you can use the Meeting Wizard to organize a meeting quickly, it is not always the most efficient way to arrange a meeting with your co-workers. Suppose you need to plan a meeting with a group of individuals, each of whom has a very tight schedule. You could use the Meeting Wizard, but what if the next available date it can find is three months away? In situations like this, it is often easier to organize a meeting using the Planner.

If your co-workers have given you Read access permission, you can view the details of their appointments. Then, if your meeting takes precedence over one of their current appointments, you can ask them to reschedule that appointment.

Your name always appears in the Attendees box located next to the Planner grid. To add names to the Attendees box and display their schedules, you can click the Invite button. If you select a busy time in the Planner, a red X appears next to the name of each busy individual in the Attendees list.

Display your co-workers' schedules

In this exercise, you display your co-workers' schedules in the Planner.

1 Click the Planner tab.

   The Planner tab becomes active.

2 Click Invite.

   The Select Attendees dialog box appears.

3 Select the names of the people helping you with this lesson, and then click Required.

   The names appear in the list of required attendees.

By default, your schedule appears in blue and the required attendees' schedules appear in gray.

4 Click OK.

   Bars appear in the Planner, indicating your co-workers' busy times. Your screen should look similar to the following illustration.

Co-worker's schedule

Your schedule

Request Meeting button

Request a meeting using the Planner

In this exercise, you schedule and request a meeting using the Planner.

1 Drag to select an empty time period of two hours in the current week.

   The selected meeting time appears highlighted.

2   Click Request Meeting.

A meeting request form appears. The time and date of the proposed meeting appear at the top of the form, and your co-workers' names from the Attendees list appear in the To field.

3   In the Subject field, type **Pecos television campaign**

4   In the message area, type **Can we meet to review the storyboards for our first commercial spot?**

5   Click the Send button.

The meeting request is sent. The selected time slots are blocked out in your Planner, indicating that the meeting has been added to your schedule.

Send

TIP   You can show or hide your co-workers' schedule information by clicking their names in the Attendees list. A checkmark in front of a name indicates that the person's schedule information is displayed in the Planner. An X in front of a name means that the selected time period conflicts with an appointment in the person's schedule. If there is no checkmark or X, the person's schedule is not displayed. You can also collapse or expand the list of attendees for a category by clicking the button to the left of the category name.

Changing Meetings

Your meeting is scheduled, but what if you need to change your plans or invitees have unlisted appointments? When someone declines a meeting or asks if you could reschedule it, you can easily make changes.

Reschedule a meeting

In this exercise, you change a meeting time and notify attendees of the changes.

1   Click the Daily tab.

The Daily tab becomes active.

2   Click the "Pecos television campaign" meeting, and then drag the top border down two time increments.

The meeting is now scheduled to start one hour later. A message appears, asking if you want to notify attendees of the change.

3   Click Yes.

The original meeting request form appears.

4   Click Send.

The new meeting time is sent to your co-workers. They can accept or decline the request.

> **NOTE**   If you'd like to build on the skills that you learned in this lesson, you can perform the exercises presented in the following section, One Step Further. Otherwise, skip to "Finish the lesson."

One Step Further: Viewing Your Mail from Schedule+

> **IMPORTANT**   In order to perform this exercise, one of your co-workers has to accept the rescheduled "Pecos television campaign" meeting and include a message with his or her response.

When you have scheduled a meeting, you can get a quick overview of who has accepted or refused by opening the Appointment dialog box and displaying the Attendees list. But what if one of your attendees has included a text message with the response? To read the message, you will need to open it using Exchange.

View mail from Schedule+

In this exercise, you open the Microsoft Exchange Inbox from Schedule+ and view a message.

1   Be sure that you are in Daily view.

2   On the Schedule+ toolbar, click the View Mail button.

View Mail

Microsoft Exchanges starts. The Viewer window opens, and the contents of your Inbox are displayed. If you are prompted to choose a profile, select Chris Adams.

3   In the Inbox folder, double-click the "Pecos television campaign" message from your co-worker.

The message opens. Your screen should look similar to the following illustration.

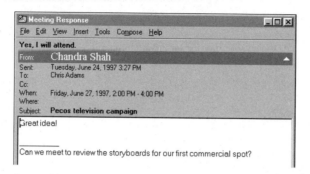

4   Read the message, and then close the "Pecos television campaign" window.

Finish the lesson

Follow these steps to delete the practice messages you created in the lesson.

1   Delete the practice messages you used in this lesson and that are still stored in your Inbox and Sent Items folders.

2   In Schedule+, delete the two meetings you created for this lesson. If you're prompted to send a cancellation notice, click No.

3   In Schedule+, on the File menu, click Exit And Log Off.

    If you choose Exit And Log Off in Exchange, you will also exit Schedule+.

Lesson Summary

To	Do this
View your schedule in the Planner	Start Schedule+, and click the Planner tab.
Display schedule details in the Planner	Use the right mouse button to click a busy time slot. Select a name.
Set access permissions	On the Tools menu, click Set Access Permissions. Click Add. Select a name from the address list, click Users, and then click OK. Select a name from the list of users. In the Permission Details area, click the User Role down arrow. Select an access permission, and then click OK.

To	Do this	Button
Schedule a meeting using the Meeting Wizard	On the Schedule+ toolbar, click the Meeting Wizard button. Follow the steps to select attendees, a location, and any resources, and specify a duration, a time, and a day for the meeting. Click Finish.	
Send a meeting request	In the Planner, click Request Meeting. In the Subject field, type the subject of the meeting. In the message area, add any important information. Click the Send button.	
View responses to a meeting request	In the Daily view, double-click the left border of the meeting appointment. Click the Attendees tab, and review the list of attendees and their responses. Click OK or Cancel.	
Display another person's schedule in the Planner	In the Planner, click Invite. In the Select Attendees dialog box, select a name, and then click Required or Option.	
Request a meeting using the Planner	Be sure that the names of your chosen attendees appear in the Attendees list in the Planner. Select a time period. Click Request Meeting. Enter the subject and a short message in the meeting request form. Click the Send button.	
Reschedule a meeting	In the Daily view, click the meeting appointment, and then drag the top border to a new time. Click Yes to notify the attendees of the change. Add any information to the meeting request form, and then click the Send button.	

For more information about	On the Help menu, click Microsoft Schedule+ Help Topics, click the Index tab, and then type
Viewing schedules in the Planner	**Planner tab**
Setting access permissions	**Permissions**
Using the Meeting Wizard	**Meetings** *or* **Meeting Wizard**
Scheduling meetings	**Meetings**
Sending meeting requests	**Mail** *or* **Meetings** *or* **Meeting Request Form**
Viewing responses to a meeting	**Mail** *or* **Meetings** *or* **Meeting Response Form**

Part

4

Review &
Practice

Estimated time
30 min.

You will review and practice how to:

- Schedule appointments in the Appointment Book.
- Edit and customize appointments.
- Create and organize a To Do List.
- Create and maintain a Contact List.
- Schedule meetings with co-workers on your network.

Before you complete this book, you can practice the skills you learned in Part 4 by working through the steps in this Review & Practice section. You will open your Microsoft Schedule+ file, add several appointments, and edit those appointments to reflect new information. You will also add a new project to your To Do List, create several tasks for the project, and update your Contact List. Finally, you will use the Planner to schedule a meeting with a co-worker.

Scenario

You are still searching for an administrative assistant. You want to schedule several interviews and coordinate them with the rest of your schedule. To prepare for the interviews, you decide to add some relevant tasks to your To Do List and prioritize them. You also want to review and update your Contact List. Finally, you arrange a meeting with the Human Resources director to discuss a new hire package for the selected candidate.

249

Step 1: Schedule Appointments in the Appointment Book

You are ready to schedule initial interviews with two applicants for the administrative assistant position. In this step, you add the interviews to your Appointment Book.

The dates in these exercises are set to 1999 to avoid any confusion with your real appointments.

1 Start Schedule+, and change the date to Monday, February 22, 1999.

2 Schedule an appointment from 10:00 A.M. to 11:00 A.M. Call the appointment "Interview with Jennifer Kennedy."

3 Schedule an appointment from 3:30 P.M. to 4:30 P.M. Call the appointment "Interview with Melissa Engels."

For more information on	See
Starting Schedule+	Lesson 10
Go to specific dates	Lesson 10
Creating appointments	Lesson 10

Step 2: Edit and Customize Appointments

Your dentist's office calls to remind you that you have an appointment for your six-month check up; the appointment conflicts with Jennifer Kennedy's interview. In this step, you reschedule the interview and add the dental appointment to your Appointment Book as a private engagement.

1 Change the start time of your appointment with Jennifer Kennedy to 1:00 P.M.

2 Schedule an appointment from 9:30 A.M. to 10:30 A.M. and call it "Six-month dental check up."

3 Add the Lakeview Medical Center location to the "Six-month dental check up" appointment.

4 Make the "Six-month dental check up" appointment private.

For more information on	See
Editing appointments	Lesson 10
Making appointments private	Lesson 10

Step 3: Create and Organize a To Do List

To prepare for your upcoming interviews, you want to familiarize yourself with the applicants' background and skills, and outline the topics to discuss during the interviews. In this step, you add these tasks to your To Do List.

1 Switch to the To Do List. Insert a project, and call it "Assistant Interviews."

2   Add three tasks to the Assistant Interviews project: "Review applicant resumes," "Draft interview questions," and "Call Joe Pecos about lunch."

3   Move the "Call Joe Pecos about lunch" task to the None project.

4   Change the priority of the "Review applicant resumes" task to 1 and the priority of the "Draft interview questions" task to 2.

5   Group the tasks by priority.

For more information on	See
Inserting a project	Lesson 11
Creating and editing tasks	Lesson 11
Setting priorities	Lesson 11
Grouping tasks	Lesson 11

Step 4: Create and Maintain a Contact List

To help you in your search, you consult the career counseling center at the local university to see if they can recommend any candidates. In this step, you add the name of the placement coordinator to your contact list and update some other contact information that you entered previously.

1   Switch to the Contacts view.

2   On the File menu, point to Import, and then click Schedule+ Interchange.

3   Open the Contacts.sc2 file from the Exchange 5.0 SBS Practice\R&P4 folder to import the practice Contact List.

4   Add the career counseling contact using the following data:

Field	Data
First Name	Joanne
Last Name	Mason
Address	310 Graduate Hall
City	Seattle
State	WA
Postal Code	98112
Title	Placement Coordinator
Company	State University
Department	Career Counseling
Phone Number	(206) 555-5627

5 Display the data for Barbara Hinkle. Add the fax number (408) 555-1288 and add the birthday January 22, 1951.

6 Group the Contact List by company.

For more information on	See
Adding a contact	Lesson 11
Editing a contact	Lesson 11
Organizing the Contact List	Lesson 11

Step 5: Schedule a Meeting with Co-Workers on Your Network

You think you have found an excellent candidate for administrative assistant position. You want to discuss a competitive new-hire package with the Human Resources director so that you can offer the applicant more incentive to accept the position. In this step, you schedule a meeting with the Human Resources director.

 IMPORTANT You'll need to recruit some help from a co-worker on your network to complete this exercise.

1 Switch to the Planner. Display your co-worker's schedule in the Planner. (Hint: Click the Invite button above the Attendees list, and then use the Required button.)

2 Select an empty time period of 90 minutes in the current week, and then request a meeting with your co-worker.

3 In the Subject field on the meeting request form, type **Administrative Assistant**. In the message area, type **I would hate to lose Jennifer Kennedy to a better offer. Can we discuss an expanded benefits package for her?** Send the meeting request.

4 After your co-worker responds to your meeting request, view the response using Exchange.

For more information on	See
Working with the Planner	Lesson 12
Requesting a meeting	Lesson 12
Viewing responses to a request	Lesson 12

Finish the Review & Practice

Follow these steps to delete the practice messages and appointments you created and used in this Review & Practice.

1 Delete the appointments you created in this Review & Practice.

2 In the To Do List, group the tasks by Project. Delete the Assistant Interviews project and the "Call Joe Pecos about lunch" task.

3 In the contact grid, delete the Fitch & Mather, Healthy Food Store, and State University categories. Change the Group By setting to None.

4 Open the Inbox. Delete the "Administrative Assistant" message.

5 If you are finished using Schedule+ for now, on the File menu, click Exit.

The Schedule+ file closes.

6 If you are finished using Microsoft Exchange for now, on the File menu, click Exit And Log Off.

You are logged off Microsoft Exchange, and the Viewer window closes.

Appendix

Additional Configurations and Setups   257

Additional Configurations and Setups

Computers, operating systems, e-mail services, and Exchange client and server software can be configured to interact in various ways. This book focuses on the Exchange 5.0 Client, the most recent version of Microsoft Exchange, configured to run under the Windows 95 or the Windows NT version 4.0 operating system, on a computer connected to a network on which a Microsoft Exchange 5.0 Server is installed. However, if your computer and software configurations are different, you might still be able to use parts of this book by adjusting some of the exercise steps. The purpose of this appendix is to help you adapt the book to your situation. Keep in mind that this appendix discusses only the major differences between some of the possible configurations and the ones used as a standard in this book. This appendix should be used as a starting point for further adjustments and is fairly technical in content.

IMPORTANT This book is designed for use with Microsoft Exchange 5.0, which is vastly different and more full-featured than the Exchange program that comes with the Windows 95 or Windows NT version 4.0 operating system. When we use the term "Exchange" in this book, we are referring to an Exchange 5.0 Client connected to an Exchange 5.0 Server that is functioning as your mail server.

The exercises in this book assume that a mailbox has been set up for you by your system administrator and that you are working with others in a networked environment, such as a local area network (LAN). To be able to perform Parts 2 through 4 of this book, you must be using the Exchange 5.0 Client with an Exchange 5.0 Server.

Using Exchange with a Different Configuration

You can use this book even if your configuration is different from the one used as the standard in this book.

If You're Using a Different Operating System

The Microsoft Exchange 5.0 Client can run on several platforms, including Apple Macintosh, Microsoft Windows 3.1, Microsoft Windows for Workgroups 3.11, Microsoft Windows NT 3.51, and MS-DOS. Only the Windows, Windows NT, and MS-DOS operating systems are discussed here.

Windows 3.1 or Windows for Workgroups 3.11

If you are using Windows 3.1 or Windows for Workgroups 3.11, you can easily follow the lessons in this book. However, you should allow for slight variances, such as screen elements that are unique to each operating system. You will also need to substitute different tools where appropriate. For example, you should use File Manager when this book mentions Windows Explorer or Windows NT Explorer. Also, if a toolbar button is not available, you should look for an equivalent menu command. In addition, Windows 3.1 and Windows for Workgroups 3.11 filenames are limited to eight characters; therefore the names of the practice files and folders might be truncated. A list of naming conventions is available in the Win31.txt file located on the practice disk that comes with this book.

Windows NT 3.51

If you are using Windows NT version 3.51 instead of version 4.0, you can work through all the lessons in this book as they are presented; and, because Windows NT supports long filenames, you will be able to use the practice files as is.

However, you should allow for slight variances, especially for screen elements that are unique to each operating system. For example, in Windows NT 3.51, your computer name might appear in the title bar of each window. You will also need to substitute different tools where appropriate. For example, you should use File Manager when this book mentions Windows Explorer or Windows NT Explorer. Also, if a toolbar button is not available, you need to look for an equivalent menu command.

MS-DOS

If you are using MS-DOS, you can complete only those exercises presented in Part 1, which deals with basic messaging features. The advanced messaging functions covered in Parts 2 through 4 are not included in the MS-DOS client. Supplemental programs, such as Microsoft Exchange Forms Designer and Microsoft Schedule+, are not available with the MS-DOS client. Also, the practice files furnished with this book can't be used when running the MS-DOS client.

If You're Using a Different Version of the Exchange Client

If you are using the Exchange program that is included with Windows 95 and Windows NT version 4.0, you will be able to work through Part 1 with some modifications to the steps. You will, however, when asked to address a message to someone in the global address list, have to substitute an Internet address or your own address. Because a practice personal address book is provided on the disk accompanying this book, you will still be able to use the fictitious names at Fitch & Mather.

If You're Using a Different Information Service

Information services are tools that you can use to deliver messages and take advantage of the capabilities and features of Exchange. For example, Microsoft Mail, CompuServe, The Microsoft Network, and Internet Mail are all information services. Just as there are different information services, there are different ways of connecting to a mail server. You might be using Exchange with an Internet Service Provider (ISP) as your mail server or dialing up and connecting to your mail server at work using Remote Mail. The possibilities and variables are too great to cover in an appendix, however—this book focuses on the Exchange 5.0 Client used with the Exchange 5.0 Server. If your configuration is different, you will only be able to use this book and its exercises as a guide.

If you use the Exchange Client with an information service other than the Exchange 5.0 Server, you might not be able to take advantage of certain features.

Additional Setup Procedures

If you use a configuration that is different from the standard configuration used in this book, you might have to perform one or both of the following procedures.

Setting Up an Information Service in Exchange

Before you can use an information service, such as Microsoft Mail, you must first add the service to your Microsoft Exchange profile. Your profile contains settings that define how you can use Microsoft Exchange with other information services.

You might have an account with The Microsoft Network or CompuServe and want your mail from those services to be delivered to the same location as your other messages. When you set up The Microsoft Network or CompuServe to work with Microsoft Exchange, your messages are routed through your Microsoft Exchange Inbox.

NOTE To initiate mail transfer with information services, such as The Microsoft Network or CompuServe, you can use the Deliver Now Using command on the Tools menu.

Add the Microsoft Mail information service

In this exercise, you add the Microsoft Mail information service to your profile to practice adding an information service.

 IMPORTANT Before beginning this exercise, you should log off Microsoft Exchange.

1   Click the Start button, point to Settings, and then click Control Panel.
2   Double-click the Mail And Fax icon or the Mail icon.
3   Click Add.

The Add Service To Profile dialog box appears.

 TROUBLESHOOTING If you do not see Microsoft Mail in the list of available services, you will have to install it using the Microsoft Exchange Setup program. To do this, click Start, point to Settings, and then click Control Panel. Double-click the Add/ Remove Programs icon. On the Install/Uninstall tab, click Microsoft Exchange, and then click Add/Remove.

4   In the Available Information Services list, click Microsoft Mail, and then click OK.

The Microsoft Mail dialog box appears.

5   Type the path to your postoffice, and then click OK.
6   Click the Logon tab, type your mailbox name, press TAB, and then type your password.
7   Click the Delivery tab. Be sure that the Enable Incoming Mail Delivery check box and the Enable Outgoing Mail Delivery check boxes are selected, and then click OK.
8   Close any open dialog boxes.

Setting Up the Practice Files for Windows 3.1 and Windows for Workgroups 3.11

In addition, Windows 3.1 and Windows for Workgroups filenames are limited to eight characters; therefore, the names of the practice files and folders might be truncated (shortened). A list of naming conventions is available in the Win31.txt file located on the practice disk that comes with this book. You can refer to this list to correctly identify which folder contains the appropriate files for each lesson.

Set up the practice files for Windows 3.1 and Windows for Workgroups 3.11

If you are using Windows 3.1 or Windows for Workgroups 3.11, before you can use the practice files, you need to perform the following setup instructions.

1   In the Program Manager window, on the File menu, click Run.

   The Run dialog box appears.

2   Type **a:setupw3** (or **b:setupw3** if the practice disk is in the B drive), and then press ENTER.

   The practice files are copied to your C drive in a folder called EXCHAN~1.0SB.

 IMPORTANT   Before you can begin the lesson exercises, you must decompress the practice files for that lesson by using Microsoft Expand (a program that comes with Windows and is usually located in the C:\Windows folder). To use this program, create a new folder on your hard disk, such as C:\SBS. From the MS-DOS prompt, switch to the folder where the files you wish to decompress are located, and then type **EXPAND** *<filenames>* **C:\SBS**. This expands the files into the C:\SBS folder. You should not change the filename extensions of any of the files you expand.

This glossary contains definitions of terms used in *Microsoft Exchange 5.0 Step by Step*. For definitions of additional terms, see the online glossary in Microsoft Exchange Help.

Address Book   A list containing all the available addresses on your network. The Address Book consists of at least two address lists: your organization's global address list and your personal address book.

attachment   A file, such as a spreadsheet, that is included in a message. An attachment is identified in an open message by an icon and the filename of the attachment. When you double-click the icon, the file opens in the program in which it was created. Messages with attachments are identified by a paper clip icon in the folder contents list.

AutoAssistant   A feature in Exchange that automatically processes and responds to your incoming mail, even if Exchange isn't running on your computer. AutoAssistants include the Inbox Assistant and the Out Of Office Assistant. *See also* Inbox Assistant; Out Of Office Assistant; rule.

AutoReply   A text message that you set up, using the Out Of Office Assistant, to inform people that you are away from your office. Your AutoReply message is automatically sent to anyone who sends you a message. Only one AutoReply message is sent to each person, regardless of the number of messages the person sends to you during your absence.

AutoSignature   Formatted text and graphics that can be used as a closing signature in outgoing messages.

blind carbon copy (Bcc)   A copy of a message that is sent to recipients listed in the Bcc box. When the original message is sent, the recipients listed in the To or in the Cc box are not aware that the message has been copied to additional recipients.

browser   *See* Web browser.

carbon copy (Cc)   A copy of a message that is sent to recipients listed in the Cc box. Carbon copy recipients are usually people who should be aware of the contents of the message, but don't necessarily have to respond directly or take action.

client   The software installed on your computer that you use to connect to the Microsoft Exchange Server. Microsoft Exchange and Microsoft Schedule+ are client software.

client-server network   A group of workstations connected to a central computer or server.

delegate   A person who has permission to manage or send messages on your behalf. Permissions are granted by you or by the system administrator. *See also* permission.

Delivery Receipt   A notification to the sender that indicates when the recipient received a message.

dial-up connection   A connection between an offsite computer and a Microsoft Exchange Server using software, a modem, and a telephone line.

Dial-Up Networking   The Windows 95 or Windows NT accessory you use to connect two computers that each have a modem. Using Dial-Up Networking, you can establish a continuous dial-up connection to the Microsoft Exchange Server.

distribution list (DL)   A list, created by the system administrator, that is used to send messages to a group of recipients. Distribution lists are part of the global address list and are available to all users in an enterprise.

domain server   A central computer, such as in a Microsoft Exchange enterprise, that verifies your username and password when you log on to the network.

download   To transfer a file from a remote computer to your local computer. Downloading can be performed on network computers or through a telecommunication system.

electronic mail   Notes, messages, and files sent between computers that have telecommunication or network services. Also referred to as e-mail.

e-mail   *See* electronic mail.

embed   The process of inserting an object from a source program into a destination document. When you double-click the object in the destination document, the source program opens, and the object can be edited. *See also* link.

enterprise   *See* Microsoft Exchange Server Enterprise.

event   An activity or special occasion associated with a specific day, but not a specific time, in your Microsoft Schedule+ schedule.

filter   The process of selectively displaying specific items, such as tasks that are not completed or are overdue. You use a filter to define which items you want to display.

folder   A container in which document and program files are stored. *See also* mailbox folder.

folder contents list   The right half of the Viewer window where the contents of an open mailbox folder are displayed.

folder forms library   A collection of forms stored in or associated with a public folder. Anyone with access to the public folder can use the forms located in a folder forms library.

folder view   A view that you use to group, sort, and filter messages contained in a folder, typically used for public folders. *See also* personal view; view.

folders list   The left half of the Viewer window where your mailbox folders are displayed.

form   An electronic format used to perform messaging tasks. For example, you enter message text using the New Message form and read messages using the Read Message form. You can use the Microsoft Exchange Forms Designer to modify existing forms or create your own. *See also* Microsoft Exchange Forms Designer.

Forms Designer   *See* Microsoft Exchange Forms Designer.

global address list   A directory of all the Microsoft Exchange users and distribution lists created and maintained by a system administrator. The global address list can contain public folder names. *See also* personal address book.

group   The process of displaying items contained in a mailbox folder by specific categories.

HTML (HyperText Markup Language)   A set of rules used to format World Wide Web pages. HTML includes methods of specifying text characteristics (bold, italic, etc.), graphic placement, links, and so on. A Web browser, such as Internet Explorer, must be used to properly view an HTML document.

hyperlink   An object, such as a graphic or underlined text, that represents a link to another location in the same file or in a different file and that, when clicked, brings up a different Web page. Hyperlinks are a key element in HTML documents. *See also* HTML; jump; link.

Inbox   A built-in folder in Windows 95 and Windows NT where your incoming messages are received and stored.

Inbox Assistant   An AutoAssistant that you use to automatically process incoming mail. You can use the Inbox Assistant to automatically delete, forward, move, or copy messages that you receive. *See also* AutoAssistant.

information service   A tool used to access information in Microsoft Exchange and other messaging programs, such as Microsoft Mail, CompuServe, or The Microsoft Network.

information store   A container where a related set of folders is stored. When you install Microsoft Exchange, the Personal Folders information store is created automatically on your hard disk and contains all your Exchange folders. *See also* personal folder.

Internet   A vast communication system that connects many different online services and other computer networks throughout the world.

Internet address   The address of a recipient outside your Microsoft Exchange enterprise. You store custom addresses in your personal address book. The following format must be used to send a message to a custom address: *[emailaddresstype:emailaddress]*.
For example, two custom addresses for Chris Adams at Fitch & Mather are as follows: [SMTP:chrisa@fitch&mather.com] *or*
[x400:c=us;a=;p=fitch & mather;o=fitch&mather;s=chrisa]

intranet   A self-contained network that uses the same communication protocols and file formats as the Internet. An intranet can, but doesn't have to, be connected to the Internet. Many businesses use intranets for internal communications. *See also* Internet.

jump   An underlined word or phrase in online Help or on a Web page that displays additional information when clicked. *See also* hyperlink; link.

keyword   A password that is created by the Microsoft Exchange Server security software, and is obtained from your system administrator during the setup procedure for advanced security.

library   A folder where custom and standard forms are stored for easy access. Different types of libraries are available to an entire organization, to specific groups of users, or to an individual user. A library is also sometimes referred to as a registry.

link   [1]*See* hyperlink. [2]To copy an object, such as a graphic or text, from one file or program to another so that there is a dependent relationship between the object and its source file. Also refers to the connection between a source file and a destination file. Whenever the original information in the source file changes, the information in the linked object is automatically updated. *See also* embed.

mailbox   The container for your incoming and outgoing messages, which includes the Deleted Items, Inbox, Outbox, and Sent Items folders. The contents of your mailbox are stored on a Microsoft Exchange Server computer.

mailbox folder   A folder stored in your mailbox on a Microsoft Exchange Server. Mailbox folders include built-in, offline, public, and personal folders.

Meeting Wizard   A step-by-step guide that helps you schedule a meeting in Schedule+. Based on your responses to questions about meeting attendees, location, equipment, duration, day, and time period, a meeting is set up automatically.

message area   The area of a form, such as the New Message form or Read Message form, in which you type or read the message text.

message header   The area of a form, such as the New Message form or the Read Message form, in which information about the sender, the date sent, the recipient, and the subject is located.

Microsoft Exchange Forms Designer   A Microsoft Exchange component that you can use to create your own forms or to modify existing forms.

Microsoft Exchange Server Enterprise   A linked set of client computers and Microsoft Exchange Server computers that provide workgroup services to your organization. An enterprise can be worldwide, nationwide, or within a building, depending on the size of your company and how the enterprise is set up.

Microsoft Office   An integrated family of business programs.

moderated folder   A public folder that has one or more designated moderators to review incoming messages before they are posted.

offline   The state during which your computer is not connected to a network or to a Microsoft Exchange Server.

offline folder   A folder that you use for messaging activities when you work offline in Microsoft Exchange. Offline folders include the Deleted Items, Inbox, Sent Items, and Outbox folders, and are synchronized with your mailbox folders when your computer is connected to the Microsoft Exchange Server.

organization forms library   A set of forms stored on a Microsoft Exchange Server computer. Anyone with access to the server can use the forms in an organization forms library. *See also* library.

Out Of Office Assistant   An AutoAssistant that you use to automatically notify people who send you messages that you are away from the office. *See also* AutoAssistant.

password   A unique series of characters that you type to gain access to a restricted network system, an electronic mail system, or a protected folder or file. Passwords are used to protect the information stored on a computer.

permission   Authorization to perform actions such as creating public folders, viewing schedule information, or sending messages for another user. Some permissions must be set by the system administrator while others can be set by individual users. *See also* delegate.

personal address book (PAB)   An address list with a PAB filename extension that contains usernames as well as public and personal distribution lists that you frequently use. *See also* global address list.

personal distribution list (PDL)   A type of distribution list that you create to send messages to a group of recipients. Personal distribution lists are stored in your personal address book.

personal folder   A folder that you create and that is typically located on your computer hard disk. Personal folders are often used for backing up other folders, archiving old files, and working with information offline.

personal forms library   A set of forms stored in your own mailbox. Only you and people to whom you grant access can use the forms contained in a personal forms library. *See also* library.

personal view   A view that you use to group, sort, and filter messages contained in a folder. Microsoft Exchange includes four predefined personal views. *See also* folder view; view.

private   An appointment, task, or contact in Microsoft Schedule+ that is hidden from other users and is identified by a key symbol.

private folder   A folder stored on a shared network computer that has not been designated as available to other users and can be opened only by the user who created it.

profile   A set of information services used to configure Microsoft Exchange and other messaging programs so that you can gain access to your mailbox.

public folder   A shared folder located on a Microsoft Exchange Server computer. Public folders can contain custom forms, rules, and views, as well as permissions used to define who can view and use the public folder.

public folder forms   *See* folder forms library.

Read Receipt   A notification that indicates that a recipient opened a message.

Remote Mail   A window in Microsoft Exchange that you use to send and download message headers while working remotely. You can also use Remote Mail to connect to the Microsoft Exchange Server, send messages that you composed offline, and synchronize offline folders.

route   To send a file to several other users sequentially or all at once. The Microsoft Exchange routing function is available on the File menu of each Microsoft Office program.

rules   A set of conditions and actions that help you organize the information contained in Microsoft Exchange. Conditions for each rule define to whom the rule applies and what actions will be performed on each item.

seal   A security feature to ensure that only the recipients to whom you sent a message can open that message. To open sealed messages, the recipient must provide his or her own security password and be registered in a Exchange security enterprise.

server   A central computer on certain types of networks to which all computers on the network are connected and through which users can obtain shared network resources. *See also* domain server.

sign   A security feature to ensure that messages are not tampered with after being sent. A signed message is encrypted with a digital signature, and the sender must use a security password.

sort   The process of reordering text or numbers in ascending or descending order, alphabetically, numerically, or by date.

synchronize   To merge the contents of offline folders with mailbox folders located on your Microsoft Exchange Server. Any changes you make while working offline are matched to the server to make the folders identical in content.

system administrator   The person or persons responsible for maintaining the Microsoft Exchange Server Enterprise and the global address list.

tentative appointment   An appointment that you can track in your Schedule+ Appointment Book but that does not appear as a busy time slot when other users view your schedule using the Planner. A tentative appointment appears dimmed in your Appointment Book.

Undeliverable Receipt   A notification to the sender that indicates that a message was not delivered to one or more of its recipients.

view   A combination of settings for displaying the contents of a folder.

Viewer   The main window in Microsoft Exchange. It is composed of the folder list on the left side and the folder contents list on the right side.

Web browser   Software that interprets and displays documents formatted for the World Wide Web, such as HTML documents, graphics, or multimedia files.

World Wide Web   The collection of available information on the Internet that is connected by links so that you can jump from one document to another. Also referred to as the Web, WWW, and W3.

A

access permissions
  defined, 84, 146
  delegating to co-worker, 84–87
  for Inbox folder, 84–87
  list of levels, 84–85
  minimum, 84
  predefined, 84–85
  and public folders, 146, 147–48
  and schedules, 202, 236–38
  setting for public folders, 152–53
additional configurations, 257–59
Address Book
  adding entries to, 14
  checking names against, 38
  creating distribution lists, 14
  defined, 7
  downloading for use offline, 90–91
  global address list, 7–9, 90–91, 175
  personal address book, 11–12
  viewing through a Web browser, 175–76
addresses
  global list, 7–9, 90–91, 175
  personal list, 11–12
  saving from incoming messages, 40–41
addressing messages, 7–9, 11–12
aligning form fields, 140
anniversary dates
  adding to Contact List, 224
  viewing in Appointment Book, 225
annual events, 204
answering messages, 35–37
applications. *See* **sample applications**
Appointment Book. *See also* **schedules**
  adding appointments in, 196
  adding events in, 204–5
  anniversary dates in, 225
  birthdays in, 225
  changing appointment information, 196
  changing date displayed, 196
  changing date of appointment, 198–200
  changing display colors, 207–8
  changing number of days displayed, 206–7
  changing work day times, 207
  Contacts view, 221
  customizing view, 206–7
  Daily view, 195
  Date Navigator, 195

Appointment Book, *continued*
  overview, 195–96
  personal dates in, 225
  Planner view, 234–35
  printing schedule, 205–6
  scheduling tasks, 220–21
  To Do List, 213–14
  viewing recurring tasks, 227–28
  Weekly view, 206–7
  workgroup uses, 202
appointments. *See also* **Appointment Book**
  canceling, 204
  changing, 197–200, 201–2
  creating, 195–96
  deleting, 204
  printing schedule, 205–6
  private, 202–3
  recurring, 200–201
  setting reminders, 201–2
  tentative, 203
attachments
  vs. embedded objects, 21–22
  and file formats, 22, 24
  finding, 51–52
  forwarding, 38
  overview, 24
  printing, 53
  receiving files as, 38–39
  saving, 38–39
  sending files as, 24–25
  when to use, 22
AutoAssistants
  Inbox Assistant, 69–72
  Out Of Office Assistant, 80–83
automatic message replies, 80–82
AutoReply
  canceling rules, 84
  creating from Web browser, 182–84
  disabling, 82, 184
  setting up, 80–81
  testing, 81–82
AutoSignature
  creating, 73–74
  editing, 74
  formatting, 73–74
  inserting automatically, 74
  inserting into messages, 73

AutoSignature, *continued*
overview, 72–73
testing, 74

B

Bcc box. *See* **blind carbon copies (Bcc)**
birthdays
adding to Contact List, 224
viewing in Appointment Book, 225
bitmap images, embedding, 23–24
blind carbon copies (Bcc)
defined, 25
and "reply to all" responses, 36
sending, 25–26
browsing. *See also* Web browser
messages, 33–35, 67
World Wide Web, 168
built-in folders, 5, 31–32, 46
bulletin boards. *See* public folders

C

calendar. *See* Appointment Book; Planner
carbon copies (Cc)
blind (Bcc), 25–26, 36
defined, 25
replying to all recipients, 36–37
sending, 12
Cc box. *See* carbon copies (Cc)
checking spelling, 18–20
client computers, xvii, 167–68
client-server-based systems, xvii, 167–68. *See also*
Microsoft Exchange Server
Clipboard, 111
collapsing folders, 47, 64, 66
colors, changing in Schedule+, 207–8
columns,
adding, 48
grouping, 157–58
resizing, 49
restoring defaults, 49
specifying for custom views, 156–57
completed tasks, 214, 217–18
composing messages, 6–9
Contact List
adding contacts, 221–23
adding personal dates, 224
creating, 221–26

Contact List, *continued*
customizing, 225–26
editing information, 223
grouping contacts, 225–26
importing for practice, xxvi–xxvii
overview, 213, 221
viewing personal dates in Appointment Book, 225
contacts
adding personal dates, 224
adding to Contact List, 221–23
grouping in Contact List, 225–26
private, 223–24
viewing personal dates in Appointment Book, 225
continuous dial-up connection, 89, 99–100
conventions used in this book, xxix–xxx
copying, practice files to Inbox folder, 30
courtesy copies. *See* carbon copies (Cc)
co-workers
accepting meeting requests, 241
access to public folders, 146, 152–53
access to schedules, 202, 236–38
delegating Inbox access, 84–87
displaying schedules in Planner, 242, 243
distributing documents, 113–14
in global address list, 8
notifying of meeting changes, 244–45
planning of meetings, 233–45
responses to meeting requests, 241–42
revising documents online, 113–17
routing documents, 113–14
selecting meeting attendees, 238
sending files from Word, 109
sending meeting request forms, 240–42
customizing
Microsoft Schedule+, 206–8
sample applications, 132–34
toolbars, 53–54
view of messages, 67–69

D

dates
changing appointment details, 198–200
changing display in Schedule+, 196
personal, adding to Contact List, 224
delegates
defined, 84
granting Inbox access, 84–87

delegates, *continued*
    restricting access, 84–85
    testing access, 87, 88
Deleted Items folder
    changing to work like Recycle Bin, 40
    defined, 5, 31
    emptying, 39
    retrieving messages from, 39
    viewing, 40
deleting
    appointments, 204
    folders, 46
    form fields, 133
    messages, 39–40
    practice files, 26–27
    toolbar buttons, 54
Delivery Receipts, 16, 34
detailed tasks, 215–16
dial-up connection, 89, 94, 99–100
Dial-Up Networking, 94, 99–100
digital signatures, 100, 102–3
distribution lists (DLs), 13. *See also* personal
    distribution lists (PDLs)
documents
    distributing to co-workers, 113–17
    editing, 108–9
    embedding in messages, 22–23
    linking Excel workbook data to Word, 110–12
    opening, 108, 110
    reviewing revisions, 114–17
    revising online, 113–17
    saving, 108
    sending to co-workers, 109
    sending vs. routing, 113
    updating linked data, 112
domain server, defined, xvii
downloading, 90–91, 95, 96–97

E

EFP files, 131, 135
electronic mail. *See* e-mail
e-mail. *See also* messages
    advantages of, 3
    defined, xviii
    Internet addresses, 15
    using Word as editor, 117–19

embedding
    vs. attaching, 21–22
    files in messages, 22–24
    when to use, 22
employees. *See* co-workers
encrypting messages, 100, 102–3
enterprises. *See* Microsoft Exchange enterprise
EPF files, 101
events
    adding to Appointment Book, 204–5
    anniversary, 224
    birthdays, 204, 224, 225
    defined, 204
    printing schedule, 205–6
Excel. *See* Microsoft Excel
Exchange 5.0 SBS Practice folder, xxiii
expanding folders, 46, 47, 64, 65, 66

F

**Favorites folder, adding public folder shortcuts
    to, 160–61**
fields
    adding, 134, 140–41
    aligning, 140
    changing font, 132
    customizing, 132–33
    deleting, 133
    resizing, 133
files. *See also* documents
    attaching, 24–25
    embedding vs. attaching, 21–22
    inserting in messages, 22–25
    practice, xxix–xxx
    sending from Word, 109
filtering
    defined, 75
    messages, 75–76
    tasks, 219–20
finding messages, 49–52
folder applications, defined, 130. *See also* Post
    forms
folder contents list
    defined, 5, 6
    viewing messages, 31–32
folder forms library, defined, 136
folder list, defined, 5, 6

Index

folders. *See also* **public folders**
  adding columns, 48
  built-in, 5, 31–32, 46
  checking properties, 147–48
  creating in Inbox, 47, 70–71
  customizing view, 67–69
  deleting, 46
  exploring in Viewer window, 31–32
  filtering messages, 75–76
  finding messages, 49–52
  grouping messages, 64–67
  information stores for, 46
  moderated, 161–63
  moving messages among, 47–48
  offline, 91, 92–93
  organizing, 46–48
  private, 46
  recovering after deletion, 46
  synchronizing, 96, 98–99
folder views, 67, 156–58
fonts
  for AutoSignature entries, 73–74
  for customized forms, 132
form applications, defined, 130. *See also* **Send
  forms**
forms. *See also* **Post forms; sample applications;
  Send forms**
  creating from scratch, 138–41
  modifying samples, 131–35
  overview, 130
Forms Designer. *See* **Microsoft Exchange Forms
  Designer**
forwarding attachments, 38
forwarding messages
  using New Message form, 37–38
  using Out Of Office Assistant, 83–84
FW. *See* **forwarding messages**

G

global address list
  addressing messages, 7–9
  defined, 7
  downloading for use offline, 90–91
  viewing through a Web browser, 175
graphics
  adding to forms, 133–34
  embedding in messages, 22–24

grouping
  contacts, 225–26
  messages, 64–67, 68
  tasks, 219

H

help, with practice files, xix, xxviii
HTML files, 208–9
hyperlinks, navigating messages using, 168
hypertext markup language (HTML) files, 208–9

I

icons
  for advanced security messages, 101
  for embedded objects, 23
  for folders, 46–47
  for information stores, 46–47
  for priority levels, 33
  for types of messages, 33–34
Inbox Assistant, 69–72
Inbox folder
  browsing through messages, 33–35
  collapsing categories, 64, 66
  copying practice files into, 30
  creating subfolders, 47, 70–71
  customizing view, 68–69
  defined, 5, 31
  delegating access to, 84–87
  deleting, 46
  expanding categories, 64–66
  filtering messages, 75–76
  grouping messages, 65–66
  reading messages in, 32–33
  setting rules 69–72
  sorting messages in, 44–46
  viewing contents list, 5, 6, 31
  viewing from Schedule+, 245–46
information service, 259
information stores, 46, 87
installing
  Microsoft Exchange Forms Designer, 130
  Post forms in public folders, 151–52
  practice files, xxii–xxiii
  Send forms in libraries, 136–37
  WordMail, 118

Internet. *See also* Web browser
    adding addresses to Address Book, 15
    defined, 4, 167

L

laptop computers, configuring to work
        offline, 89–91
libraries
    defined, 136
    folder forms, 136
    installing new forms in, 136–37
    organization forms, 136
    personal forms, 136–37
linking
    defined, 110
    editing linked data, 112
    Excel workbook data to Word documents, 110–12
log files, 98
logos, adding to forms, 133–34
Lotus Organizer, switching from, xvi

M

Mail. *See* Microsoft Exchange; Microsoft Mail
    mailbox. *See also* Mailbox Viewer
    accessing through a Web browser, 169–78
    advanced security for, 100, 101–2
    delegating access to, 84–87
    list of built-in folders, 5, 31
    viewing folder contents, 31–32
Mailbox Viewer
    accessing, 168
    exploring, 171
meeting request forms
    creating, 240
    response options, 241
    sending, 240
    using in Planner, 244
    using with Meeting Wizard, 240
    viewing responses, 241–42
meetings
    planning, 233–45
    rescheduling, 244–45
    scheduling using Meeting Wizard, 238–40
    scheduling using Planner, 242–44
    sending request forms, 240–42
    setting up, 236–45
    verifying details, 240–41
Meeting Wizard, 238–40

message area, defined, 6, 7
message headers
    defined, 6, 7
    for sent messages, 32
    using to differentiate messages, 31
    using to sort messages, 44
    viewing in Remote Mail window, 95
messages
    accessing through a Web browser, 172–78
    addressing using global address list, 7–9
    addressing using personal address book, 11–12
    advanced security for, 100, 101–2
    arrival notification, 32
    assigning priority, 17
    attaching files to, 24–25
    automatic replies to, 80–82
    browsing, 33–35, 67
    checking when offsite, 93–96
    checking spelling, 18–20
    creating, 6
    deleting, 39–40
    editing text, 17–18
    encrypting, 100, 102–3
    exploring using hyperlinks, 168
    filtering, 75–76
    finding, 49–52
    forwarding, 37–38
    grouping, 64–67
    identifying read vs. unread, 31
    moving among folders, 47–48
    opening, 32
    printing, 52
    read vs. unread in Inbox folder, 5, 6
    replying to, 35–37
    requesting receipts, 16
    retrieving after sending, 10
    sealing, 100, 103
    selecting, 48
    sending, 10–16, 25
    sending objects, 22–24
    sending to multiple recipients, 12–16
    sending using distribution lists, 13–16
    sent by delegates, 88
    signing electronically, 100, 102–3
    simple sorting, 44–46
    sorting into groups, 64–67
    templates for, 118–19
    viewing list of, 31–32
Microsoft, contacting, xix, xxiii

Microsoft Excel
  editing linked workbook data, 112
  embedding workbooks in messages, 22–23
  linking workbook data to Word documents, 110–12
Microsoft Exchange. *See also* **Microsoft Exchange Server**
  accessing through a Web browser, 169–79
  and practice files, xxi–xxviii
  quitting, 27
  spelling checker, 18–20
  switching from version 4.0, xvi
  synchronizing folders, 96, 98–99
  user profiles, xxiii–xxv
  viewing Inbox from Schedule+, 245–46
  working offline, 89–100
Microsoft Exchange enterprise, defined, xvii, 7
Microsoft Exchange Forms Designer
  creating forms from scratch, 138–41
  defined, 130
  installing, 130
  main window, 131
  modifying forms, 131–35
  starting, 131
  toolbox, 131
Microsoft Exchange Server
  connecting automatically, 99
  connecting to, 93–96
  continuous dial-up connection, 89, 99–100
  defined, xvii
  Internet connectivity, 168
  IP address, 168, 169
  logging off, 27
  logging on, xxv, 5
  postoffice, as a, xviii
  public folders on, 146–49
  remote mail properties, 95
  and use of rules, 69
  and Web browser, 168, 169–70
Microsoft Mail
  as an information service, 260
  switching from, xvi
Microsoft Office
  integrating Exchange with, 107–19
  linking documents between applications, 110–12
  routing documents, 113–14
  sending documents from Word, 109
Microsoft Schedule+
  customizing, 206–8
  importing Contact List, xxvi–xxvii

Microsoft Schedule+, *continued*
  overview, 193
  planning meetings, 233–45
  starting, 194–95
  using Appointment Book, 194–206
  using Contact List, 221–26
  using To Do List, 241–21
  viewing Exchange Inbox from, 245–46
Microsoft Visual Basic, 136
Microsoft Word
  editing documents, 108–9
  as e-mail editor, 117–19
  embedding documents in messages, 22–23
  linking Excel workbook data to documents, 110–12
  modifying message templates, 118–19
  opening documents, 108, 110
  routing documents, 113–17
  saving documents, 108
  sending files from, 109
  starting, 108
modems, 89, 94
moderated folders, 161–63
moving
  appointments to different days, 200
  messages among folders, 47–48
  sent messages, 10

N

names
  adding to Address Book, 14–15
  adding to distribution lists, 14–15
  checking against Address Book, 38
  in global address list, 7–9
  saving incoming message addresses, 40–41
  sorting messages by, 45, 46
naming folders, 47
Navigation Bar, 169, 170
New Message form, 6, 36, 159
New Post form, 153
Normal view, 68, 69, 156

O

objects, embedding in messages, 22–24
offline. *See also* **Remote Mail**
  as working mode, 89–100
  folders, 91, 92–93

opening
 e-mail messages, 32
 Excel workbooks, 110–11
 public folders, 147
 sample applications, 131
 Word documents, 108, 110
organization forms library, defined, 136
OST files, 90
Outbox folder
 defined, 5, 31
 moving messages to, 10
 retrieving sent messages from, 10
Out Of Office Assistant
 processing messages automatically, 80–83
 using from Web browser, 182–84

P

passwords, 100, 101–2.
permissions. *See* access permissions
personal address book (PAB)
 adding distribution lists, 14
 adding names, 14–15
 addressing messages, 11–16
 changing sort order, 46
 defined, 11
 for practice, xxiv, 11
 saving incoming message addresses, 40–41
 setting properties, 46
 viewing names, 41
personal distribution lists (PDLs)
 adding names, 14–15
 creating, 14
 defined, 13
 using, 14–16
 viewing properties, 16
personal folders, defined, 46. *See also* folders
personal forms library, 136–37
personal views
 creating, 68–69
 defined, 67
 vs. folder views, 67
 predefined, 68
 using, 69
pictures. *See* graphics
Planner
 defined, 234
 scheduling meetings using, 242–44
 viewing schedule in, 234–35

Post forms
 defined, 130
 designating for use, 152
 installing, 151–52
 using, 154–55
 viewing, 155
 and Web browser, 181–82
practice files
 copying into Inbox folder, 30
 corrections for, xix
 deleting after finishing lessons, 26–27
 folders for, xxiii
 help with, xix, xxviii
 importing Contact List, xxvi–xxvii
 importing personal address book (PAB), xxv–xxvi
 installing, xxii–xxiii
 overview, xix
 uninstalling, xxvii
 using, xxiii
predesigned forms, defined, 130
printing
 attached files, 53
 blank schedule pages, 206
 messages, 52
 schedules, 205–6
priority
 assigning to messages, 17
 assigning to tasks, 218
private appointments, 202–3
private contacts, 223–24
private folders, 46
profiles
 changing settings, xxv
 creating for practice, xxiii–xxiv
projects. *See also* tasks
 adding tasks to, 215–17
 adding to To Do List, 214
public folders
 accessing through a Web browser, 179–82
 adding items to, 158
 checking access permissions, 147–48
 checking for posts, 181–82
 creating, 150
 defined, 46, 146
 designating forms for use, 152
 designing views, 156–58
 developing, 149–53
 and forms library, 136
 installing forms in, 151–52

public folders, *continued*
  opening, 147
  overview, 146, 149
  permissions overview, 146
  and Post forms, 130, 151–52
  posting information, 153–59
  replying to posted items, 159
  setting access for co-workers, 152–53
  shortcuts to, 160–61
  uses for, 153–54
  viewing contents, 148–49
Public Folders Viewer, 168, 179–80

R

reading messages, 32–33
Read Receipts, 16
receipts
  attaching to messages, 16
  defined, 16
  requesting for all messages, 17
  undelivered, 25, 33
recurring appointments, 200–201
recurring tasks
  creating in To Do List, 227
  viewing in Appointment Book, 227–28
refreshing messages in Web browser, 170, 173
registered mail. *See* receipts, attaching to
    messages
registries. *See* libraries
reminders, 201–2
remote communication, 89–100
Remote Mail
  copying messages, 96, 97
  defined, 91, 93
  deleting messages, 96, 97
  downloading messages, 96–97
  marking messages, 96–97
  retrieving messages, 96–97, 97
  unmarking messages, 96
  viewing message headers, 93
replying
  automatically, 80–82
  to e-mail messages, 35–37
  to items in public folders, 159
responding to messages, 35–37
revisions, document
  accepting and rejecting, 116–17
  reviewing, 114–17

revisions, document, *continued*
  soliciting from co-workers, 113–17
routing documents, 113–14
routing slips
  asking for document return, 114
  creating, 113–14
  editing, 114
  saving for later distribution, 114
rules
  canceling, 84
  conflicts between, 82
  defined, 69
  disabling, 71
  editing, 72
  and Microsoft Exchange server, 69
  order of processing, 70
  setting up for Inbox Assistant, 69–70
  setting up for Out Of Office Assistant, 83–84
  testing, 71–72

S

sample applications. *See also* Post forms; Send
    forms
  customizing, 132–34
  defined, 130
  modifying, 132–34
  opening in Forms Designer, 131
saving
  attachments, 38–39
  new Send forms, 135, 141
  Word documents, 108
SCD files, 195
Schedule+. *See* Microsoft Schedule+
schedules. *See also* Appointment Book
  and access permissions, 236–45
  preparing for World Wide Web, 208–9
  printing, 205–6
  viewing co-workers, 242, 243
  viewing in Planner, 234–35, 240–41, 242, 243
sealing messages, 100, 103
searching for messages, 49–52
security, advanced, 100, 101–2. *See also* access
    permissions
selecting messages, 48
Send forms
  adding fields to, 134, 140–41
  adding graphics to, 133–34
  changing fonts, 132

Send forms, *continued*
    changing window title, 135
    creating from sample applications, 130–35
    creating from scratch, 138–41
    customizing fields, 132–33
    defined, 130
    installing in libraries, 136–37
    modifying, 132–34
    saving, 135, 141
    using, 137, 159
sending
    documents from Word, 109
    forms, 137
    messages, 10–16, 25, 176
servers, 167. *See also* Microsoft Exchange Server
shortcuts, creating for public folders, 160–61
signatures. *See* AutoSignature; digital signatures
signing messages, 100, 102–3
sorting messages, 44–46. *See also* grouping,
    messages
spelling checker, 18–20
spreadsheets. *See* workbooks
starting
    Forms Designer, 131
    Microsoft Exchange, xxv, 5
    Microsoft Schedule+, 194–95
    Microsoft Word, 108
synchronizing folders, 96, 98–99
system administrator, defined, xxvii

T

tasks
    adding to To Do List, 215–16
    assigning priorities, 218
    assigning to projects, 215, 217
    completed, 214, 217–18
    detailed, 215–16
    editing, 216–17
    end dates for, 215, 216
    filtering, 219–20
    grouping, 219
    organizing, 218–21
    recurring, 227–28
    scheduling in Appointment Book, 220–21
    viewing list, 214
templates
    creating, 118
    modifying in Word, 118

templates, *continued*
    saving, 119
tentative appointments, 203
text-only format (TXT), for attached messages,
    22, 24
tiling windows, 30
To Do List. *See also* tasks
    adding projects, 214
    adding tasks, 215–16
    creating, 214–18
    editing tasks, 216–17
    organizing tasks, 218–21
    overview, 213
    viewing, 214
toolbars
    adding buttons, 53–54
    customizing, 53–54
    restoring to default settings, 54
    in Viewer window, 6

U

Undelivered Receipts, 25, 33, 34
URLs, 168, 169
user profiles
    changing settings, xxv
    creating for practice, xxiii–xxiv

V

Viewer window. *See also* WebView
    built-in folders in, 5, 31–32
    defined, 5
viewing
    from Schedule+, 245
    mailbox contents list, 31–32
    messages using a Web browser, 167–68
    public folder contents, 148–49
views, folder. *See also* personal views
    customizing, 67–69
    defined, 67
    personal vs. public folder, 67

W

Web browser
    checking for new messages using, 177, 184
    checking for new posts using, 181–82
    defined, 167

Web browser, *continued*
    logging onto Exchange from, 169–70
    organizing messages, 172–75
    using Out Of Office Assistant, 182–84
    using to create AutoReply, 182–84
    using to create posts, 181
    using to create public folders, 180
    viewing Exchange Address Book, 175–76
    viewing public folder contents, 179–80
    viewing schedules, 208–9
WebView
    defined, 168
    Mailbox Viewer, 168, 170, 171
    Public Folders Viewer, 168, 179–80
windows, tiling, 30
Windows 95, installing practice files, xxii–xxiii
Windows Explorer, 30
Windows NT, installing practice files, xxii–xxiii
wizards
    Forms Designer Wizard, 131
    Form Template Wizard, 139
    Meeting Wizard, 238–40

Word. *See* Microsoft Word
WordMail
    editing templates, 118
    enabling as e-mail editor, 118
    installing, 118
    saving modified templates, 119
    selecting template to use, 118
workbooks
    editing linked data, 112
    embedding in messages, 22–23
    linking data to Word documents, 110–12
    opening, 110–11
    receiving as attachments, 38–39
workgroups. *See* co-workers
World Wide Web. *See also* Web browser
    accessing Exchange mailbox, 169–78
    creating schedules for viewing, 208–9
    defined, 167
    Microsoft Press address, xix, xxiii
    practice file corrections, xix

Take
productivity
in stride.

Microsoft Press® *Step by Step* books provide quick and easy self-paced training that will help you learn to use the powerful word processor, spreadsheet, database, desktop information manager, and presentation applications of Microsoft Office 97, both individually and together. Prepared by the professional trainers at Catapult, Inc., and Perspection, Inc., these books present easy-to-follow lessons with clear objectives, real-world business examples, and numerous screen shots and illustrations. Each book contains approximately eight hours of instruction. Put Microsoft's Office 97 applications to work today, *Step by Step.*

Microsoft® Excel 97 Step by Step
U.S.A. $29.95   ($39.95 Canada)
ISBN 1-57231-314-5

Microsoft® Word 97 Step by Step
U.S.A. $29.95   ($39.95 Canada)
ISBN 1-57231-313-7

Microsoft® PowerPoint® 97
 Step by Step
U.S.A. $29.95   ($39.95 Canada)
ISBN 1-57231-315-3

Microsoft® Outlook™ 97 Step by Step
U.S.A. $29.99   ($39.99 Canada)
ISBN 1-57231-382-X

Microsoft® Access 97 Step by Step
U.S.A. $29.95   ($39.95 Canada)
ISBN 1-57231-316-1

Microsoft® Office 97 Integration
 Step by Step
U.S.A. $29.95   ($39.95 Canada)
ISBN 1-57231-317-X

Microsoft Press® products are available worldwide wherever quality computer books are sold. For more information, contact your book retailer, computer reseller, or local Microsoft Sales Office.

To locate your nearest source for Microsoft Press products, reach us at mspress.microsoft.com, or call 1-800-MSPRESS in the U.S. (in Canada: 1-800-667-1115 or 416-293-8464).

To order Microsoft Press products, call 1-800-MSPRESS in the U.S. (in Canada: 1-800-667-1115 or 416-293-8464).

Prices and availability dates are subject to change.

***Microsoft**·Press*

Get quick, easy answers—anywhere!

Microsoft® Excel 97 Field Guide
Stephen L. Nelson
U.S.A. $9.95 ($12.95 Canada)
ISBN 1-57231-326-9

Microsoft® Word 97 Field Guide
Stephen L. Nelson
U.S.A. $9.95 ($12.95 Canada)
ISBN 1-57231-325-0

Microsoft® PowerPoint® 97 Field Guide
Stephen L. Nelson
U.S.A. $9.95 ($12.95 Canada)
ISBN 1-57231-327-7

Microsoft® Outlook™ 97 Field Guide
Stephen L. Nelson
U.S.A. $9.99 ($12.99 Canada)
ISBN 1-57231-383-8

Microsoft® Access 97 Field Guide
Stephen L. Nelson
U.S.A. $9.95 ($12.95 Canada)
ISBN 1-57231-328-5

Microsoft Press® Field Guides are a quick, accurate source of information about Microsoft Office 97 applications. In no time, you'll have the lay of the land, identify toolbar buttons and commands, stay safely out of danger, and have all the tools you need for survival!

***Microsoft*Press**

The
Step by Step
Practice Files Disk

The enclosed 3.5-inch disk contains timesaving, ready-to-use practice files that complement the lessons in this book. To use these files, you'll need Microsoft Exchange 5.0 and either the Microsoft Windows 95 operating system or version 4 of the Microsoft Windows NT operating system.

Before you begin the *Step by Step* lessons, read the the section of the book titled "Installing and Using the Practice Files." There you'll find a description of each practice file and easy instructions for installing the files on your computer's hard disk.

Please take a few moments to read the license agreement on the previous page before using the enclosed disk.

Register your Microsoft Press® book today, and let us know what you think.

At Microsoft Press, we listen to our customers. We update our books as new releases of software are issued, and we'd like you to tell us the kinds of additional information you'd find most useful in these updates. Your feedback will be considered when we prepare a future edition; plus, when you become a registered owner, you will get Microsoft Press catalogs and exclusive offers on specially priced books.
Thanks!

I used this book as
- ⬤ A way to learn the software
- ⬤ A reference when I needed it
- ⬤ A way to find out about advanced features
- ⬤ Other_____

I consider myself
- ⬤ A beginner or an occasional computer user
- ⬤ An intermediate-level user with a pretty good grasp of the basics
- ⬤ An advanced user who helps and provides solutions for others
- ⬤ Other_____

I purchased this book from
- ⬤ A bookstore
- ⬤ A software store
- ⬤ A direct mail offer
- ⬤ Other_____

I will buy the next edition of the book when it's updated
- ⬤ Definitely
- ⬤ Probably
- ⬤ I will not buy the next edition

The next edition of this book should include the following additional information:
1 •_____
2 •_____
3 •_____
The most useful things about this book are_____
_____

This book would be more helpful if_____
_____

My general impressions of this book are_____
_____

May we contact you regarding your comments? ⬤ Yes ⬤ No
Would you like to receive a Microsoft Press catalog regularly? ⬤ Yes ⬤ No

Name_____
Company (if applicable)_____
Address_____
City_____State_____Zip_____
Daytime phone number (optional) (_____)_____

Please mail back your feedback form—postage free! Fold this form as described on the other side of this card, or fax this sheet to:
Microsoft Press, Attn: Marketing Department, fax 206-936-7329

FOLD THIS FLAP TOWARD CENTER AND TAPE TO OPPOSING FLAP

FOLD HERE

BUSINESS REPLY MAIL
FIRST-CLASS MAIL   PERMIT NO. 53   BOTHELL, WA

POSTAGE WILL BE PAID BY ADDRESSEE

NO POSTAGE
NECESSARY
IF MAILED
IN THE
UNITED STATES

MICROSOFT PRESS
MICROSOFT® EXCHANGE 5.0
STEP BY STEP
PO BOX 3019
BOTHELL   WA   98041-9946

FOLD HERE

FOLD THIS FLAP TOWARD CENTER AND TAPE TO OPPOSING FLAP